The Yahwist's Landscape

The Yahwist's Landscape

Nature and Religion in Early Israel

Theodore Hiebert

New York   Oxford
OXFORD UNIVERSITY PRESS
1996

Oxford University Press

Oxford   New York
Athens   Auckland   Bangkok
Calcutta   Cape Town   Dar es Salaam   Delhi
Florence   Hong Kong   Istanbul   Karachi
Kuala Lumpur   Madras   Madrid   Melbourne
Mexico City   Nairobi   Paris   Singapore
Taipei   Tokyo   Toronto

and associated companies in
Berlin   Ibadan

Library of Congress Cataloging-in-Publication Data
Hiebert, Theodore.
The Yahwist's landscape : nature and religion in early Israel /
Theodore Hiebert.
p. cm.
Includes bibliographical references and index.
ISBN 0-19-509205-8
1. J document (Biblical criticism) 2. Nature—Biblical teaching.
I. Title.
BS1181.4.H54   1995
222'.106—dc20   95-11578

1 3 5 7 9 8 6 4 2

Printed in the United States of America
on acid-free paper

To my parents,
Rachel Wiebe Hiebert and Waldo Daniel Hiebert,
who gave me an appreciation for the Bible;
and to our children,
Nicholas Sharpe and Mary Claire,
who will inherit the world we leave to them.

Preface

This study of the role of nature in biblical religion is motivated by two developments. One of these is the new interest in nature and the human place within it in Western religious traditions, prompted by the environmental crisis. Historians, ethicists, and theologians have begun to uncover the intellectual legacy of Western culture regarding nature and to assess its strengths and weaknesses as a resource for an enlightened ecological ethic. Since the Bible stands at the origin of Western traditions, its perspectives on the natural world have been subjected to close scrutiny by environmentalists and biblical scholars alike, who are often rather quick to blame or defend biblical points of view. This study is intended as a contribution to the ongoing task of uncovering, and making available to its heirs, the biblical legacy regarding the natural world and its significance in religious thought.

The other development that motivated this study is a growing personal dissatisfaction with the traditional approach to nature in biblical scholarship. This uneasiness first arose out of my dissertation work on Habakkuk 3, an elaborate account of God's appearance in the form and phenomena of the thunderstorm. How was one to account for such a vivid presentation of nature as a medium of revelation within a religion, so I had been taught, that embraced history and rejected nature as the realm of divine activity? As an aberration? A vestige of nonbiblical thought?

This dissatisfaction grew as I realized that the results of modern biblical scholarship, to which those with a renewed interest in nature in the West's religious traditions would turn for information, were based on a prohistory, antinature presentation of biblical religion, which did not consider texts like Habakkuk 3 of crucial significance. When one turns to scholarship on nature in biblical religion, one invariably confronts two widespread assumptions: ancient Israel originated in the desert, and its religion was stamped with an historical consciousness that marginalized the world of nature. Often, these two assumptions have been regarded as interrelated, and almost always they have shaped the content of exegetical and theological analyses of biblical perspectives on nature. Both seemed to me to be, at best, overstatements of the case and, at worst, misconceptions of the biblical environment and biblical thought.

The purpose of this study then is to lay open as carefully as possible the presuppositions that have shaped traditional scholarship on the role of nature in biblical religion, examine the anthropological and philosophical sources of these presuppositions, and test them against the details of a substantial and influential biblical text. The text selected for that purpose contains the oldest narrative traditions in the opening books of the Bible, a set of stories modern scholars have traditionally attributed, in their final form at least, to the Yahwist, a great narrator of the Israelite monarchy. The narratives attributed to the Yahwist have been influential in the development of scholarly approaches to nature in the Bible, and they have been of great interest as well to contemporary readers exploring the legacy of environmental values in Western traditions.

Throughout this study, I have kept two audiences in mind. One of these is biblical scholars, since I am criticizing in this study a number of traditional scholarly assumptions, and I am proposing a different approach to conceptualizing nature in biblical religion and a different way of interpreting certain biblical texts. The other audience is nonbiblical scholars who are interested in the values regarding nature in the West's religious traditions. With this audience in mind, I have tried to place the most technical data and the majority of the references to the history of biblical scholarship in the endnotes, where it is available to those who wish to pursue these matters further. I believe biblical scholarship should be more available to a broad audience, especially on a topic of such wide popular interest, but it is a difficult challenge to write for specialist and generalist alike. I do not think I have always been successful, but I hope both audiences will find something here to enrich their reading of these biblical narratives.

The basic research on which this study is based was funded by an American Schools of Oriental Research/National Endowment for the Humanities Postdoctoral Research Fellowship at the W. F. Albright Institute of Archaeology in Jerusalem, and by a grant from the Endowment for Biblical Research, Boston. A number of my colleagues, Frank Cross, Paul Hanson, Jo Ann Hackett, John Huehnergard, and Gordon Kaufman, have read parts of the manuscript and have made suggestions that have forced me to bring more rigor and clarity to the line of argument within this study. Throughout this project, Timothy Weiskel, director of the Harvard Seminar on Environmental Values, has been a provocative and supportive conversation partner. I am thankful to Brian Murphy and Margaret Studier, who have done more than their share to put this manuscript into readable form. Finally, I am indebted to my wife, Paula Sharpe Hiebert, who has given a tremendous amount of her own time and energy to discuss these ideas with me and to provide enough encouragement and time for me to put them together in this way.

Cambridge, Massachusetts   T. H.
December, 1994

Contents

Abbreviations

AB	*Anchor Bible*
ABD	*Anchor Bible Dictionary.* 6 vols. Edited by D. N. Freedman. New York: Doubleday, 1992.
AJSL	*American Journal of Semitic Languages and Literature*
ANET	*Ancient Near Eastern Texts Relating to the Old Testament.* 3rd ed. Edited by J. B. Pritchard. Princeton: Princeton University, 1969.
BA	*Biblical Archaeologist*
BAR	*Biblical Archaeology Review*
BASOR	*Bulletin of the American Schools of Oriental Research*
BDB	F. Brown, S. R. Driver, and C. A. Briggs, *Hebrew and English Lexicon of the Old Testament.* Oxford: Clarendon, 1952.
CBQ	*Catholic Biblical Quarterly*
CTA	*Corpus des tablettes en cunéiformes alphabétiques.* A. Herdner. Paris: P. Geuthner, 1963.
ER	*Encyclopedia of Religion.* Edited by M. Eliade. New York: Macmillan, 1987.

GKC   *Gesenius' Hebrew Grammar.* Edited by E. Kautzsch, translated by
           A. E. Cowley. Oxford: Clarendon, 1910.

HTR   *Harvard Theological Review*

ICC   *International Critical Commentary*

IDB   *Interpreter's Dictionary of the Bible.* 4 vols. Edited by George
           Buttrick. Nashville: Abingdon, 1962.

IDBSup   *Supplementary volume to IDB.* Edited by Keith Crim. Nashville:
           Abingdon, 1976.

JAOS   *Journal of the American Oriental Society*

JB   *Jerusalem Bible*

JBL   *Journal of Biblical Literature*

JCS   *Journal of Cuneiform Studies*

JJS   *Journal of Jewish Studies*

JNES   *Journal of Near Eastern Studies*

JPSV   Jewish Publication Society Version

JTS   *Journal of Theological Studies*

KAI   *Kanaanäische und aramäische Inschriften.* H. Donner, W. Röllig.
           Wiesbaden: Otto Harrassowitz, 1971.

KJV   King James Version

NAB   *New American Bible*

NEB   *New English Bible*

NRSV   New Revised Standard Version

TDOT   *Theological Dictionary of the Old Testament.* Edited by G. J.
           Botterweck and H. Ringgren. Translated by John T. Willis. Grand
           Rapids, Mich.: Eerdmans, 1974.

TWAT   *Theologisches Wörterbuch zum Alten Testament.* 4 vols. Edited
           by G. J. Botterweck and H. Ringgren. Stuttgart: W. Kohlhammer,
           1970–72.

VT   *Vetus Testamentum*

VTSup   *Vetus Testamentum*, Supplements

ZAW   *Zeitschrift für die alttestamentliche Wissenschaft*

ZDPV   *Zeitschrift des deutschen Palästina-Vereins*

The Yahwist's Landscape

1

The "Problem" of Nature
in the Bible

In both the popular consciousness and the enduring achievements of Western culture, the world of nature is remembered and represented as a familiar part of the biblical story. Biblical images of nature have, in fact, become a standard feature of the Western imagination. One of the now famous examples of this phenomenon in popular culture was the recitation of Genesis 1 on the first moon voyage. To express their amazement at the natural beauty of the planet earth floating in space as a small blue sphere, the Apollo 8 astronauts chose to read, out of all the nature literature of Western culture, the biblical story of creation.

Almost as well-known to many as this creation story are the vivid natural images painted in the poetry of the psalmists, who claimed that the heavens declare the glory of God. The Twenty-third Psalm, probably the most beloved poem in the Bible, is full of natural scenes and contains what may be the most familiar image of God in Scripture: "The Lord is my Shepherd." Other nature images come to mind. When God gives Moses the law, it is on a mountain in the midst of a dark cloud full of thunder and lightning. When God speaks to Job, the divine speech comes from the whirlwind and contains the greatest survey of the wonders of wild nature in the Bible. All in all, the concrete details of the biblical environment—its flocks of sheep and goats, vineyards and olive orchards, farmers sowing and harvesting grain, lush oases and vast deserts, donkeys and caravans of camels; its sacred mountains, vivid thunderstorms, and harsh droughts—have etched themselves into the literature and art of the West and into the minds of Jews and Christians, religious and nonreligious alike.

Nature As a Problem

Yet when one turns to those who have examined this topic in most detail one finds a different picture. In the history of biblical scholarship, on the one hand, and in recent literature on the environment and Western religious values, on the other, nature has commonly been presented as a problem in the Bible. Biblical scholars and environmentalists have questioned whether the world of nature has any significant value within biblical thought and whether, in fact, serious attention to it does not stand in some conflict with the core dogmas of biblical religion.

These reservations about the role of nature in biblical thought are not the result of shared contexts, goals, or methods of interpretation, or of any close cooperation between biblical scholars and environmentalists. The respective cultural settings and constituencies of these scholarly circles are very different in most respects, as are their lines of argumentation. Certainly little collaboration has taken place. Environmental writers seldom take advantage of the years of biblical scholarship on the topic that has preceded their interest in it. Yet both parties have come to regard nature as a problem in the Bible, and their arguments are not entirely dissimilar. In fact, their presuppositions and attitudes about biblical life and thought intersect at important points. To understand their common claim that nature is a problem in biblical religion, to understand the similarities and differences in their defense of this claim, and ultimately to evaluate its basic merit, the views of biblical scholars and environmental writers must be briefly reviewed.

The Problem in Biblical Interpretation

History versus nature The judgment by twentieth-century biblical scholars that nature in the Bible is a problem is based on several widely held convictions. To illustrate these, we may start with a classic essay by Gerhard von Rad, appropriately titled "The Theological Problem of the Old Testament Doctrine of Creation."[1] The thesis of this essay is stated succinctly in the opening sentence: "The Yahwistic faith of the Old Testament is a faith based on the notion of election and therefore primarily concerned with redemption." By "redemption" von Rad is referring to the salvation or well-being of humans, of the whole human race at one level, but even more precisely, of a particular people that the God of the Bible has chosen or elected for a special relationship. It is this divine-human relationship, according to von Rad, about which biblical religion is primarily concerned.

By contrast, the nonhuman world is a secondary concern. "How far is the idea of Yahweh as Creator a relevant and immediate conception, over against his redemptive function?" asks von Rad. After surveying the biblical accounts of creation in Genesis and the references to creation and nature in the Psalms and Prophets, he arrives at a largely negative answer. In all of these texts, according to von Rad, "the creation of the world by Yahweh is not being considered for its own sake, nor as of value in itself. On the contrary . . . it performs only an ancillary function. It provides a foundation for the message of redemption, in that it stimulates faith. It is but a magnificent foil for the message of salvation."[2] Nature has been reduced to a stage, magnificent though it may be, for the great human drama about which the Bible is primarily concerned.

Basic to von Rad's conclusion that creation is a theological problem are two conceptions that typify standard treatments of nature in the Bible. The first is the presumption of a sharp dichotomy between redemption and creation, that is, between the realm of human culture and history on the one side and the world of nonhuman nature on the other. Redemption and creation, history and nature, are regarded as distinct conceptual categories, each relatively unique and self-contained in its own right. They may be separated from one another, discussed in relative isolation, and variously compared or contrasted. In all of this, history and nature are not only assumed to be meaningful modern categories, intelligible to the contemporary interpreter and reader alike, but they are also believed to be appropriate for penetrating the ancient mentality of biblical writers. In a disarming statement, von Rad reveals at once the well-defined modern philosophical distinction between history and nature that underlies his analysis and its potentially questionable value for understanding ancient thought. "We are struck," he writes about the writings of the exilic prophet Second Isaiah, "by the ease with which two doctrines, which to our way of thinking are of very different kinds, are here brought together."[3]

A second conception prominent in von Rad's essay and common in biblical scholarship more generally is the judgment that these two realms, now distinguished from one another, do not share equally in the biblical drama. One of them, the realm of human culture, dominates biblical religion. It is the primary and, for all practical purposes, exclusive concern of biblical authors. The redemption of the human race, and of the people of God in particular, surpasses all other interests. By consequence, the realm of nonhuman nature recedes into the background and becomes less important. The world of creation is, as von Rad puts it, everywhere in the Bible "subordinated to the interests and content of the doctrine of redemption," at times "altogether swallowed up in the doctrine of redemption."[4] Thus nature is not only separated from human culture, but it is regarded as subservient to it.

Together, these two conceptions provide the basic framework for most of what has been written by biblical scholars about nature in biblical thought during the last century. Both are prominent in the work of another influential biblical theologian, G. Ernest Wright, whose scholarship may be used to fill out this picture further. Like von Rad, Wright viewed nature and history as distinct spheres and believed human history to be the central concern of biblical writers. This view of nature and history in fact was regarded by Wright as "the one, primary irreducible datum of biblical theology."[5]

For Wright biblical theology was based exclusively on the history of the people of God. "Biblical theology is first and foremost a theology of recital," wrote Wright, "in which Biblical man confesses his faith by reciting the formative events in his history as the redemptive handiwork of God. The realism of the Bible consists in its close attention to the fact of history and of tradition because these facts are the facts of God."[6] Within such a religion that claimed "history as the arena of God's activity," nature lost its inherent significance. "Nature was not an independent object," according to Wright, "it was instead a handmaiden, a servant of history."[7]

Wright saw biblical religion, by virtue of its preoccupation with the historical process, as sharply distinguished from the religions of its environment. The religion of the Bible represented to Wright "an utterly unique and radical departure from all contemporary pagan religions."[8] He described the radical difference between biblical religion and other religions in the following way.

> Natural religion in Biblical times analyzed the problem of man over against nature. In the struggle for existence the function of religious worship was that of the integration of personal and social life with the natural world. . . . The life of the individual was embedded in society and society was embedded in the rhythm and balance of nature which was the realm of the gods. . . .
>
> In the faith of Israel, even in the earliest preserved literature, there is a radical and complete difference at every significant point. The Israelite did not analyze the problem of life over against nature. The latter plays a subordinate role in the faith, except as it is used by God to further his work in society and history. Instead, the problem of life is understood over against the will and purpose of the God who had chosen one people as the instrument of his universal, redemptive purpose. . . . Here then is an utterly different God from the gods of all natural, cultural and philosophical religion. He is no immanent power in nature nor in the natural process of being and becoming. The nature of his being and will is revealed in historical acts.[9]

From Wright's analysis emerge two further conceptions characteristic of traditional treatments of nature in the Bible. One is that the Bible's emphasis on history and its subordination of nature is distinctive in the ancient world. At its origins in ancient Israel, biblical religion, according to Wright, represented a new vision of reality different from all others. On the one side are Israel's neighbors, regarding the world through the lens of nature, identifying divine power and will with natural phenomena, and grounding their liturgy and worship in nature's rhythms and orders. On the other side is Israel, viewing the world through the lens of human history, associating God with human culture, its social institutions and political events, and reciting within its worship its formative historical experiences. The ancient world could be divided neatly according to Wright, with natural religions on the one side and historical religion, found only in the Bible, on the other.

A second and related conception is Wright's view that this distinctiveness of biblical religion represented an intellectual and theological breakthrough in ancient Near Eastern thought. The kind of breakthrough involved has been described in various ways. For Wright, this breakthrough meant the drastic shift from viewing human life as confined by the unchanging cycles of nature to viewing human experience as a meaningful process en route to a goal; from accepting society as bound to the status quo and its hierarchical structures to embracing social evolution and human justice; from practicing rites of sympathetic magic insuring one's physical security to reciting God's saving acts on behalf of the poor and oppressed.[10] According to Wright's scheme, nature was not just the neutral background for the real drama of human redemption, but the realm of a complex of beliefs and behaviors super-seded by and antithetical to biblical religion. The world of nature is thus not merely peripheral to biblical religion but potentially perilous to it as well.

For H. and H. A. Frankfort, who edited a widely used study of ancient Near Eastern thought entitled *Before Philosophy: The Intellectual Adventure of Ancient Man,* Israel's rejection of nature and acceptance of history as the realm of religious reality represented an advance that could be phrased in more philosophical terms. It was the initial step in "the emancipation of thought from myth."[11] Whereas ancient Near Eastern societies functioned in the framework of "mythopoeic thought," in which subject and object—the realm of nature and the realm of humanity, or the natural world and the divine—were not distinguished from one another, biblical culture made the first move toward speculative thought, which stands behind modern science, by distinguishing God from nature and identifying history, not cosmic phe-nomena, as full of divine meaning and purpose. Biblical thought thus repre-sented the first stage of a journey away from myth, to be completed in its entirety by the later Greek philosophers.[12]

As this brief survey of several key scholarly figures shows, the view of nature in recent biblical interpretation has been predicated upon four simple conceptions: (1) nature and history are distinct categories, (2) biblical reli-gion was grounded in history rather than nature, (3) in this regard biblical religion was distinct from other ancient religions that were grounded in na-ture, and (4) the Bible's historical consciousness was an advance in the evo-lution of human thought. The natural consequence of such a stress on his-tory as the center of biblical religion is the marginalization of the world of nature as a significant concern. The result is the characterization of nature as a problem.

This scheme and its conclusions have been widespread and highly influ-ential in the biblical scholarship of the twentieth century. By way of illustra-tion, a few other representatives of it may be cited. A good place to begin is with H. Wheeler Robinson, the author of a classic and often-cited essay en-titled "The Hebrew Conception of Nature." The essay begins with a contrast between Babylonian and Israelite deities:

> They [the Babylonian gods] were nature-deities, with all the ethical limitation which this implies; He [Israel's God] was above Nature, as its Creator and Con-troller according to a moral purpose.... The primary conception of Yahweh which made such progress possible cannot have been itself a development from natural phenomena. Its inspiration was derived from the very different realm of human

history. Yahweh's ultimate relation to things is a derivative from His primary relation to men.[13]

Sigmund Mowinckel, a scholar known for his vigorous and sympathetic exploration of the ancient Near Eastern cosmogonic motifs that were incorporated into Israelite worship, is nevertheless decisive about Israel's historical distinctiveness. In his discussion of the enthronement festival, the centerpiece of his study of the Psalms in Israelite worship, he asserts that

> something new was added to the festival in Israel. This derived partly from the contrast between Yahweh and the local deities of nature and fertility and partly from the historical influence on Israelite religion of their experience of Yahweh in a decisive historical hour. . . . On the whole this historical character is a really fundamental feature of the religion of Israel. . . . This is what has made Israelite religion something essentially different from the 'natural' religions and 'nature-religions' of the Near East.

The line between history and nature and between Israel and its neighbors is very sharply drawn here, and its consequence for understanding Israelite worship is precisely described: "The reality re-experienced through the cult is no longer first and foremost the cyclical course and renewal of nature, but the historical 'facts of salvation.' The facts of salvation, 'recalled' and repeated by means of the festival, were removed from the sphere of natural religion (fertility and so on) to the world of historical reality."[14]

The observations on the character of Israel's God in two commentaries on the Book of Genesis may also be cited. Umberto Cassuto, in his discussion of the creation narratives, makes a clear distinction between the God of Israel pictured in them and the gods of Israel's neighbors. "Then came the Torah and soared aloft, as on eagle's wings, above all these nations," he wrote. "Not many gods but one God . . . not a deity associated with nature and identified with it wholly or in part, but a God who stands absolutely above nature, and outside of it."[15] In a more recent commentary, Nahum Sarna expresses a similar portrait of the creation narratives.

> The theme of creation, important as it is, serves merely as an introduction to the book's central motif: God's role in history. The opening chapters are a prologue to the historical drama that begins in Chapter 12. . . . The God of Genesis is the wholly self-sufficient One, absolutely independent of nature, the supreme, unchangeable Sovereign of the world who is providentially involved in human affairs. He is, therefore, Lord of history.[16]

This centering of biblical religion on the historical process and the consequent marginalization of the world of nature within it has been described by James Barr as one of the reigning orthodoxies of our age. "Historians of theology in a future age will look back on the mid-twentieth century and call it the revelation-in-history period," he writes. "No single principle is more powerful in the handling of the Bible today than the belief that history is the channel of divine revelation."[17] This principle is as operative among historians of religion as among biblical theologians. When the religion of the Bible

is considered in broader comparativist contexts, it is invariably characterized as uniquely historical. The great comparativist Mircea Eliade, for example, drew a sharp division between natural—primordial, cyclic, archetypal—
and historical views of reality, and he saw in Israelite thought the first decisive
rejection of the former and adoption of the latter. In this regard he found the
roots of the austere historical consciousness of modernity in the Hebrew
Bible.[18]

Two studies of sacred space in which Israelite thought is examined in a
broader comparative context might be noted by way of further illustration.
Hans J. Klimkeit introduces an analysis of Egyptian thought on this topic by
way of the traditional dichotomy: "We can, to a certain degree, contrast the
space-oriented mythical thinking of Egypt with the historical thinking of the
Old Testament. . . . [Israel] has its special position on account of the great
historical deeds of Yahweh, not on account of its *geographical* environment,
or the geographical factors of its *Lebensraum*. Whereas Israel . . . thinks historically in terms of time, Egypt thinks more geographically, in terms of space
[author's emphasis]."[19] Robert L. Cohn, who goes a long way toward breaking down this dichotomy in his studies of sacred space in biblical thought,
nevertheless starts his work with the traditional assumption: "It remains true
that for Israel, history, conceived as a purposeful sequence of divine-human
encounters, served as the organizing principle for communicating the Israelite experience of Yahweh in the Hebrew Bible."[20]

The desert versus the sown This view of biblical religion as historical rather
than natural in character has often been related to a view of the precise physical environment in which it came into being. This is the view that the desert
was ancient Israel's native environment and that Israel's earliest culture was
the pastoralist economy of nomadic shepherds. According to this view, Israel's
consciousness of nature—even more, its central religious and cultural tenets—
can only be understood in the context of desert nomadism. As Israel's formative environment, the desert and the specialized pastoral nomadism connected with it left an indelible stamp on all later generations. Though Israel
may have settled among Canaanite farmers and taken up their way of life, its
desert pastoralist origins gave Israel the distinctive religious consciousness
that was to characterize its thought and set it apart from its agrarian neighbors.

This view of Israel's origins was presented as forcefully by Albrecht Alt
as by any twentieth-century scholar. In a series of essays in the 1920s and
1930s, Alt analyzed the beginnings of Israel in terms of its desert origins and
the effects of this landscape on Israelite life and thought. Alt defended a theory
of the Israelite settlement as a peaceful infiltration into the arable zones of
the Canaanite hills by nomadic pastoralists from the surrounding deserts.[21]
He argued for the origin of Israel's religion in the desert experience of Israel's
ancestors before their settlement among Canaanite farmers.[22] And he proposed an interpretation of Israelite law that connected its original and distinctive features to this desert setting in which Israel was born.[23] For Alt,
Israelite thought, from its early perception of God as a deity bound to tribal

groups to its unique forms of law, bore the lasting imprint of its desert origins and could be clearly differentiated on this basis from the thought of the ancient Canaanite farmers among whom Israel settled and whose ways it slowly assimilated, though not without intellectual conflict and tensions.

In his essay on the origins of Israelite religion, "The God of the Fathers," Alt argued that the deity worshipped by Israel's earliest ancestors possessed an historical character that was to be directly associated with the desert nomadism of those who worshipped him. "The seeds of a completely different development from that of local and nature gods were implanted at the very inception of [Israel's] cult, " Alt claimed.

> The god was not tied to a greater or lesser piece of earth, but to human lives, first that of an individual, and then through him to those of a whole group. . . . The gods of this type of religion show a concern with social and historical events which most other primitive numina either lack altogether or possess only to a much more limited degree. This makes it even more appropriate to the way of life of nomadic tribes.[24]

According to Alt, this historical consciousness, forged in the furnace of the desert and its ancestral deities, later became the distinctive feature of Israelite Yahwism, even while Yahwism assimilated some characteristics of the nature gods of its Canaanite neighbors:

> Everything that we recognized as truly characteristic of these gods—their association with particular groups of men, families, clans, or tribes, their providential oversight over the fortunes of their worshippers in the desert, and where they had settled, their concern with social and historical events—all this recurs, only on a higher level and over a much wider field, in the character of Yahweh as the God of Israel. . . . The idea that Yahweh rules over the nation as a whole and over its history, is clear and precise from the beginning, and is the most distinctive characteristic of the religion of Israel.[25]

This conception of Israelite religion as distinctively historical on account of its desert origins was popularized for a generation of students in the widely read introduction to ancient Near Eastern thought, *Before Philosophy: The Intellectual Adventure of Ancient Man.* In their concluding chapter on the unique aspects of Hebrew and Greek thought, H. and H. A. Frankfort relate Israel's rejection of natural phenomena and acceptance of history as the revelation of God to a formative desert period. According to the Frankforts, we may best

> understand the originality and the coherence of their speculations if we relate them to their experience in the desert. . . . The Hebrews, whatever their ancestry and historical antecedents, were tribal nomads. . . . It seems that the desert as a metaphysical experience loomed very large for the Hebrews and colored all their valuations. . . .
>
> The organized states of the ancient Near East were agricultural; but the values of an agricultural community are the opposite of those of the nomadic tribe, especially of the extreme type of nomads of the desert. . . . For, wherever we find reverence for the phenomena of life and growth, we find preoccupation with the

immanence of the divine and with the form of its manifestation. But in the stark solitude of the desert, where nothing changes, nothing moves (except man at his own free will), where features in the landscape are only pointers, land marks without significance in themselves—there we may expect the image of God to transcend concrete phenomena altogether. . . .

. . . The doctrine of a single, unconditioned, transcendent God rejected time honored values, proclaimed new ones, and postulated a metaphysical significance for history and for man's actions.[26]

It was Israel's "metaphysical experience" of the desert, according to this line of thinking, that led it to dissociate divine reality from natural surroundings and identify it instead with peoples and their movements, that is, with human history.

Such a view of Israel's desert origins has typified biblical scholarship both earlier and later than Alt, its most formidable spokesman.[27] An illustrative example is the classic study of Israel's social institutions by Roland de Vaux.[28] This study of the familial, civil, military, and religious institutions that characterized sedentary Israelite society throughout its national life is prefaced by an introduction entitled "Nomadism and Its Survival." It begins with the following assertions: "At the beginning of their history the Israelites, like their ancestors before them, lived as nomads or semi-nomads, and when they came to settle down as a nation, they still retained some characteristics of that earlier way of life. Consequently any study of Old Testament institutions must begin with an investigation into nomadism. . . . Naturally, such a life entails a distinct pattern of society, and enjoins a code of behavior all of its own."[29] Following these assertions, de Vaux spells out the implications of such a viewpoint for his interpretation of Israel's tribal structure and legal system, both of which betray, according to de Vaux, their desert origins. These classic and influential statements by Alt and de Vaux are only two of the many that have been made in the past century claiming the desert as Israel's native environment and associating Israel's distinctive religion with it.[30]

This standard view of Israel's origins is based on several crucial conceptions of ancient environments and their related economies. The first is the belief that ancient Near Eastern environments and cultures can be neatly divided into separate spheres, the desert and the sown as they are sometimes called. On the one side is the arid or semiarid desert with its specialized pastoralists practicing a nomadic life-style to provide pasture for their herds. On the other side is the arable land of the humid zones, with its sedentary farmers cultivating the soil of their ancestral estates. Such a dichotomy has customarily pictured each environment with its related economy as relatively autonomous, self-contained, and independent of the other, so that conflict between them is to be expected as a logical consequence of their differences.

A second conception is that biblical culture and thought in their origins are to be associated exclusively with one of these settings, desert nomadism, while the culture and thought of the societies of the Bible's environs—in particular the Canaanites but also the Mesopotamians and Egyptians, for example—are to be associated rather with sedentary agricultural life. Thus biblical society could be clearly distinguished from those of its neighbors by virtue of its unique way of life and natural environment.

A third conception basic to this standard reconstruction of Israel's origins is the notion that nomadic pastoralism represents a more primitive stage of societal development than sedentary agriculture. Forces of social and historical change naturally encourage the evolution from herding to cultivation: nomadic pastoralists customarily settle down and become sedentary farmers. Though Israel, from the time of its settlement in the Canaanite hill country at the beginning of the Iron Age, was clearly an agrarian society, its real roots were to be connected with an earlier nomadic stage of cultural development.

The prevailing view within biblical interpretation during the last century of the place of biblical society in its natural environment and of its attitude toward the natural world in which it found itself is thus based on two foundational dichotomies that have often been considered related and mutually reinforcing—one philosophical and the other geographical. On the one hand is the well-defined distinction between nature and history and on the other hand the clear-cut division between the desert and arable land. Together they have provided the intellectual framework for the widely held view of Israel as a desert society that conceived out of its nomadic existence an historical consciousness new in the history of religions, whereby the natural world was devalued and stripped of its sacred significance.

The Problem in Ecological Literature

Such a presentation of biblical religion resonated well with the Western mood in the middle decades of the twentieth century. The preoccupation with history and human redemption, which was considered biblical religion's distinctive genius and primary concern, was regarded as the ultimate source of the modern commitment to human dignity and social justice. This was certainly the case for G. Ernest Wright, who viewed the nature religions of the ancient Near East as bound up by nature's unchanging cycles and as defenders of the status quo and of entrenched political power. By contrast, he saw in the historical consciousness of biblical thought a dynamic spirit embracing the new and moving toward a goal, the first force in ancient religion for revolution and social change.[31]

It is a conception that has subsequently been taken up into the literature of liberation theology. J. Severino Croatto, in his *Exodus: A Hermeneutics of Freedom,* makes the same contrast Wright did. Ancient religions that sought to align human life with the orders of the cosmos bound their adherents into its ceaseless and unchanging rhythms. In them humans were not free. "Mythic persons," claims Croatto, "are not free, creators in the sense of being aware of a vocation; rather, they are subject to the cosmos." By contrast, in biblical religion

> history displaces the cosmic. God is visualized in human events more than in the
> phenomena of the physical world. . . . Now human beings do not need to associate
> themselves with the rhythms of the cosmos to imbibe the sacred. . . . The rela-

tionship between God and humans is no longer cosmic, but rather dialogical, within a historicity in which human beings are responsible for a destiny but where they are also challenged by the prophets or by the Gospel. Thus we understand that human beings created in the image of God are free.[32]

The desacralization of nature that was a major component of this reconstruction of biblical religion also fit the modern Western mood. It was identified as the ultimate source of the scientific mentality that had freed society from primitive superstitions and had produced new and remarkable technologies. By removing God from nature, according to this view, biblical religion had reduced it to an object rather than a subject, to neutral matter that was no longer reverenced but that could now be dispassionately examined and manipulated. Accepted widely in theological circles, this viewpoint was described succinctly by Harvey Cox in his best-seller, *The Secular City*. Cox argued that biblical religion "opened nature for science" by breaking the integral connection between the human race, the gods, and the cosmos that defined the ancient religious systems of Sumer, Babylon, and Egypt. By separating nature from God and from society, the biblical view of creation began the "disenchantment process," as Cox called it, whereby nature was freed from its religious overtones and perceived in a matter-of-fact way. "This disenchantment of the natural world," wrote Cox, "provides an absolute precondition for the development of modern science."[33]

With the appearance of the environmental crisis in the final decades of the twentieth century, this traditional conception of biblical religion found itself in an entirely new and less friendly world. What had been considered unquestionably admirable within it suddenly came under direct criticism and was for the first time characterized as seriously problematic. How this came about can best be seen by looking at a few representative pieces of ecological literature that have been motivated by the environmental crisis and that are concerned with uncovering the values that have produced it.

One of the earliest and most widely discussed statements of this kind was a speech delivered by the historian Lynn White, Jr., to the American Academy for the Advancement of Science in 1966, published the next year for a broad popular audience in the journal *Science*.[34] Entitled "The Historical Roots of Our Ecologic Crisis," White's essay set the stage for subsequent discussions in a number of important respects. In the first place, White argued that the source of the environmental crisis lies not just in science and technology but in deeply held attitudes and values toward the world of nature. Furthermore, he endeavored to show how contemporary values derive from the West's religious heritage, a heritage that goes back ultimately to the Bible and its stories of creation at the beginning of Genesis. Finally, White delivered a rather scathing indictment on the biblical worldview. In its creation accounts, White saw a dualistic perspective and an anthropocentric bias that disturbed him. According to White, the biblical stories of creation set humans apart from nature and pictured them as superior to it, sharing in large part God's own transcendence over it by being created in the divine image. The physical creation for its part was made solely "to serve man's purposes" and was placed under human dominion. The result, in White's opinion, was the familiar Western notion "that it is God's will that man exploit nature for his proper ends."[35]

While White demonstrates no knowledge of the history of biblical scholarship on the texts or issues he discusses, it is not hard to recognize the parallels between his critique and the results of biblical scholarship. White's "dualism of man and nature" is conceptually parallel to the dichotomy between history and nature that has played such a major role in the standard treatments of nature in biblical interpretation. And his focus on anthropocentrism—the centering of the narrative on human well-being—corresponds closely to scholarly descriptions of biblical religion as primarily concerned with human history and redemption. For White such an image of the cosmos and the human place within it is untenable in an ecological age. In the Bible's unusual preoccupation with human affairs and its objectification of the world of nature lie the seeds, in White's opinion, of the anthropocentrism of Western society and of its exploitation of the physical environment.

This characterization of the biblical approach to nature is prominent also in the writings of Thomas Berry, a cultural historian who has been at the forefront of the ecological movement in the United States for many years. Biblical religion, as Berry understands it, was so strongly oriented toward a deity who transcends nature and enters into a relationship with a covenant people that it rendered the natural world "despiritualized and desacralized. . . . The very purpose of Genesis," he claims, "was to withdraw Israel from the Near Eastern orientation. Whatever the benefits of such diminishment of the divine in the natural world, it rendered the world less personal, less subject; it became something seductive, more liable to be treated as object." For Berry, biblical traditions are so absorbed with human redemption and so "radically oriented away from the natural world" that they have become "dysfunctional" and must be set aside and replaced by a new story of the universe.[36]

In a chapter entitled "The Problem of Nature in Theology"—there is the word "problem" again—that introduces his book, *Theology of Nature,* George Hendry traces the West's attitudes toward nature back to the Bible as well. After asking "why the world of nature was dropped from the agenda of theology," Hendry surveys major Western thinkers from Augustine to Kant to Barth and discovers "the concentration of theology on the theme of God and the soul, or God and man." But does not this focus, he asks, "faithfully reflect the central emphasis of the Bible?" He believes it does, quoting in his defense Gerhard von Rad's essay with which this chapter began. "In Israel's faith history is always the primary field of the action of God," writes Hendry, "and his action in nature is secondary and instrumental to it. . . . The location of the creation story at the beginning of the canonical Scriptures gives a misleading impression of Biblical faith; for this is not where Biblical faith begins. Biblical faith begins with the God of the people, not with the God who created the heavens and the earth."[37]

Such a view that the devaluation of nature in Western thought can be traced back to the Bible and its historical orientation has become standard in literature on values and the environment. Paul Santmire calls it "the critical ecological wisdom," and it has become a largely unquestioned truism in environmental circles.[38] To illustrate, we may take a *Newsweek* article on ecology and religion in which columnist Kenneth Woodward describes Genesis as "designed to desacralize nature." He proceeds from this to the more general claim that "in the religions of the West, the world of nature—from planets to plankton—has little theological significance . . . what matters is human redemption, not divine creation."[39] The echoes of Gerhard von Rad and G. Ernest Wright are unmistakable here, and they illustrate the extent to which the view of nature in the Bible that has characterized biblical scholarship is reflected—whether self-consciously and by design, or not—in the current discussion on the environmental values embedded in Western religious traditions.

Rethinking the Problem

This then is the prevailing view toward nature in the Bible that one finds in traditional scholarship, a view that rests on crucial dichotomies regarding Israel's environment and theology. It has been accepted by contemporary theologians as the starting point for Western philosophical thought about the natural world, and it has found its way, through one means or another, into much environmental literature. The validity of this view of Israelite religion depends in the first instance on how well it explains the details of the biblical text itself. That is, in fact, the central aim of this book: to submit this traditional view of Israelite religion to a reexamination based upon the textual data of one important and influential biblical author, the Yahwist. The core of this book, chapters 2, 3, and 4, are devoted to this task. But before this study of the Yahwist is undertaken, the presuppositions that lie behind this traditional view of nature in the Bible must be examined briefly in their own right.

Reexamining Presuppositions

History versus nature The conception that biblical religion was primarily concerned with human history and only secondarily with the natural world rests on several key suppositions popular in the age that gave rise to modern biblical scholarship. One of these was the supposition that nature and history were distinct and useful categories for analyzing ancient religions. Another was that human culture had evolved from religions of nature to religions of history. Both were characteristic of eighteenth- and nineteenth-century German idealism, represented most prominently by the great philosopher G. W. F. Hegel, which had a major influence on early modern biblical scholarship. Hegel's writings in particular have influenced biblical scholars, many of whom are indebted to his categories of thought and some of whom quote him directly in their defense.

As an idealist, Hegel was heir to a long tradition in Western philosophy and theology, represented by such figures as Plato in classical antiquity and

Descartes and Kant in the enlightenment. With its dualism between mind and matter, idealism had divided the world into two metaphysically distinct orders, the spiritual and the material, and had placed ultimate value on Mind and Spirit. In his own adaptation of this philosophical tradition, Hegel developed a view of the history of religion as a dialectical process passing through three stages: (1) the religion of nature, in which God or Spirit is identified directly with nature; (2) the religion of spiritual individuality, in which Spirit is distinguished from nature; and (3) absolute or revealed religion, in which the Spirit-Nature dichotomy is overcome in the incarnation of Christ.[40]

Within this scheme, the religions of the ancient Near East exemplified for Hegel the first stage of religious development, the religions of nature. Ancient Israel, for its part, played a major role in the second stage. Israelite religion, according to Hegel, divided the world sharply between the natural and the spiritual and in the process "undeified" and devalued nature while moving toward a religion of humanity and freedom. The split between spirit and nature in this second stage of religious development is expressed by Hegel in strong language:

> This Power which has potential being, Nature, is now degraded to the condition of something powerless, something dependent relative to the underived Power, or, to put it more definitely, it is made a means. Natural things are deprived of their own independent existence. Hitherto they had a direct share in Substance, while now they are in the subjective Power separated from substantiality, distinguished from it, and are regarded as only negative. . . . Nature is represented as thus entirely negated, in subjection, transitory.[41]

Within this second stage of religious development, according to Hegel, humanity stands with God over nature: "Man is exalted above all else in the whole creation. He is something which knows, perceives, thinks. He is thus the image of God in a sense quite other than that in which the same is true of the world. What is experienced in religion is God, He who is thought, and it is only in thought that God is worshipped."[42]

Key elements in Hegel's philosophy of religion—his dichotomy between Nature and Spirit, his concept of evolutionary development from a religion of nature to a religion of humanity, and his assignment of ancient Israel to a central role in both—had a distinct influence on biblical scholarship in the modern era. Julius Wellhausen, whose classic reconstruction of Israelite religion provided the starting point for twentieth-century scholarship, contrasted natural and historical religion and saw in Israel's own literature a development from a religion of nature—or something very close to it—in the older sources to a religion of history in the later Priestly Writings. In the process, according to Wellhausen, Israelite religion became "denaturalized" and finally came to represent an absolute "negation of nature."[43]

Other scholars, down into the twentieth century, in particular those wishing to emphasize the sharp break with natural religion in ancient Israel, have enlisted in their support the views of Hegel. G. Ernest Wright, for example, quotes Hegel prominently in defense of his argument that Israel broke from its ancient Near Eastern milieu with its transcendent deity, its concerns for human history, and its demotion of nature to the status of "a mere creature."[44] Mircea Eliade, to cite another important figure, goes so far as to discern "a parallel between Hegel's philosophy of history and the theology of history of the Hebrew prophets," in that both value the invisible event of history as a manifestation of the will of God over against "the viewpoint of traditional societies dominated by the eternal repetition of archetypes."[45]

The conceptual world of Hegelian idealism has thus provided the categories and language for much of the traditional biblical scholarship that has emphasized Israel's new historical consciousness and its subordination of nature. The question raised by this fact is whether the idealistic tradition in Western philosophy, especially in its Hegelian form, provides the appropriate framework for analyzing biblical thought, a conceptual system that antedated the earliest forms of idealism. Such a question can only be properly answered by a reexamination of biblical texts with this particular issue as the focus of attention. At this point it is sufficient to point out how conspicuously traditional treatments of nature in the Bible have drawn on idealistic categories regnant in the age in which they were conceived and developed.

At the same time, a word might be said here about the potential problems of using Hegelian thought to analyze the biblical conception of nature. The biblical Hebrew language possesses no terms comparable to the modern words "nature" and "history," which divide reality into two independent and unified realms. This does not necessarily mean that ancient Israel did not in some fashion reflect upon the realities represented by these terms, but it does raise the question whether Israel organized its universe by these categories. One finds in Israelite literature words for the earth and its features and for political entities and social institutions, but no words that divide these matters conceptually and absolutely into two different spheres and orders of reality as do the modern words "nature" and "history."

A brief look at the word *spirit*, a term that played a major role in Hegel's thought and that he regarded as the antithesis of nature, provides just a single illustration of the potential difficulty of applying Hegel's categories to biblical thought. "Spirit," *rûaḥ* in biblical Hebrew, does not divide between spiritual and natural, between mind and matter. *rûaḥ*, a widely used term, can be employed for the common wind, for the breath of human beings, and for the being of God. It moves so easily across the boundaries Idealists have drawn between spiritual and material that one is often at a loss to translate it in modern terms that rely so heavily on idealistic categories. In Genesis 1:2, where the *rûaḥ 'ĕlōhîm,* "Spirit of God," hovers over the waters before creation, are we to understand it as the physical wind of God, or as the spiritual presence of God, or are these categories not operative or, on the other hand, interrelated in Israelite thought?

Toward the end of his career, Gerhard von Rad, one of the greatest proponents of Israel's unique historical worldview, expressed some misgivings about the interpretation of the Hebrew Scriptures that stressed history to the exclusion of nature. While by no means abandoning his staunch historicist approach, von Rad opened his new discussion with the observation that "the greater part of what the Old Testament has to say about what we call Nature has simply never been considered. If I am right, we are nowadays in serious danger of looking at the theological problems of the Old Testament far too much from the one-sided standpoint of an historically conditioned theology."[46]

In the course of his article, von Rad recognized in rather disarming fashion the modern and anachronistic character of the concepts of "history" and "nature." Noting that the use of this vocabulary puts the issue in contemporary philosophical dress, he asserted that "the Old Testament draws no such distinction between Nature and history, regarding them as one single area of reality under the control of God." Such notions as nature and history are "merely vast ciphers, so many images projected" onto reality. Consequently, "anyone who wishes to see the world in some measure as Israel saw it must first rid his mind of both mythical and philosophical ways of thinking. It is much easier said than done!"[47]

Indeed. Yet von Rad himself considered this an unavoidable endeavor. He put before biblical scholars the following observation and ensuing challenge:

> The religion of Israel was intensely interested in the world, which it saw in direct and immediate relation to God. It was no less fascinated by the phenomenon of the world than by the phenomena of a "history" [notice now the quotation marks] wholly directed by God. Are we not then confronted at this point with an exegetical task similar to that which we have already in part performed in respect of the Old Testament theology of history?[48]

Von Rad is here asking for no less than a new study of the biblical view of nature, a study that would not only retrieve neglected texts but reexamine the philosophical assumptions that have controlled past interpretations. Coming just three years before Lynn White's essay regarding the ecological bankruptcy of biblical traditions in 1967, von Rad's remarks raised many of the same issues. Together these two essays have set a new agenda for biblical studies that has only begun to be addressed.

Some have already seriously questioned the common conception that biblical religion is uniquely preoccupied with history. Bertil Albrecktson, for example, has argued, on the basis of a comparison of biblical texts with other ancient Near Eastern documents, that Israel's association of divine activity with human history is not a unique phenomenon but one shared widely with its neighbors.[49] And James Barr has questioned the conception that history itself is as foundational to biblical revelation and religion as is often claimed.[50] Such figures as Rolf Knierim and H. H. Schmid have, in programmatic essays, more directly addressed von Rad's concern for a reconsideration of nature in biblical thought, and they have argued that it was a much larger and foundational concern than traditionally believed.[51]

What such studies have begun to expose are the inadequacies of traditional idealistic categories as a framework for describing the character of biblical religion. And by consequence they have questioned the accuracy of the picture of biblical religion constructed on the basis of these categories. It is increasingly being recognized that the obsession with history and the problem with nature in traditional scholarship may be more in the nineteenth-century idealist agenda than in the texts of the biblical authors themselves. What is now necessary are new readings of substantial biblical texts in which the old presuppositions can be systematically reexamined and a new approach to the study of nature in the Bible may be fashioned.

The desert versus the sown In order to do this properly, the presuppositions about the actual biblical environment, which have predominated in traditional biblical interpretation, must also be reexamined. These presuppositions—that biblical society originated in the desert as a pastoral and nomadic culture—are crucial because they have been so closely associated with claims for the Bible's special historical consciousness and its disregard for nature. The Bible's desert origins have frequently been believed to have placed a distinctive stamp on biblical thought and life that was never fully lost.

The traditional idea that Israel originated in the desert rests, as has been observed, on several key assumptions: that pastoral nomadism is an autonomous phenomenon to be sharply differentiated from sedentary agriculture, and that it represents an earlier stage of cultural development than farming. Both of these assumptions, in fact, are characteristic of anthropological theories regnant in the nineteenth and early twentieth centuries, when the now standard reconstruction of early Israelite history was developed by biblical scholars. Based upon analogies with later more developed and independent forms of pastoralism reliant upon riding animals, such as camels and horses, pastoralism in antiquity was considered by early anthropologists as an autarkic enterprise. Furthermore, it was believed to be a primitive stage of cultural development. According to the tripartite theory of social development widespread in early anthropological study, human culture evolved naturally in unilinear fashion through three stages: from hunting and gathering to herding to cultivation.[52] Such a view of cultural evolution is old and widespread, going back at least to Aristotle's pupil Dicaearchus, who held that humans had evolved from shepherds to farmers.[53]

On the basis of new archaeological, zoological, and botanical evidence accumulated since the 1950s, combined with new comparative anthropological data, this traditional conception of pastoralism in antiquity has been seriously questioned and new hypotheses proposed in its stead.[54] It now appears unlikely, for example, that at the time of Israel's origins pastoralism was the autonomous, economically self-sufficient, culturally distinct phenomenon presumed by early anthropologists and by biblical scholars who proposed the older reconstructions of Israel's beginnings. Pure pastoral nomadism emerged only later in the Levant with the domestication of riding animals in the late second and early first millenia B.C.E., the period when Israel had already become a landed political entity.[55]

Sheep and goat pastoralism in antiquity was always closely integrated

with sedentary agriculture in some way. In fact, it is better to think of ancient societies existing on a continuum from intensive cultivation to intensive pastoral activity than to imagine them as pure forms of one or the other.
In his summation of the various treatments of this topic collected in *Pastoralism in the Levant,* Richard Meadow observes that "the dichotomy drawn
between the desert and the sown is an oversimplification. While these categories may be enshrined in the literature of the region, focus on normative
values tends to obscure how relationships were actually played out on the
ground."[56]

Groups specializing in pastoralism certainly could exist, but they were
never isolated from agriculture. Within these groups, a limited cultivation
of grains is normally practiced, but in a more secondary role than in typical
agrarian settings. Furthermore, because of the specialized character of their
economy, such pastoralists are actually more, rather than less, dependent on
the world of sedentary agriculture for their survival. Their own need for car-
bohydrates and agricultural products, for pastures for their herds in arable
zones during the dry season, and for markets for their animals and animal
products demands a close symbiotic relationship to their agricultural neighbors. "The more specialized pastoral nomadism becomes," according to
Emmanuel Marx, "the more it is integrated into the social fabric of a complex urban civilization."[57] Because of this symbiotic relationship, and without the riding animals necessary to cover the vast distances of the desert,
specialized sheep and goat pastoralists regularly inhabit the semiarid zones
contiguous with arable land as well as the pasture lands unsuited for cultivation within the arable zones themselves. They are not pure nomads but possess a sedentary base from which herds are moved in rather confined and
regular patterns to exploit seasonal pasturage. This type of specialized pastoralism is therefore commonly referred to as seminomadic or transhumant
pastoralism.[58]

Such pastoralists have always been a minority in ancient Near Eastern
society. By far the more typical form of pastoralism in the Levant is one sub-
sumed in a multipurpose household as a subsidiary part of a mixed economy
based on the cultivation of grains and fruits. In this form, animal husbandry
is part of a sedentary village society and is closely integrated with cultivation
as one component of a single subsistence agrarian economy. Raising animals
in this context enriches the agricultural economy with animal products—
milk, meat, wool, leather—and hedges the risks of subsistence farming
through diversification.[59]

The implication of these newer reconstructions of pastoralism in antiquity is that an accurate description of any ancient Mediterranean society,
including that of early Israel, cannot be made by categorizing it in terms of
the traditional dichotomy between agriculture and pastoralism. A valid description must instead rest on a nuanced assessment of the forms, the balance, and the ratio of one to the other in a particular society, place, and time.
The traditional view of Israel's origins as an autonomous pastoral society of
nomads at home in the desert is ruled out by the realities of ancient Mediter-

ranean economics. The realistic question that emerges from the new data is the following: in what proportion did early Israel combine herding and cultivation in its economy? Or, for our purposes in this study, exactly where on the pastoral-agricultural continuum are Israel's ancestors to be placed?

Just as the independence of pastoralism in the ancient Near East has been questioned by new archaeological and anthropological data, so has the traditional notion that pastoralism antedates agriculture. In the actual history of the evolution of human culture in the ancient Near East from food-extracting societies—hunters and gatherers—to food-producing societies—herders and farmers—the domestication and cultivation of plants predates by several millennia the domestication and herding of animals. When it did emerge, pastoralism did not develop out of hunting, as early anthropologists thought, but came into being as a secondary offshoot of sedentary cultivation, which itself appears to have provided the indispensable conditions for the domestication of animals to take place at all.[60]

Changing economic, political, demographic, and environmental conditions may of course press any particular society from a more intensive pastoral economy to a more intensive agricultural one. But the reverse may also be true.[61] Such a process of change is more complex and subtle than imagined by those who thought of human, and Israelite, evolution as a unilinear development from herding to farming. There appears now to be no evidential basis for the traditional view that nomadic pastoralism represents an early stage of cultural development out of which sedentary agriculture naturally and expectedly emerges, as was once assumed by proponents of Israel's nomadic origins.

A critique of Israel's origins in desert pastoralism in much this same vein has been pursued already for some years by a school of scholars, in particular George Mendenhall and Norman Gottwald, who regard Israel's beginning as a peasant revolt by indigenous peoples rather than as the infiltration of desert pastoralists.[62] Mendenhall began his critique of the older peaceful immigration and military conquest theories of Israel's settlement of the hill country by a reexamination of the assumption that Israel's ancestors were originally pastoralist nomads. He claimed that the "sharp contrast" between nomadic pastoralists and sedentary villages assumed by biblical scholars did not conform to observations of the actual practice of pastoralism in the Middle East; that the modern Bedouin in any case, dependent as they are on the camel, are not a good analogy for reconstructing Israel's origins; that such cultural traits as tribalism were not necessarily reflections of nomadism; and that the biblical text itself presented Israel's ancestors, both before and after the flood, as villagers and farmers whose pastoralism was pursued in this context.[63]

Gottwald has carried this critique much further by a more thorough analysis of pastoralism in antiquity and by a more detailed reappraisal of biblical texts in this light. "To employ pastoral nomadism as an explanatory model for early Israel," writes Gottwald, "is to go wrong from the start."[64] For both scholars, the critique of pastoral nomadism is part of the larger sociological and ideological agenda that aims to defend a view of the birth of

Israel as a revolt against oppressive political structures. Whether or not this theory of Israel's origins can be sustained over the long run, the critique of traditional conceptions of pastoral nomadism that it incorporates has done much to undermine outdated notions of ancient environments and econo- mies.[65] The traditional view of Israel's origins in the desert as nomadic pastoralists, based on views of pastoralism widely accepted in the eighteenth, nineteenth, and early twentieth centuries, when modern historical study of the Bible came into its own, have now by and large been abandoned by archae- ologists and anthropologists as inadequate or inaccurate.

Thus the two presuppositions that have led to the view of nature as a problem in the Bible—Israel's desert origins and its unique historical con- sciousness—are both problematic in and of themselves. They reflect ways of looking at the environment and religion that were popular in the eighteenth and nineteenth centuries when modern biblical scholarship originated but that, when reexamined, have serious if not fatal flaws as models for describ- ing ancient societies. It is obvious that an adequate picture of biblical reli- gion can only be reconstructed with linguistic and conceptual tools more amenable to the actual economies and ideologies of biblical antiquity. The most recent archeological and anthropological data and reconstructions of ancient environments must replace outmoded nineteenth-century notions of the desert versus the sown as the backdrop for analyzing the biblical envi- ronment. And a new language must be found to move beyond the dualism present in the idealistic division between spirit and matter, history and nature, for analyzing the biblical view of nature.

Rereading Biblical Texts

This can only be accomplished, of course, within the context of a reexami- nation of the biblical texts themselves. Many new investigations by biblical scholars into the place of nature in biblical literature have in fact already appeared. Primarily responses to the criticism of the Bible by environmen- talists, these new studies have created a new genre of biblical interpretation on nature themes in biblical texts. Too numerous to mention, these studies have made an admirable start at reviving dormant texts and themes, provid- ing fresh readings of familiar material, and calling into question old ap- proaches and habits of interpretation.[66]

The study of the Yahwist's epic in this volume builds upon and extends these studies in several ways. In the first place, its scope is new: it represents the systematic analysis of the thought of a single, but substantial, biblical au- thor. Most past studies have been much more specific or much more gen- eral. On the one hand, essays on nature in the Bible have focused on such crucial, but very short, texts as the command to exercise dominion in Gen- esis 1:26–28, undoubtedly the most widely discussed verses in recent writ- ing on nature in the Bible. While essential, these studies are necessarily lim- ited by their narrow scope, which excludes from detailed analysis the larger textual and ideological context of the verses in question. The almost exclusive preoccupation with the creation accounts in discussions of nature in the Bible, as if the creation of the natural world in Genesis 1–2 exhausts its significance for biblical thought, represents the same kind of circumscribed focus.

On the other hand, essays on nature in the Bible have been expansive and far-reaching, covering the biblical view of nature as a whole within the boundaries of a single article. Such studies have the merit of striving for a broad synthesis, but they are limited in several respects in what can be accomplished. Little detailed exegesis of texts is possible in such a format. And a level of generality is required that cannot do proper justice to the differences in perspective among the Bible's authors or to the nuances within a single writer.

The kind of analysis needed to carry the discussion of nature in the Bible beyond the results of current work is the study of individual biblical authors in a comprehensive and systematic fashion. Such a study is narrow enough in scope to allow for a detailed analysis of texts and encourage attention to the distinctive perspectives of a particular writer, thereby avoiding the homogenizing of biblical views. At the same time, this kind of study is broad enough in scope to allow for the examination of a pattern of thought encompassing various dimensions of the human-nature relationship. While such a study is still far from a complete and systematic treatment of the entire range of biblical thought on the topic of nature, it is the necessary next step that must be taken on the way to such a goal.

Another respect in which this volume extends current discussions is its special attention to the presuppositions that have underlain modern scholarly work on nature in the Bible and its concern to submit these presuppositions to a new, critical review within the process of biblical interpretation. Defenses of the Bible in response to the criticisms in recent ecological literature are more frequently aimed at precise points of interpretation than they are at major, foundational assumptions. In fact, an irony is present in much recent biblical scholarship designed to defend and rehabilitate the place of nature in the Bible in that it rests on the same presuppositions about nature and history that have led to the "problemizing" of nature in biblical thought. In order to break new ground, these old presuppositions must be more carefully uncovered and more seriously reexamined in the process of rereading biblical texts.

The Yahwist as a source for study For this study of nature in biblical religion, the writer whose work provides the primary source is the Yahwist. The selection of the Yahwist deserves an explanation, both for the general audience, which may not be familiar with this author, and for the scholarly audience, for whom the Yahwist's existence is no longer the foregone conclusion it once was.

After Julius Wellhausen's influential synthesis at the end of the nineteenth century, in which he described the authorship and development of the literature in the first five books of the Hebrew Scriptures, a broad scholarly consen-

sus developed around the view that these books are composite in character.[67]
Traditionally attributed to a single author, Moses, these books came to be regarded, according to the hypothesis that Wellhausen put into classic form, as
in actuality a combination of four continuous sources or documents authored
by four different writers living at different times in Israelite history. The oldest
narratives, dated variously within the monarchic period (tenth–eighth centuries B.C.E.), were attributed to the Yahwist, so named because this author prefers to use the divine name "Yahweh" (*Jahweh* in German—hence the accepted
abbreviation of the Yahwist as *J* instead of *Y*), and to the Elohist, so called because this author prefers the more general "God" (*ĕlōhîm* in Hebrew—hence
the abbreviation *E*). These old narratives, according to this "documentary
hypothesis," were later incorporated into a new edition of Israel's beginnings
prepared by Priestly Writer(s)/Editor(s) (abbreviated *P*). The Priestly Writer
gave a new focus to the older narratives, primarily by making Mt. Sinai the
focus of the narrative and adding at this place in the narrative a massive body
of ritual and social regulations that now accounts for the end of Exodus, all of
Leviticus, and the beginning of Numbers. It was recognized early that the book
of Deuteronomy was a separate source (abbreviated *D*), which has widely come
to be recognized as the introduction to the history of Israel that follows in
Joshua, Judges, Samuel, and Kings.

Of these four authors, the Yahwist, or *J*, has been identified as the figure
responsible for the oldest stories in the first five books of the Hebrew Scriptures, also known as the Pentateuch ("five books") or Torah ("law"). These
include most of the stories of the creation and the preflood eras at the beginning of Genesis, and most of the narratives of Israel's ancestors, Abraham,
Isaac, and Jacob, which make up the remainder of the book. Also attributed
to the Yahwist are the majority of the accounts of Israel's escape from Egypt
and wandering in the wilderness in the books of Exodus and Numbers. A
precise division of the Pentateuch into its constituent sources, highlighting
those texts that make up the Yahwist's work in particular, may be found in
an appendix at the end of this book.

The kind of redaction or compilation of traditions proposed in the documentary hypothesis is not unique to the first five books of the Bible but has
been recognized in one form or another in almost every corpus in the Hebrew
Bible and in the Christian Scriptures of the New Testament. The book of
Isaiah, for example, is believed to contain speeches from three different prophetic figures living in different periods of Israelite history: the Judean monarchy, the Babylonian exile, and the period of Persian repatriation. The recognition and treatment of such distinct sections of a larger literary corpus,
together with their respective historical and social contexts, have traditionally been considered essential for a proper understanding of the corpus's aims
and content.

The study of the Yahwist, and of the composition and completion of the
Pentateuch in general, has entered a new stage in the final decades of the twen-
tieth century, a stage full of much more ferment than in the preceding years.
On the one hand, there is a new interest in the documentary hypothesis and

in the Yahwist in particular. For years, the only book-length study of the Yahwist in English was Peter Ellis's, *The Yahwist: The Bible's First Theologian*.[68] In the last five years, three new studies of the Yahwist have appeared: Robert Coote and David Ord's *The Bible's First History*; John Van Seters's *Prologue to History: The Yahwist as Historian in Genesis* and *The Life of Moses: The Yahwist as Historian in Exodus-Numbers*; and the literary critic Harold Bloom's *The Book of J*, which has popularized the Yahwist beyond the world of academic biblical scholarship.[69] And this list does not include a number of new studies in other languages.[70]

This new interest in the Yahwist and in the traditional source analysis of the Pentateuch coincides with a new attack on the entire documentary hypothesis itself. These new critics object to its fragmentation of the Pentateuchal narrative, arguing for a more unitary approach, or they recognize its composite character but deny the existence of the traditional continuous sources, putting forward instead new proposals for the Pentateuch's constituent parts and new models for understanding its compilation.[71]

The dust from this new debate is not likely to settle soon, and in the interim some position must be assumed as a starting point for the study of Pentateuchal traditions. For the analysis in this book, that starting point is the narrative material that predates the Priestly contributions to the Pentateuch, in particular that strand within this pre-P material traditionally ascribed to the Yahwist. By the attribution of this narrative to an individual, the Yahwist, and by the use of terms like "author" and "writer" for this individual in the analysis that follows, I do not wish to imply that these narratives were created de novo by a single creative author. It is more likely that these narratives have behind them a long history of tradition and transmission, for which the designation, the Yahwist's narrative, refers to the last stage, edition, or version of this process of the handing down and recitation of Israelite traditions.

I do wish to make the case in the study that follows, however, that the non-P narratives traditionally assigned to J have a unified and cohesive orientation to the natural world. It is this unified textual perspective that I have in mind when speaking of the Yahwist, (or referring to the Yahwist as an author or writer), rather than a specific theory of the compilation or authorship of this material. I also wish to make the case that the perspective on the natural world contained in texts presumed to be Yahwistic contrasts sharply at points with that represented in Priestly texts. So, while this is not a study of the literary formation of the Pentateuch, it does provide data that can be taken into consideration for this debate as well.

The Yahwist is a particularly attractive choice among biblical writers for a reexamination of nature in biblical thought. In the first place the Yahwist's work is a narrative about origins, the origins of the world and human society as J knew it. Stories of origins such as this are customarily foundational narratives, explaining and legitimating the basic realities and values of the author's own world. Furthermore, J's account is the earliest of the Pentateuchal sources and, if dated early in the monarchy as has customarily been the case, would represent the Bible's oldest sustained reflection on God, the world, and the human place within it.[72] As such, it sets the basic parameters of the way the world was to be understood in biblical society.

By reason of its age and its prominent and defining position in the Bible, the Yahwist's work has been touted as among the most important sources of the Western intellectual tradition. With an obvious exuberance, Harold Bloom calls the Yahwist's narrative "a work that has formed the spiritual consciousness of much of the world ever since."[73] Peter Ellis called it the world's "first major theological opus" and judged the Yahwist, as the author of Israel's national epic, "more than comparable to Homer."[74] Such accolades may be somewhat extravagant, but they point to the formative and influential position the Yahwist's narratives hold in the Bible and in Western religious tradition. Some of the most familiar images of the world and of humanity in Western culture derive from these stories attributed to J. No reexamination of nature in the Bible would be complete without serious consideration of this formative body of literature.

Past readings of the Yahwist's view of nature Before embarking on this rereading of the Yahwist, a few illustrations may be provided of the way in which the old presuppositions about nature and history and about the desert and the sown have affected past scholarship on the Yahwist's work itself. Here, as in biblical interpretation more broadly, these problematic dichotomies have played an important role.

The conception of Israel as an autonomous nomadic desert culture that evolved into a sedentary agricultural society has led many scholars to see these two distinct viewpoints in J and consequently to divide J itself into two sources, one reflecting the older nomadic pastoral background and the other a later sedentary agricultural setting. Otto Eissfeld, for example, building on a tradition going back to Rudolf Smend's work, separated out from J an older stratum because he thought it preserved Israel's original nomadic setting. Eissfeld thus found in the traditional J two sources: a nomadic source he named the Lay (L) source because of its perceived primitive and secular character, and an agricultural source, J proper. Eissfeld's assumptions about the dichotomy between the desert and the sown and about the natural evolution from desert pastoralism to sedentary agriculture are clear in his discussion of the relationship between his L source and J. "It appears that the L strand in the primeval history pictured men as nomads," writes Eissfeld, "whereas J and P clearly think of them as husbandmen. . . . It is quite clear that in Israel, which became an agricultural people from being a nomadic people, an outline of their history which places nomads at the beginning must be older than one which pictures the first men as husbandmen. . . . L is no doubt giving expression in this to his enthusiasm for the nomadic ideal."[75]

George Fohrer was also convinced that the desert and the sown could be isolated as distinct perspectives within the Yahwist's work, and he too singled out a series of texts that he believed represented a nomadic perspective. He called this source N, the Nomadic Source Stratum. In contrast to

Eissfeld, however, he connected this nomadic source with a later revival of the older nomadic ideal that arose as a reaction to sedentary agricultural society, with its questionable Canaanite character. "The whole presentation," he claimed, "can best be understood as a reaction and reply on the part of conservative nomadic circles to J's enthusiasm for settled civilization. . . . The author of this source stratum comes from the mileau of a cattle-raising society faithful to Yahweh, which opposed or rejected Canaanite civilization and the Palestinian civilization of Israel with its Canaanite traits."[76] While not all have been convinced by such a bifurcation of the Yahwist's work, some form of it is not uncommon in detailed exegetical treatments of J's narratives. Rudolf Smend's isolation of nomadic and agricultural sources behind J's story of the Garden of Eden, for example, has appealed to many later exegetes, such as Claus Westermann, who appropriates it in his exhaustive commentary on Genesis.[77]

The way in which this dichotomy between the desert and the sown has played into the related dichotomy between history and nature may be illustrated from Peter Ellis's study of the Yahwist. While not dividing J into constituent nomadic and agricultural sources, as had Eissfeld, Fohrer, and others, Ellis saw in J an admiration for the nomadic existence of early Israel, symbolized for example in the shepherd Abel, and a hostility toward sedentary Canaanite society, symbolized for example in the farmer Cain. Connected with these two settings, according to Ellis, were two kinds of religion, the religion of Yahweh, in which the deity was interested in humans and entered into covenants with them, and the religion of Baal, in which a nature deity was worshipped through fertility rituals. In this contrast between the historical religion of Israel and the nature religion of Canaan could be perceived, according to Ellis, "the broad, theological outline of the saga as a whole: namely, the rise of chosen, covenanted Israel and the covenanted Davidic dynasty and their conquest of the forces of anti-God in the world, represented by the fertility religion of the Canaanites in the time of the Yahwist."[78]

Just how normative—and how arbitrary in its actual application—this nature–history dichotomy has been in analysis of the Yahwist may be illustrated further by describing the use made of it by Julius Wellhausen at the end of the nineteenth century. For Wellhausen, in contrast to Ellis's later views, J was rather solidly on the nature side of this division. According to his reconstruction of Israelite religion from Pentateuchal traditions, Israel's religion evolved from a natural to a historical one. In its earliest stage, represented by the Yahwist's work, Israelite religion was based in agriculture, that is in nature and its seasonal cycles. In the next stage of religious development, reflected in Deuteronomy (D), a new historical consciousness arose and was combined with the older agricultural orientation of J. Later, in the final stage of Israelite religion, found in the Priestly (P) stratum, the connection with nature was severed and life and religion became exclusively bound up with history. Thus J was regarded as a witness to a primitive stage of Israelite religion in which nature played a major and formative role.[79]

One can see in these illustrations both the longevity and the influence of the traditional presuppositions about the desert and the sown and about nature and history in the interpretation of the Yahwist's work itself. Other examples could be mentioned here, but they will be reserved for discussion when the specific texts they bear upon are brought up for analysis in the chapters that follow.

Rereading the Yahwist This study then represents an attempt to take a new look at the Yahwist's view of nature. It is new in approach because it does not take the traditional, anachronistic, and clearly problematic presuppositions about the desert and the sown and about nature and history as its starting point. In place of the old anthropological models of desert shepherds and sedentary farmers, more recent archaeological and anthropological data on the environments and economies of the ancient Near East will be employed as a context for interpretation. Furthermore, the Yahwist's thought will be discussed in language that does not presuppose the post-biblical, idealistic categories of matter and spirit, of nature and history that have played such a dominant role in reconstructions of biblical religion.

This study is new in another sense as well, because it makes nature its central focus. Interpreters have invariably commented upon this aspect of J's narratives. They could hardly avoid it because the natural environment is such a prominent part of J's stories. But they have done so only in passing and as a secondary concern. Their comments about it are usually brief, disconnected, and unexamined. They have not considered the natural world crucial, nor have they tried to describe its role in the Yahwist's narratives and ideology in a systematic and synthetic fashion. This is a direct consequence, of course, of the widespread view that the world of nature is a peripheral concern in a religion absorbed with human redemption.

The following study of the Yahwist's work has been divided into three sections according to the major parts of the overall narrative itself. The first section, in chapter 2, deals with the Primeval Age, the period from the creation of the world to the great flood, which brought about a new beginning for the world and its human civilization. While this is the shortest of the major parts of J's work, it will, for several reasons, be given the most attention. In the first place, its well-known stories—Adam and Eve in the Garden of Eden, Cain's murder of Abel, and Noah's Ark and the Great Flood—have captured the imagination of later generations in a way that other parts of the narrative have not and have thus played a much larger role in subsequent thought than their brief scope might suggest. Second, these stories, while brief, describe the very beginnings of the world and humanity and are therefore especially foundational for later reality. They provide a unique window into the Yahwist's own conceptions about the very essence of things. Third, because they come at the beginning of the Yahwist's work, these stories introduce the reader to certain basic facts and points of view present throughout the work that deserve, at the outset, some fuller introductory comments.

The second section of this study, in chapter 3, deals with the Ancestral Age, the period from the great flood to the settlement of Israel's ancestors in

Egypt. This part of the Yahwist's work, describing Israel's ancestors as residents of the Canaanite hill country that was to become the heartland of biblical Israel, is both the longest and the most significant part of the epic. It centers J's narrative geographically and ideologically. The third section of this study, in chapter 4, treats the Mosaic Age, the period during which Israel's ancestors are to be found in the south, first in Egypt and then in the Sinai desert. This is an age of exile.

In the analysis of each of these parts of the Yahwist's work, two issues, directly related to the two kinds of presuppositions that have controlled biblical interpretation, will be of primary concern. First, the environment presupposed by the narrative will be investigated. If the dichotomy between nomadic pastoralism in the desert and sedentary agriculture in arable zones is a misleading model for understanding ancient environments and ways of life, what alternative setting might better describe that assumed by the Yahwist's narratives? Based on a more realistic assessment of ancient environments and on the details of the stories themselves, how might one reconstruct the Yahwist's actual landscape?

Each chapter will also investigate the Yahwist's attitudes toward that landscape. In this regard, J's view of the relationship between human culture and the world of nature will come under special scrutiny. If the dichotomy between nature and history is more at home in the Idealist tradition and its particular Hegelian expression in the last two centuries than in ancient thought, what alternative mode of thought might better describe the Yahwist's point of view? Without starting from the modern dualisms that separate matter from spirit and nature from history, how might one describe the Yahwist's ideology?

The relationship between the two, the Yahwist's landscape and the Yahwist's ideology, is absolutely crucial for understanding the Yahwist's work. It is impossible to understand properly the Yahwist's attitudes toward nature without a clear conception of the precise kind of environment that contributed to their formation and in terms of which these attitudes were developed and expressed. At the same time one must be careful not to collapse the two as if the Yahwist's ideology is to be explained alone from its environment. The fallacy of such an environmental determinism can be illustrated very simply by a comparison, as is occasionally made in chapter 2, between the thought of J and P, both inhabitants of the same environment. Such comparisons reveal the great influence exercised by social factors and particular agendas in the attitudes toward nature that are expressed in their respective works.

In the final chapter of the book, chapter 5, the results of this reexamination of the Yahwist's work will be summarized. In addition, the implication of these results will be explored, on the one hand for the historical reconstruction of biblical religion and on the other for contemporary theology.

2

The Primeval Age

The Yahwist's epic begins with three of the most familiar stories in Western literature: Adam and Eve in the Garden of Eden; Cain's murder of his brother Abel; and Noah's ark, in which Noah's family and all species of animals survived the great flood. These stories are actually the primary episodes in a more detailed account of the first era of world history, a primeval age cut off from subsequent history by a catastrophic flood. This primeval age is above all an age of origins, in which the basic features of the world of nature and of human society come into existence.

Of all biblical texts, the primeval narrative has been the primary source for reflection on the biblical understanding of nature. This is as true in traditional historical scholarship as in recent treatments of biblical perspectives on nature in light of the environmental crises. The main reason for this special attention to the primeval age is its focus on the origins of the natural world. Stories of origins such as these are not just descriptions of events in the distant past but etiologies, that is, explanations of why things are as they are in the present. They are first and foremost founding stories. In the act of coming into being, the character of the world, its inhabitants, and their relation to one another is revealed and established for all time. The realities of the author's world are in such accounts of origins both explained and validated as part of a design built into the world from its very beginnings. Origin stories thereby possess, to use the words of Paul Ricoeur, a "foundational function."[1] In them, the author's basic beliefs about the world become transparent. Because of its foundational character, the primeval narrative will be given more detailed attention in this study of the Yahwist's view of nature than its modest length in the Yahwist's epic overall might otherwise suggest.

A second, less substantive, but nevertheless important reason that the primeval narrative has played such an important role in discussions about nature in biblical thought has been its prominent place at the beginning of the Bible. This narrative is by no means the only Israelite account of creation. Other texts, in particular many of the psalms, offer additional versions, some similar to those in Genesis, some quite different.[2] Yet because of the simple fact that it occurs first in the biblical story, the creation of the world described in the primeval narrative in Genesis has always had the greatest impact on both scholarly and popular discussions about nature in the Bible.

In these discussions of creation and nature in Genesis, most time and energy has been devoted not to the Yahwist's narrative but to the first account of creation in Genesis 1:1–2:4a, attributed to a later Priestly Writer (P) who prefixed it to the older Yahwistic epic. This simple editorial act, by which the Priestly Writer placed his creation account first, has had far-reaching consequences. Readers interested in the biblical view of creation have either stopped at the end of P's account, or they have read the following material through the lens of P's version. In either case, P's view of nature and the human place in it has become the standard for understanding biblical thought. No text has been quoted more frequently or discussed more avidly in recent debates on biblical religion and ecology than the Priestly account of the creation of the human race:

> God created humanity in his image; in the image of
> God he created it; male and female he created them.
> And God blessed them and God said to them, "Be
> fruitful and multiply and fill the earth and subdue it;
> rule over the fish of the sea and the birds of the sky
> and all of the animals created on the earth." (Gen
>   1:27–28)[3]

This nearly exclusive interest in the Priestly viewpoint has persisted in spite of the fact that the Priestly Writer's account is immediately followed by the Eden narrative, the opening episode of the Yahwist's epic, which represents an independent account of creation and reflects a view of the human role in nature remarkably different from that of the Priestly Writer. The Yahwist's narrative actually provides the bulk of the information about the primeval age as it is presented in the Bible. To J's cohesive account of the first age of human history, from Adam to Noah, the later Priestly Writer has added nothing new, only alternative accounts of creation (Gen 1:1–2:4a), Adam's genealogy (Gen 5:1–32), and the flood (sections of Gen 6:9–9:17). Yet the Priestly Writer's perspective on nature has dominated ancient and modern treatments of biblical thought. One of the aims of the following analysis is to rescue from relative obscurity the foundational and distinctive perspectives on nature reflected in the Yahwist's epic.[4]

The Environment of the Primeval Age:
Israelite Highland Agriculture

> *Ours is not a maritime country; neither commerce nor the*
> *intercourse which it promotes with the outside world has*
> *any attraction for us. Our cities are built inland, remote from the*
> *sea; and we devote ourselves to the cultivation of the productive*
> *country with which we are blessed.*
>
> Josephus, Apion

> *Every man takes the limits of his own field of vision for the limits*
> *of the world.*
>
> Arthur Schopenhauer,
Studies in Pessimism:
Psychological Observations

The Yahwist's account of the primeval age begins in the Garden in Eden (Gen 2:4b–3:24), the first environment the Yahwist brings to life. A lush, irrigated orchard, Eden is the setting in which plants, animals, and humans come into being. Yet this garden is a temporary location, neither the real home of the primeval heroes nor the actual world in which the Yahwist's epic is to unfold. That world lies outside the garden. And this world outside the garden provides the perspective from which the story of the Garden of Eden is told. It is to the details within the Eden story that reveal the outside perspective from which it is narrated that we turn before taking up the ecology of the garden itself.

Adam and Eve

The setting outside of the garden from which the garden is described is reflected both in the introduction (Gen 2:4b–7) and in the conclusion (3:23–24) to the story, which together provide a literary framework for the Eden narrative as a whole. This post-Eden world is also reflected in the series of divine decrees about life outside the garden, toward which the narrative momentum of the story builds (3:14–19). Of these, the final decree in which the land is cursed (3:17–19) provides the most information about the narrator's perspective outside the garden. In these key texts, from the framework and the climax of the Eden narrative, the first details of the Yahwist's principal primeval landscape emerge.

[4b] When Yahweh, God, made earth (*'ereṣ*) and sky—
[5] Before any pasturage (*śîaḥ haśśādeh*) was on the earth (*'ereṣ*),
And before any field crops (*'ēśeb haśśādeh*) had sprung up,

Since Yahweh, God, had not sent rain upon the earth (*'ereṣ*)
And there was no man (*'ādām*) to cultivate (*'ābōd*) the arable land (*'ădāmā*),
⁶ Though a spring rose from the earth (*'ereṣ*)
And watered the surface of the arable land (*'ădāmā*)—
⁷ Yahweh, God, formed the man (*'ādām*)
Out of soil (*'āpār*) from the arable land (*'ădāmā*),
And blew into his nostrils the breath of life,
And the man (*'ādām*) became a living being.
⁸ Yahweh, God, planted a garden . . . (Gen 2:4b–7).⁵

¹⁷ To the man (*'ādām*) he said, "Since you listened to your wife
and ate from the tree of which I commanded,
"Do not eat from it,"
cursed is the arable land (*'ădāmā*) on account of you;
(Only) through painful labor will you eat from it
All the days of your life.
¹⁸ Thorns and thistles will spring up for you,
and you will eat field crops (*'ēseb haśśādeh*).
¹⁹ By the sweat of your nostrils
you will eat bread
Until you return to the arable land (*'ădāmā*)
Since you were taken from it.
For you are soil (*'āpār*)
And to soil (*'āpār*) you will return. (Gen 3:17–19)

²³Yahweh sent him out of the Garden of Eden to cultivate (*'ābōd*) the arable land
(*'ădāmā*) from which he was taken.²⁴ He drove out the man (*'ādām*), and he
stationed, to the east at the Garden of Eden,⁶ the cherubim and the flaming sword
brandished to guard the way to the tree of life. (Gen 3:23–24)

The expulsion from the garden (3:23–24) and the divine decrees that
precede it (3:14–19) obviously picture life outside of Eden and have been
interpreted in this way, but the story's opening sentence (2:4b–7) has not
usually been placed into this same context. More often, it has been read as
an attempt to describe the character of the void—the nothingness, barrenness, or chaos—which preceded creation.⁷ It has sometimes even been understood as a brief remnant of a more elaborate account of creation, which once
introduced the Yahwist's epic but was later suppressed by the Priestly Writer
who substituted his own account (1:1–2:4a).⁸

Neither of these traditional interpretations explains properly the content and function of the Yahwist's first sentence. The repetition of the preposition "before" (*ṭerem*) in the opening subordinate clauses (2:5) certainly
places the listener at a time before the known world existed. Yet this is
accomplished not by describing the contours of primordial chaos but by
listing the most common and basic features of the audience's world—
pasturage, field crops, rain, cultivation—which had not yet come into being.
Precreation is thus defined by negating a list of ordinary realities. The details of this list provide no real information about the time before creation.
Rather, they outline the most basic features of the world of the storyteller.

Such a procedure is not unique to the Yahwist but is in fact a traditional ancient Near Eastern technique for introducing origin narratives. The great Mesopotamian creation epic, Enuma Elish, begins in just this fashion, listing, in a series of introductory subordinate clauses like those of the Yahwist, common aspects of the Mesopotamian culture and environment that had not yet come into being.

> When on high the heaven had not been named,
> Firm ground below had not been called by name . . .
> No reed hut had been matted, no marsh land had appeared,
> When no gods whatever had been brought into being,
> Uncalled by name, their destinies undetermined—
> Then it was that the gods were formed.[9]

The Yahwist is thus following a traditional pattern for the introduction of a narrative of origins, and there is no reason to suppose a more detailed account of divine creation or conflict ever preceded this conventional opening of the Yahwist's epic.[10]

The Eden narrative's introductory sentence thus pictures neither the garden's ecology nor the void preceding it. Its details instead provide data about the familiar world of the storyteller and the audience outside of Eden. Taken together with the divine decrees mandating the conditions for life after Eden and with the conclusion to the story describing the expulsion from the garden, these details provide the first concrete facts about the Yahwist's own landscape as it comes into existence in the primeval age.

The central feature of the Yahwist's landscape in each of these three sections of the Eden narrative is *'ădāmâ*, arable land. In the story's opening sentence, J draws the reader's attention in from the whole earth (*'ereṣ*) to focus it especially on *'ădāmâ*. *'ădāmâ* is the realm of human labor and its object (2:5), the site of irrigating water (2:6), and the material from which human and animal life are made (2:7; cf. v 19). In the divine decrees to govern life outside Eden, *'ădāmâ* is identified as the land which humans will farm to survive (3:17–19). Finally, when the first couple is expelled from the garden, it is to the *'ădāmâ* they are sent (3:23).

Traditionally translated by a general term, such as "ground" (KJV, NRSV, NEB), *'ădāmâ* is employed by the Yahwist with a more precise sense. It is J's technical term for arable land, fertile soil that can be cultivated. Whenever the human work of cultivation is mentioned in these three parts of the garden narrative, the object of cultivation is *'ădāmâ* (2:5; 3:17–19, 23). Furthermore, *'ădāmâ* is identified as the site of irrigating waters (2:6). By contrast, the word *'ereṣ* is used with a more general sense. In the story's opening phrase, where it is paired with sky (*šāmayim*, 2:4b), *'ereṣ* refers to the entire earth. In succeeding phrases it is a general designation for all regions where rainfall and vegetation are present (2:5).

This pattern of usage is typical of the Yahwist's style throughout the epic, where *'ădāmâ* is consistently used as a special term for cultivable land. Some of the clearest examples are in the stories of Cain and Abel (Gen 4:2, 3, 10,

11, 12, 14), Noah (5:29, 8:21, 9:20), Sodom and Gomorrah (19:25), Joseph's purchase of Egyptian farmland (47:18, 19, 20, 22, 23, 26), and in the Yahwist's decalogue (Exod 34:26).[11] On the other hand, *'ereṣ* is employed by J for other purposes. It is used to designate: (1) the earth as a whole (e.g., Gen 7:3, 11:1, 24:3; Exod 9:14, 34:10; Num 14:21); (2) a territory or country, as in "the land of Egypt," "the land of Canaan" (e.g., Gen 10:10, 42:5; Exod 4:20; Num 21:31), or the land promised to Israel's ancestors (Gen 12:1; Exod 34:24; Num 14:23); and (3) the ground in a general sense, in such expressions as "he bowed down to the ground" (e.g., Gen 18:2; Exod 4:3; Num 11:31).[12] In the story of Cain and Abel, *'ereṣ* is even used in conscious contrast to *'ădāmâ* in order to identify the nonarable regions to which Cain is banished (Gen 4:12, 14).

This *'ădāmâ* or cultivable soil, is presented by the Yahwist as the setting for human society. The relationship between them, between human life and arable land, is described in two ways. In the first place, the first human, *'ādām*, is described as the cultivator of *'ădāmâ*. This fact is explicitly stated in each of these three sections of the Eden narrative: when typical human life is described in the epic's opening clauses as not yet existent (2:5), when the style of life for humans outside of Eden is prescribed by divine decree (3:17–19), and when humans are assigned their role after being expelled from Eden (3:23). The archetypal human outside Eden, from whose perspective the Eden narrative is told, is the farmer, the cultivator of arable land.

But the connection between the first human being and the arable land, between *'ādām* and *'ădāmâ*, runs even deeper for the Yahwist. Not only does *'ādām* cultivate *'ădāmâ*, he is fashioned by God out of the land he farms. This point is also made by J in each of these sections of the Eden narrative: when the first human is made out of *'ădāmâ* as God's first creative act (2:7), when the human destiny to return to the *'ădāmâ* from which it was taken is spelled out in the divine decrees (3:19), and once again when the first humans are expelled from Eden (3:23). *'ădāmâ* is the beginning and the end of human life. As the first human was derived from arable soil, so all humans are destined to return to it at death.

'ādām is thus linked to *'ădāmâ* in two important respects: *'ădāmâ* is the stuff out of which *'ādām* is made and is also the primary object of his labor. And these two facts were certainly conceived by the Yahwist as closely interrelated. The primary activity of human life was believed to be related to the essential substance of the human creature. In each of the three sections of the garden narrative under consideration, this interrelationship is stressed, but nowhere is it more clearly and succinctly stated than in the conclusion of the story at the expulsion from Eden: "Yahweh, God, sent him out of the Garden of Eden to cultivate the arable land from which he was taken" (3:23). For the Yahwist, the human being from primordial time has been destined to farm the land from which he himself was formed.

This close relationship between *'ādām* and *'ădāmâ*, developed in these parts of the Eden narrative, is of course highlighted by the similarity of the terms themselves. For J and his society, as for most traditional societies, names reflect the essential nature of those who bear them, a phenomenon J will repeatedly exploit in the epic.[13] Here the possession of names from the same root, 'dm, signifies the essential identity of 'ādām and 'ădāmā. While the linguistic relationship between these terms is regularly noted, the thorough way in which they together establish the agricultural character of human existence has not been widely recognized.[14]

The center of the Yahwist's landscape, when it first comes into view in these three parts of the Eden narrative, is arable land. And human society, according to the Yahwist, derives from this land and is engaged in its cultivation. The perspective from which J presents the origin of the world is thus fundamentally agricultural. In fact, J is even more precise than this. The particular kind of agricultural environment depicted by the Yahwist's narrative is represented in additional details in these same parts of the Eden story.

One key detail is the reference, in the epic's opening sentence, to rainfall as essential for the growth of vegetation:

> Before any pasturage was on the earth,
> And before any field crops had sprung up,
> Since Yahweh, God, had not sent rain upon the earth. (2:5)

Such a detail might seem of little use for determining a specific type of agriculture, since all agriculture is ultimately dependent on rainfall. Yet when the beginning of the Yahwist's epic is compared to the beginnings of origin narratives from other cultures, this mention of rain stands out as a distinctive characteristic of J's narrative.

In the great river valley civilizations of the ancient Near East, Egypt and Mesopotamia, where agriculture was dependent on the inundation of lowlands by flooding rivers and on irrigation systems related to them, narratives focus on these phenomena rather than on the rainfall that is the ultimate source of the rising rivers. A creation text from Ur, in just such a series of introductory clauses describing not yet existent realities as those that begin the Yahwist's epic, focuses on the key phenomena of irrigation agriculture:

> In those days no canals were opened,
> No dredging was done at dikes and ditches on dike tops.
> The seeder plough and ploughing had not yet been instituted
> > for the knocked under and downed people
> No (one of) all the countries was planting in furrows.[15]

By contrast, J's reference to rain alone reflects the rain-based, dryland farming characteristic of the highlands on the shores of the Mediterranean where biblical Israel came into being. In such a setting, where irrigation was impractical, fields on mountain slopes and small intermontane valleys are completely dependent on direct rainfall to produce crops. "Rainfall," writes geographer Yehuda Karmon about these highlands, "is the decisive climatic factor in the physical existence of population and for plant life and agriculture."[16] This contrast between the dry farming of the Israelite hill country and the irrigation agriculture of its neighbors is described very specifically in Deuteronomistic tradition:

> The land which you are about to enter and take possession of is not like the land of Egypt which you left where you sow your seed and irrigate with your feet like a green garden. No, the land which you are crossing into to take possession of is a land of mountains and valleys, watered by rain from the sky. (Deut 11:10–11)

A second key detail of the Yahwist's specific agricultural ecology is the reference to particular kinds of vegetation in the Eden narrative's opening sentence.

> Before any pasturage (*śîaḥ haśśādeh*) was on the earth,
> And before any field crops (*'ēśeb haśśādeh*) had sprung up. (2:5)

Both kinds of vegetation are customarily translated with such generic terms that little can be made of them, when in fact they describe a very precise agricultural environment.

The second plant type mentioned by the Yahwist, *'ēśeb haśśādeh,* is the most important, as it is referred to again in the divine decrees as the primary food cultivated by human beings (3:18):

> Thorns and thistles will spring up for you,
> and you shall eat the field crops (*'ēśeb haśśādeh*),
> by the sweat of your brow [literally "nose"] you shall eat bread (*leḥem*).

Set apart for human consumption and placed in a parallel relationship to bread (*leḥem*) in these lines, *'ēśeb* is undoubtedly the grain from which bread is made. Thus *'ēśeb haśśādeh* can be translated literally as "grain of the field" or more idiomatically as "field crops," as I have done here. This understanding is consistent with the Yahwist's use of *'ēśeb haśśādeh* elsewhere. In the plagues of hail and locusts in the Egyptian delta, for example, it is differentiated from tree crops and directly identified as wheat and barley (Exod 9:22, 25, 31, 32; 10:12, 15).[17] Grain is in fact the field crop that, for biblical Israel, was the basis of its highland Mediterranean agriculture, as archaeological evidence and biblical references both attest.[18] "The importance of field crops in ancient Israel," notes the botanist Michael Zohary, "can be measured by the daily consumption of bread, which was the major constituent of the meal of the poor, the rich, and the king alike."[19]

The other plant type mentioned in the story's opening sentence, *śîaḥ haśśādeh,* traditionally rendered with the general "plant of the field" (KJV, NRSV, cf. *NEB*), is somewhat harder to identify since the Yahwist does not again use this expression. When *śîaḥ* is employed elsewhere in the Bible, however, it is used for vegetation that grows in semiarid and arid regions, the low bushes and dwarf-shrubs characteristic of areas that lack enough rain to support intensive agriculture (Gen 21:15 [the Elohist]; Job 30:4, 7). Since such areas typically provide pasturage for the grazing of sheep and goats in the hill country, J evidently describes here the vegetation that supports the other major part of traditional hill country farming, stock breeding. Thus *śîaḥ haśśādeh* can be translated literally as "shrubs of the field" or more idiomatically as "pasturage," as I have done above. Raising sheep and goats provided a valuable complement for grain-based agriculture by making use of grazing land unsuitable for agriculture, providing manure for the fields, contributing products for the diet (milk, cheese, meat) and other uses (wool, bone), and thus in general hedging the risks of subsistence farming through diversification.[20]

The Yahwist has, therefore, in a few concise phrases within these parts of the garden story that refer to life outside of Eden, sketched the particulars of the distinctive environment that was to become normative for the human race. It is the environment of the farmer involved in rain-fed agriculture, cultivating grain on arable soil, and raising flocks on nearby pasturage. These are the basic facts of existence characteristic of the mixed economy typical of Mediterranean agricultural societies such as biblical Israel. Images of cultivation and herding dominate not just the Yahwist's work but biblical literature as a whole. And material remains from Iron Age Israel, down to the architecture of the typical Israelite farm house, substantiate this picture of Israelite life.[21]

To a great extent, this mixed agricultural economy is dictated by its environment: the topography, the soils, and the climate of the hill country. In today's West Bank, the heartland of biblical Israel, 36 percent of the land is cultivable, 32 percent suitable for grazing herds, 27 percent too arid or rocky for either cultivation or grazing, and 5 percent natural forest.[22] While natural forest would have made up a larger percentage of the Israelite hill country in the Iron Age, the relative balance of cultivable, grazing, and arid zones would not have varied substantially. Israel's mixed agricultural economy was thus a successful adaptation to its environment and a subsistence strategy. Through diversified farming, ancient Israelites provided for a wide range of subsistence needs and shielded themselves from excessive vulnerability to any single environmental threat.

Cain and Abel

This agricultural setting, introduced in the framework of the Garden of Eden story, provides the context from which the Yahwist describes the world in the primeval age before the flood. Of the seven generations who lived in this age, the second—comprising Cain and Abel, sons of Adam and Eve—is given the greatest attention. Their story is set in, and derives much of its color and drama from, the agricultural environment that has just been described.

Most interpreters of the Cain and Abel story have understood its setting differently. Cain and Abel have usually been identified as archetypes of two distinct cultures, those of the agriculturalist and the pastoralist, one pursuing a sedentary existence on arable land, the other practicing a nomadic life-style following flocks in arid zones. Several variations of this approach have been proposed. According to one, Cain (*qayin*), who was expelled from the arable land, is to be identified as the ancestor of the nomadic, desert-dwelling people living south of the Israelite hill country and referred to elsewhere in the Bible

by the name Kenites (*qēnî* < *qayin*); while Abel is to be regarded as the ancestor of the peaceful, sedentary Israelites.[23] According to another view, the
archetypes are reversed: Abel represents the peaceful Israelite nomads who
settled in Canaan, with whom the storyteller sympathizes, while Cain represents the violent Canaanite farmers among whom they settled.[24] Still a third
approach avoids such ethnic identifications. It relates Cain and Abel rather
to a general division of labor established at the dawn of civilization between
two basic and distinct ancient Near Eastern occupations, farming and herding.[25] All three approaches assume a fundamental, sometimes antagonistic,
distinction between farmers and shepherds.

The variety of ways in which the farmer–shepherd dichotomy has been
applied to this story may itself suggest something of the arbitrariness of this
approach. Even more of a problem is the fact that this understanding of Cain
and Abel is based on a conception of ancient environments and cultures no
longer tenable, the conception that the ancient Near East could be rather simply and categorically divided between the domains of the farmer and the shepherd.[26] The weaknesses in this approach become clearest in the details of the
story itself, which reflect the same mixed agricultural economy that the
Yahwist has already described as the norm for human society after Eden.

In this story, as in those sections of the Eden narrative already examined, the focal point of the landscape is *'ădāmâ*, arable land. It is on this land
that Cain and Abel live and that their story unfolds. *'ădāmâ* is the land that
Cain cultivates (Gen 4:2) and that produces the crops he offers to God (v 3).
It is the scene of Cain's crime, literally swallowing the blood of the stricken
Abel (vv 10,11). It is the agent of Cain's curse, refusing any more to yield its
productive power to his cultivation of it (vv 11, 12). It is, all things considered, the secure home from which he is banished (v 14). This banishment
shows just how central *'ădāmâ* is to the narrative. The terrain outside of it is
viewed as unimaginably harsh, an environment unlivable for a human being.
Cain himself claims that leaving the arable land is a punishment too great
for a human to bear (v 13). Twice at this point in the narrative, once by Cain
and once by the storyteller, *'ădāmâ* is identified directly as the realm of divine
activity, and leaving it means leaving the presence of God (vv 14, 16). This
portrait of arable land reflects the perspective of one who inhabits it and who
considers the surrounding desert dreadful, dangerous, and outside the pale
of divine protection and care.

Cain and Abel, who live on this land, are typical sons of a highland
farming family engaged in both cultivation and herding. The older, Cain, is
involved, as is his father Adam, in the cultivation of the arable land, presenting as an offering to Yahweh the fruits of his harvest (3:23, 4:2–3). The
younger, Abel, takes care of the sheep and goats, offering to God the firstborn of the flock (4:2, 4). This sharing of labor is characteristic of family life
in a Mediterranean highland farming village in which subsistence is dependent both on the cultivation of fertile land and the raising of herds on less
fertile pastures near the cultivated fields. Here, as is common in such families, the older son is primarily involved in cultivation, an activity related to

his prestige as the primary heir to his father's estate. Meanwhile, the younger son is delegated to caring for the flocks, a less esteemed role in such farming families.[27]

Cain, the older brother, is the central character of the story and of primary interest to J. Abel is a secondary figure who never speaks, is regularly referred to as Cain's brother (vv 2, 8, 9, 10), and dies before he can produce descendants. Cain is the Yahwist's second Adam, the tarnished hero of the second generation. His name, *qayin,* according to his mother, means "creation/procreation" (from *qānâ*), designating him the first creation of the human race (4:1).[28] Like his father before him, he is a cultivator of arable land (*'ōbēd 'ādāmâ;* 3:23, 4:2). And like his father, he is an errant farmer, transgressing a divine command (2:16–17, 4:7). The result of disobedience is the same for both: the relationship between farmer and soil is imperiled. For *'ādām* the ground is cursed and yields its produce only to great labor (3:17–19); for *qayin* the ground refuses to produce at all (4:12).[29]

The conflict between Cain and his brother Abel is indeed archetypal, but not archetypal of conflict between shepherds and farmers. It is archetypal rather of conflict between brothers, between members of the same kinship group sharing a single social and environmental setting, that of the Israelite hill country. As such it illustrates the dire consequences of the failure to negotiate such conflict successfully. In the postflood era, kinship conflict drives the Yahwist's major ancestral narratives. The conflicts between Abraham and Lot, Jacob and Esau, and Joseph and his brothers all threaten family stability. Yet in the new age these conflicts are all in the end negotiated without bloodshed. In this light, the story of Cain's murder of his brother represents the primeval negative paradigm for conflict resolution in a kinship-based society such as biblical Israel. The punishment for the guilty is exile, the loss of status in the family and a place on the ancestral farmland.[30]

Of the factors that have directed interpreters toward the shepherd versus farmer reading of this story, two have been particularly influential. One is God's preference for Abel's animal offering over Cain's harvest offering, a fact interpreted to indicate God's approval of a pastoral life-style over an agricultural one.[31] Since J does not give the reason for God's behavior, all explanations must remain conjectures. At the same time, it is very unlikely that this behavior is meant to reflect God's preference for animal offerings and pastoral existence, since the Yahwist's decalogue prescribes offering the first harvest of arable soil together with the first lambs of the flock (Exod 34:19, 22, 26). A more likely explanation for God's behavior lies in the overall design of the narrative itself. Just as God sets up a challenge for Adam by planting and then prohibiting the tree of knowledge, so God sets up a challenge for Cain by introducing conflict and then prohibiting its violent resolution. It is the human response in which the Yahwist is interested rather than the reasons for the situation itself.

The second factor that has led to the shepherd versus farmer interpretation is Cain's banishment, which, together with the link between his name and the Kenites (*qayin/qēnî*), has suggested the story be read as an origin narrative of a group of nomadic pastoralists in the southern desert.[32] But key details in the narrative argue against this reading. In the first place, the Yahwist's etymology for Cain's name designates him as the first human procreation rather than the ancestor of a particular ethnic group. Furthermore, J does not make the connection between the ancestor and his descendants explicit by a direct reference to the later nation, which is his usual practice in etiological narratives (e.g., Gen 16:10–12; 19:37–38; 25:23, 30; 27:28–29). Finally, J's mapping out of the political relationships of his day, within Israel and between Israel and its neighbors, by means of ethnological etiologies, commences only with Noah's sons after the flood. From these three sons descend the peoples of the major areas of the Middle East with which the Yahwist is familiar: Egypt, Mesopotamia, and Syria-Palestine (Gen 10:8–19, 21, 24–30).

Cain, then, must be viewed like his father Adam as a primeval ancestor of the human race involved in the agricultural life-style of the Israelite highlands. According to the Yahwist's genealogical traditions that follow this story (4:17–26, 5:9), Cain is the ancestor of the next great figure in the epic, Noah, the first farmer after the flood (9:20). As a farmer, Cain takes his place among the Yahwist's other primeval heroes, Adam and Noah, who are also prototypical farmers. Thus J traces the human race through its farmers, two disobedient ones in the primeval era, Adam and Cain, followed finally by an obedient one, Noah, through whom Yahweh saves the human race and reestablishes agriculture in the new era after the flood (5:29, 8:20–22, 9:20). The later Priestly editor either had different genealogical traditions or was troubled by the Yahwist's connection between Cain and Noah. He cuts Cain loose and transfers Noah's ancestry to Seth, the son of Adam and Eve according to an alternate genealogy (4:25–26, 5:1–32).[33]

Cain's Descendants

Cain's descendants make up the remainder of the seven generations who lived before the flood. Their names as J lists them are Enoch, Irad, Mahujael, Methushael, and Lamech (4:17–18). Lamech in turn had four sons, one of whom, Noah, survived the flood and became the primordial ancestor of the postdiluvian era. Of these preflood generations the Yahwist offers little information. Only for Lamech's family (4:19–24) are any details provided.

Two different environments have been associated with these generations. According to one view they should be understood as the descendants of Cain, the banished nomad (4:12–16). Thus Lamech's song (4:23–24) and the specialized skills initiated by his sons—Jabal's pastoralism (4:20), Jubal's music (4:21), and Tubal-Cain's metal work (4:22)—are considered representative of the customs, arts, and crafts typical of the life of desert nomads such as the Kenites.[34] According to a second view, these preflood generations should be understood as the descendants of Cain, the city builder (4:17).[35] Thus the skills of Lamech's sons are taken to represent specializations within urban culture. Cattle breeders, musicians, and metalworkers are identified as three common guilds of city dwellers.[36]

As has been argued above, the Yahwist's Cain is above all a hill country farmer. His major role in the epic is neither as a desert nomad nor as an urbanite but rather as a representative of the agricultural way of life practiced by his father Adam. His descendants, the preflood generations including Lamech's family, should thus be considered children of Cain the farmer and residents of this same agricultural milieu. Before illustrating how this is the environment of Lamech's family, however, a word is in order about the only other detail J provides for Cain's descendents: the Yahwist's mention of a city and his attribution of it to Cain (4:17).

Though the Yahwist simply mentions the city without any descriptive or evaluative commentary, scholars have been quite ready to explain J's attitude toward it. According to one perspective, J views the city favorably, as the first achievement of civilization.[37] According to another viewpoint, J presents the city as an evil place, built as it was by the first murderer, Cain. Thus, this account of the first city is only the first salvo in a sustained anti-urban polemic carried forward throughout the Yahwist's epic as a whole.[38]

The salient fact about the Yahwist's treatment of the city in this text is his brief and neutral mention of it. By contrast to his elaborate description of the first two generations, in which agriculture is presented as the primeval occupation of the human race, this reference to the first city appears remarkably cryptic. It is a fact of the Yahwist's world, but by no means of central interest. When compared with the detailed documentation of humanity's agricultural life-style in the previous narratives, this brief, nondescript mention of a city leaves the impression that here, too, the Yahwist views the world from an essentially rural point of view.

When compared with origin narratives from the great urban cultures of antiquity, the distinctive character of the Yahwist's treatment of the city becomes clearer. In Mesopotamian traditions about the preflood era, cities dominate the landscape. The first human work at the dawn of civilization is the establishment of cities, a series of five in most accounts.[39] These cities then provide the focus for human life, functioning as economic centers that are the distribution points for agricultural goods produced by their societies.[40] The following lines from a Sumerian primeval tradition illustrate this well:

> When the royal scepter was coming down from heaven . . .
> [The king] laid the bricks of those cities in pure spots.
> They were named by name and allotted half-bushel baskets.
> The firstling of those cities, Eridu, she [Nintur] gave to
>   the leader Nudimmud
> the second, Badtibira, she gave to the Prince and Sacred One,
> the third, Larak, she gave to Pabilsag,
> the fourth, Sippar, she gave to the gallant, Utu,
> the fifth, Shuruppak, she gave to Sud.
> These cities, which had been named by names,
>   and been allotted half-bushel baskets,
> dredged the canals, which were blocked with purplish (wind-borne) clay,
>   and they carried water.
> Their cleaning of the smaller canals established abundant growth.[41]

The character of Mesopotamian civilization, centered in the city and the king and dependent on irrigation agriculture, is clearly outlined in this text. For Mesopotamian scribes, the preflood era was the period in which the urban civilization that typified their culture had been founded. By comparison, the Yahwist's presentation of the primeval age is decidedly nonurban. His first two heroes are farmers, not kings, and they inhabit the rural, agricultural environs that typified biblical Israel. The contrast between these two landscapes and their points of view could hardly be sharper.

Lamech's family, the only other primeval generation about which J provides any details, fits comfortably into, and reflects particular aspects of, the same nonurban agricultural milieu represented by its ancestors Adam and Cain. Both Lamech and his most important son Noah are farmers, as was Cain. This is the only conclusion that can be drawn from Lamech's brief speech at Noah's birth: "This one will give us relief from our work, from the painful labor of our hands, from the ground which Yahweh has cursed" (Gen 5:29).[42] In these words, which repeat the vocabulary of the original curse on the land and of Adam's charge to cultivate it (3:17), Lamech identifies himself too as a struggling farmer. He also connects the destiny of his son Noah with this same agricultural enterprise.

Before we look at Noah, the farmer who provides the transition from the old age to the new, Lamech's other sons deserve attention. The first of these, Jabal, is identified as the ancestor of those who reside in tents and own livestock (4:20).[43] Owning herds and living in tents are characteristic of a wide range of environments and economic life-styles. Yet the focus on herds and tents here seems to indicate that J considers Jabal the ancestor of specialized pastoralists who are characteristically seminomadic. Such groups have been a constant feature of the Middle Eastern landscape, exploiting the semiarid terrain contiguous with the more humid agricultural land, terrain that is suitable for grazing livestock but not for intensive agriculture. The modern Bedouin in the Judean Desert and Negev are only the most recent manifestation of a phenomenon that can be traced back into antiquity. The economy of such groups is not self-sufficient and independent of sedentary society, but exists in a symbiotic relationship with it. The specialized character of herding makes pastoralists dependent, in fact, on nearby farmers for food and material goods. Pastoral nomads have never represented a major proportion of the Middle Eastern population. They have always been a peripheral minority, in the modern era representing no more than 10 percent of the total populace.[44]

These features of specialized pastoralists fit well with their position in the Yahwist's primeval genealogies. Their close relationship to the neighboring agricultural society, as well as their status as a specialized, peripheral minority are all captured in their position as descendants of one of Lamech's less important sons, Jabal. The specialized pastoralist is thus viewed as an offshoot, related to but less important than, the dominant agricultural society reflected in the Yahwist's main characters, Adam, Cain, Lamech, and Noah.

Another of Lamech's sons, Tubal-Cain, is identified as a metalworker (4:22). Forging metal is an occupation in varied cultures, from the nomadic to the urban to the rural agricultural society of the Yahwist. Since the description of Tubal-Cain's work in the original Hebrew is somewhat difficult and awkward, translators have retreated for the most part to the relative safety of a general and neutral English rendering such as that of the JPSV: "who forged all implements of copper and iron."[45] However, if the Hebrew term *ḥōrēš* is translated in its familiar sense of "plowman," Tubal-Cain's occupation may be rendered as "the blacksmith for all who plow with bronze and iron (*lōṭēš kol-ḥōrēš nĕḥōšet ûbarzel*)."[46] He would thus represent the ancestor of village blacksmiths, those who forged and sharpened the metal plow points used by Iron Age highland farmers. Whatever the exact translation of Tubal-Cain's work, there is no doubt that he was a blacksmith, a specialization which is just as indigenous to the agricultural village in the Israelite hill country as it is to desert nomadism or to the urban economy. It was a specialization of the rural economy that provided an essential service for the Iron Age farmer.[47] In the case of Tubal-Cain, as in Jabal's case, J has located the origin of a specialized skill important to the mixed economy of highland agriculture among the sons of Lamech, the last farmer of the primeval age.

Lamech's other son, Jubal, provides no further information about the Yahwist's environment, but, as the ancestor of those who play stringed instruments, he may be of particular interest to the Yahwist (v 21). While Jubal's descendants are usually understood as musicians in a general sense, J could be referring to a particular kind of musician, the epic singer or bard. Jubal's lyre (*kinnôr*) is regularly mentioned in conjunction with the kind of song (*šîr*) that relates Israel's epic story (Exod 15:1–18; cf. Judges 5). Thus the Yahwist may here be tracing back to the primeval age the art of epic song, the practitioners of which he may count among his own ancestors.[48]

Among the sons of the last farmer of the primeval age is thus found the origin of several specialized occupations that figure prominently in the highland agricultural society represented by their father Lamech. The members of Lamech's family represent the origins of neither nomadic nor urban culture, but further define aspects of the agricultural milieu depicted in the careers of the major primeval figures. Among these figures is Lamech's most well-known son, Noah, who, like his father and ancestors, is a prototypical hill country farmer. His story, as told by the Yahwist, is strongly shaped by this basic fact.

Noah

At his birth, Noah's destiny is linked to the practice of agriculture. In his birth announcement, Noah's name is derived, by way of one of the Yahwist's folk etymologies, from the verb *nḥm*, "comfort, bring relief."

> [Lamech] called his name Noah (*nōaḥ*), "This one will bring us relief (*yĕnaḥămēnû*) from our work and the painful labor (*'iṣṣābōn*) of our hands, from the arable land (*'ădāmā*) which Yahweh has cursed" (*'ērĕrāh*). (5:29)

The relief Noah is expected to deliver is the alleviation of the dreadful toil of subsistence farming initiated by the divine curse on arable land at the beginning of the primeval age. Indeed, Lamech's announcement of Noah's name and his purpose in life draws heavily on the original announcement of this curse.

> Cursed (*'ārūrā*) is the arable land (*'ādāmâ*) on account of you [*'ādām*],
> Through painful labor (*'iṣṣābōn*) will you eat from it. (3:17)

Noah was born to turn back this curse and to moderate the arduous character of agricultural labor in the primeval age.

This is the very assignment that Noah accomplishes upon his emergence from the ark after the flood. In the Yahwist's conclusion to the flood story (8:20–22), Noah's first act in the postflood age is to construct an altar and to place upon it whole burnt offerings (*'ōlōt*; v 20). Upon inhaling the pleasing aroma of this offering, God responds to Noah's act in two ways. And both responses have a direct bearing on dryland farming in the new age. First, in an explicit reference to Genesis 3:17, God decides "not to curse arable land (*'ādāmâ*) again"—or "not to continue to curse arable land" (both translations are possible)—on account of *'ādām* (here used with its generic meaning, "the human race"), nor will he again strike down all its life (v 21). Thus, *'ādāmâ*, arable land, is relieved of its debilitating curse.

In the second response to Noah's offering, God decrees the regular occurrence of the seasonal cycle that determines the rhythm and success of highland agriculture:

> For all the earth's days
> Planting grain (*zera'*) and harvesting grain (*qāṣîr*),
> Cold season (*qōr*) and hot season (*ḥōm*),
> Summer harvest (*qayiṣ*) and autumn harvest (*ḥōrep*),
> Day and night
> Shall not cease. (v 22)

In this decree are listed the major occasions of the agricultural year in the Israelite hill country: the sowing of grain in the fall (*zera'*) and its harvest in the spring (*qāṣîr*), the harvest of summer fruit, including primarily grapes and figs (*qayiṣ*) and the autumn harvest of olives (*ḥōrep*). Commonly mentioned in biblical texts, these events are directly paralleled in an ancient agricultural calendar from the Solomonic city of Gezer. It is the only document, from the Bible or other sources, that provides a systematic record of the entire Israelite agricultural year. A much briefer, but still useful, parallel is found in a list of times for prayer from the Rule of the Community at Qumran. The similarity in terminology and sequence of the seasons between Genesis 8:22 and these extrabiblical agricultural calendars can be seen in Table 2.1.

The planting of grain (*zera'*), after the arrival of the first good rains in the late fall (November and December), is the first event in the agricultural year mentioned by the Yahwist in this short survey. It is followed by the grain harvest (*qāṣîr*), the first harvest in the highlands that occurs in the spring.

Table 2.1 The Agricultural Year in Genesis 8:22, the Gezer Calendar, and the Community Rule

Months	Gen 8:22[a]	Gezer Calendar[b]	Community Rule[c]
November December	*zera'*, "planting grain"	*yrhw zr'*, "two months of planting grain"	*mw'd zr'* "the time of planting grain"
January February		*yrhw lqš*, "two months of growth"[d]	*lmw'd dš'* "to the time of vegetation"
March		*yrh 'sd pšt*, "a month of cutting flax"	
April	*qāṣîr*, "harvesting grain"	*yrh qṣr š'rm*, "a month of barley harvest"	*mw'd qṣyr*, "the time of harvesting grain"
May		*yrh qṣr wkl*, "a month of grain harvest and measuring"[e]	
June July		*yrhw zmr*, "two months of cutting"[f]	
August	*qayiṣ* "summer harvest"[g]	*yrh qṣ* "a month of summer harvest"	*lqyṣ* "to the summer harvest"
September October	*hōrep*, "autumn harvest"[h]	*yrhw 'sp*, "two months of ingathering"	

[a]Two other biblical texts describe the agricultural year schematically as a series of three episodes roughly parallel to Genesis 8:22. Leviticus 26:5 refers to planting grain (*zera'*), threshing grain (*dayiš*; i.e., the grain harvest), and the grape harvest (*bāṣîr*). Amos 9:13 refers to the one plowing (*hōrēš*) and sowing grain (*mōšēk hazzāra'*), the one harvesting grain (*qōṣēr*), and the one crushing grapes (*dōrēk 'ānābîm*).

[b]The Gezer Calendar actually begins with *yrhw 'sp*, the olive harvest in the autumn, before proceeding through the list as given. The adjustment made here, to compare it with Genesis 8:22, in no way alters its agricultural sequence, just the point at which one starts its description. On the Gezer Calendar and ancient Israel's agricultural year, see Oded Borowski, Agriculture in Iron Age Israel (Winona Lake, IN: Eisenbrauns, 1987) 31–44. Important studies, among the many on the Gezer calendar, are those by W. F. Albright, "The Gezer Calendar," *BASOR* 92 (1943) 16–26, whose translation appears in *ANET* (320); and by S. Talmon, "The Gezer Calendar and the Seasonal Cycle of Ancient Canaan," *JAOS* 83 (1963) 177–87.

[c]Col. 10, line 7. The text in The Community Rule actually begins with the grain harvest (*mw'd qṣyr*). The adjustment made here for a comparison with Genesis 8:22, as with the Gezer Calendar, in no way changes the basic pattern of the seasons listed. The text was published in Millar Burrows, John C. Trevor, and William H. Brownlee, *The Dead Sea Scrolls of St. Mark's Monastery*, Vol. II, Fasc. 2: *Plates and Transcriptions of the Manual of Discipline* (New Haven: American Schools of Oriental Research, 1951). On the relationship between this text and the Gezer Calendar, see Talmon, 183–87.

[d]The meaning of this line and the following one have occasioned a great deal of debate. Since the term *lqš* occurs in only a single biblical context, Amos 7:1, and even there needs to be clarified by the author, its identification has been difficult. And some have claimed that

Both barley (in April) and wheat (in May) make up this harvest, a fact reflected in the mention of a grain harvest (*qṣr*) in these two successive months in the Gezer Calendar.

The harvest of fruit follows in the summer and early fall. In this case, as with the cereal harvest, the more detailed Gezer calendar breaks down the fruit harvest into its successive stages. The cutting (*zmr*) of June and July likely refers to the grape harvest, the summer fruit (*qṣ*) of August to the fig harvest in particular (pomegranates also ripened at this time), and the ingathering ('*sp*) of September and October to the olive harvest. The Community Rule from Qumran uses the general designation *qyṣ*, "summer fruit," for the entire fruit harvest, while the Yahwist refers to it in two phrases: *qayiṣ*, the summer harvest of grapes, figs, and pomegranates; and *ḥōrep*, the autumn harvest of olives.

The reference to planting grain (*zera'*), harvesting grain (*qaṣîr*), the summer harvest (*qayiṣ*), and the autumn harvest (*ḥōrep*) in Genesis 8:22 thus prescribes the regularity of the major episodes in Israel's agricultural year. The additional terms, *qōr* and *ḥōm*, literally "cold" and "heat," probably refer to the two climatic seasons of the Mediterranean agricultural year, the cold rainy season, at the beginning of which grain is planted and at the end of which it is harvested, and the hot dry season, when the fruit harvests take place.[49] The final pair of terms, day and night, simply completes the list of the recurrent cycles that structure the farmer's life. Thus has Noah in his first act of the new age, by the first offering devoted to God on the first altar, fulfilled the destiny given him at birth. His righteousness and devotion have moved God to terminate the curse on arable land and to stabilize the agricultural seasons and their harvests.

The termination of the divine curse on arable land ('*ădāmâ*) through Noah's act of devotion is the first major evidence that the Yahwist considered the flood to be the end of the primeval age. Until this point, arable land

---

pšt, "flax," was neither grown in ancient Israel nor harvested at this time. For a survey of the major proposals, see Borowski, *Agriculture*, 34–35.

ᵉThe identification of the letters of the final term in this line, *wkl*, has been difficult. See Borowski's discussion of the debate, *Agriculture*, 36.

ᶠThe root *zmr* is connected with vine tending in the Bible (Lev 25:3, 4; Isa 5:6) and may refer to harvesting the vineyard, rather than pruning it (see also, Isa 18:5; Num 13:23). For this interpretation of the Gezer Calendar see Borowski, *Agriculture*, 36–38 and A. Lemaire, "*Zāmîr* dans la tablette de Gezer et le Cantique des cantique," *VT* 25 (1975) 15–26.

ᵍ*qayiṣ* is used in the Bible both for summer fruit (Amos 8:1, 2) and for the season in which fruit is harvested (Amos 3:5). It appears to have a particular connection with figs, since it occurs in parallelism with the early fig (*bikkûrâ;* Mic 7:1) and is coupled with vintage (Mic 7:1; Jer 48:32). In one case *qayiṣ* occurs in a list between the produce of the vine, wine, and the olive tree, oil, just the sequence of the Gezer Calendar (Jer 40:10).

ʰ*ḥōrep* is often paired with *qayiṣ* in the Bible to refer to the winter season following the summer season (Ps 74:17; Zech 14:8; Amos 3:15). It is used more specifically in Proverbs 20:4, as here in Genesis 8:22, to refer to the autumn harvest just before planting (cf. Job 29:40 where it is used figuratively for maturity).

lies under the divine curse (3:17, 4:11, 5:29); but once the curse is removed after the flood (8:21), arable land is never again so described in the epic. The conception of curse, and with it blessing, is employed by J in the rest of the epic, starting with Noah's sons (9:25–27), but henceforward to describe the relationships between political groups. The fact that Noah is the Yahwist's first righteous hero (7:1), and that he builds the first altar (8:20), only adds to this impression that he stands at the beginning of a new age.

The first thing Noah does after building the altar and making a sacrifice, according to the Yahwist, is to plant a vineyard (9:20). He becomes thereby the first and prototypical farmer of the new age: 'iš hā'ādāmâ, "the man of the arable land," as J calls him (v 20). As has already been noted, fruit growing is a standard part of highland Mediterranean agriculture. Together with cereal production and herding, fruit crops—foremost among them, grapes, figs, and olives—represent an essential element of the mixed agricultural economy practiced by Israelite farmers. Noah's vineyard is thus typical of the agricultural milieu that has provided the backdrop for the Yahwist's depiction of the first human life in the primeval age.

While Noah's agricultural work places him in the same rural highland environment of his primeval ancestors, the farmers Adam, Cain, and Lamech, much attention has been devoted in the interpretation of this text to explaining the particular mention of a vineyard. Some, influenced by Noah's drinking and the questionable deeds that follow, have regarded the vineyard story as disapproval of the excesses of alcohol or other reprehensible practices of sedentary Canaanite farmers.[50] This cannot be the Yahwist's point of view, however. For J, Noah is humanity's first righteous ancestor (Gen 7:1) and nothing in the story actually compromises this fact. The only unrighteous act in the story is Ham's, for which his line, in particular Canaan, is duly cursed (9:22–26). At the story's conclusion, Noah delivers the divine blessings and curses that establish the relationships between his sons and their descendants in the new age. Noah's drinking of wine is characterized by the Yahwist with the same term used later to describe the celebrative drinking of Joseph and his brothers (šākar; Gen 43:34), though modern translators perpetuate a distinction that implicates Noah alone (e.g., NRSV: Gen 9:20, "become drunk"; 43:34, "be merry").[51]

A more compelling explanation for Noah's vineyard is to identify it as a stage in the development of human civilization, and to impute to the Yahwist thereby a concept of the evolution of agriculture.[52] At first glance, the evidence for such a view seems quite appealing. Human life starts in a garden, which could represent a hunting and gathering stage, proceeds at the expulsion from Eden to the domestication and cultivation of grains, and then to the mixed economy of grain farming and the domestication and herding of sheep in the generation of Cain and Abel. These developments are followed by urbanization and emerging specializations such as specialized pastoralism and metalworking. Finally, the vine—and possibly other fruit species—is domesticated by Noah and grown for its produce. This evolutionary view is supported by a common translation of v 20: "Noah, the man of the soil, was the first to plant a vineyard."[53]

All in all, this is not a bad chronological survey of the development of food production in antiquity, which moved from hunting and gathering to the domestication of grains (c. 7000 B.C.E.), then animals (c. 5000), then fruit trees and vines (c. 3000). But, in the end, this in fact does not appear to be the Yahwist's view nor the plan by which he has structured the primeval age. Adam is, according to the Yahwist, not a hunter-gatherer, but a farmer who is commissioned to cultivate (*'ābad*) even in the garden itself (Gen 2:5, 7, 15). When he leaves Eden, his occupation does not change but only takes on the genuine character of grain based Mediterranean farming that was to characterize his descendants throughout the primeval age and be reinstituted by Noah in the new age after the flood. Herding is a part of the picture throughout, being reflected in the Yahwist's initial reference to pasturage (2:5), in the leather clothing made for Adam and Eve (3:21), in Abel's work (4:2), in Jabal's specialized practice of it (4:20), and in Noah's animal sacrifice (8:20).

Noah's vineyard, in like manner, reflects a dimension of highland farming already referred to earlier in the primeval narrative. Both the fig tree (3:7) and the olive tree (8:11), the other major fruit crops of Mediterranean agriculture, have already been mentioned. They are probably not to be taken as wild examples of their species but as part of the familiar landscape of the hill country farmer. As for the translation of Genesis 9:20, no simple solution exists. The translation, "Noah was the first to plant," demands an infinitive form of the verb, *nāṭa'*, "plant," just as in English, when in fact v 20 contains a converted imperfect form, indicating an action consecutive to Noah's "beginning" (*wayyāḥel*). As it stands, the text requires a translation something like, "Noah, a man of the arable land, made a beginning and planted a vineyard."[54] That is, when Noah began his agricultural labors after the flood, he planted a vineyard. Such a statement does not attribute the first vineyard to Noah.

This concept that the known world came into being in its entirety at the beginning of time—this lack of concern for periodization—has been understood to be a characteristic of the Yahwist more generally, notably in the use of the divine name. In contrast to the Priestly Writer and the Elohist, who believe the divine name was revealed only at the time of the Exodus (E, Exod 3:14–15; P, Exod 6:2–3) and so do not use it until then, the Yahwist, as his scholarly title suggests, uses the divine name Yahweh from the beginning of time as if it were from the first the designation by which Israel's ancestors referred to God. The same contrast between the Yahwist's lack of interest in periodization and the Priestly Writer's great concern for it can be seen in the treatment of the human diet during the primeval age. The Yahwist considers stock-raising—presumably for its meat along with dairy products and wool—a part of farm life from the beginning, although the Priestly Writer makes it clear that people before the flood were strictly vegetarian (1:29–30). Only after the flood were people in P's narrative granted the permission to eat meat (9:2–4).

Thus for the Yahwist, Noah's work represents a restoration rather than a revolution of agricultural practice. Just as kingship must again be lowered from heaven after the flood in Sumerian tradition,[55] so the practice of agriculture must be reinstituted for the Yahwist. When the Yahwist describes Noah planting (*wayyiṭṭa'*; 9:20) a vineyard, he may in fact see this as a reenactment of Yahweh's planting (*wayyiṭṭa'*; 2:8) the garden, the only other instance in which J has employed the verb "plant" (*nāṭa'*) in the epic.

A factor that may have something to do with the Yahwist's particular interest in the vineyard is his southern orientation, his interest throughout the epic in the southern hill country and its prominent tribe, the tribe of Judah. While grapes are grown throughout the Mediterranean and throughout the highlands of ancient Canaan, the hill country south of Jerusalem has been known in particular, in ancient and modern times alike, for its vineyards.[56] When vineyards are mentioned later in the epic, in the tribal blessings the Yahwist has incorporated (Gen 49:11–12, regarding Judah) and in the story of the exploration of Canaan (Num 13:23), they are located in the southern hills. Noah may be instituting the kind of agriculture especially characteristic of the Yahwist's own region of the country.

Perhaps more important, however, are the narrative demands of the story itself. The differences in agricultural detail among various stories in the Yahwist's primeval narrative have to do with the unique character and narrative demands of each story rather than any attempt to represent the evolution of human culture. In this particular case, the produce of the vine is essential for the plot of the story, which results in the curse on Canaan and blessing on Shem, its ultimate concern.[57] Taken together, the agricultural details from the Yahwist's primeval narrative reveal the distinctive features of the highland agriculture practiced by biblical Israel, an agricultural life-style instituted with the first generation of human beings, carried on by their descendants, and reestablished by Noah, the first farmer of the new age.

The flood itself, which divides the old and new ages, is described by the Yahwist from the perspective of this same agricultural setting. A common ancient Near Eastern tradition, the flood narrative reflects in its various tellings the environments of its narrators. The Mesopotamian version, for example, describes the great deluge from the perspective of the urban society practicing irrigation agriculture in the great Euphrates River valley. Its hero, Utnapishtim, lives in a city surrounded by irrigation canals and constructs his ship from the reeds of the riverine marshlands.[58] By contrast, the Yahwist's hero is a highland farmer, and the flood is attributed to constant heavy rains of the kind that sweep across the hill country of biblical Israel during the winter wet season (Gen 7:4, 12; 8:2). Throughout the flood story, the Yahwist focuses, as always, on arable land, 'ādāmā, (Gen 6:7; 7:4, 23; 8:8, 13b). And the olive tree, from which Noah's dove tears off a branch, is a characteristic species of Israelite agriculture.

The Yahwist may even envision Noah's ark coming to rest in the Canaanite highlands following the flood. Upon opening the door of the ark, the first thing Noah sees is the dried surface of arable land (*pĕnê hā'ădāmā;*

13b). By planting a vineyard, he establishes in the hill country a typical species of highland agriculture. In the next major episode of the new age, the Yahwist pictures the early postflood generations moving eastward (*miqqedem*) to build the tower of Babel (Babylon) in Mesopotamia (11:1–2).

In these details, the Yahwist's flood story differs not only from its Mesopotamian counterparts, but from the other Israelite account of the flood attributed to the Priestly Writer. For the Priestly Writer the flood is a cosmic event, not a heavy rain in the hills. The waters above and below the earth rush out upon the world (7:11)—always designated by the general term "earth" (*'ereṣ*) for P—returning it to the chaos that preceded creation (1:1–2). According to P, the orders established at the origin of the cosmos, according to his account of creation (1:1–2:4a), disintegrate in this catastrophe. Afterward, his hero disembarks on the distant mountains of Ararat (8:4; the Assyrian Urartu) far to the northeast.

The Yahwist's version of the flood story illustrates a style of thought that infuses his narrative of primeval time. His thinking always begins with his own particular ecological niche and moves out from this local, concrete, and familiar terrain. Even in J's enumeration of animal life this style is apparent. Whenever he lists animals—whether those that were created (2:19), died in the flood (6:7, 7:23), found refuge in the ark (7:2–3), or were offered to the deity after the flood (8:20)—the Yahwist begins with the animals that live nearby in the field and that creep on the ground and concludes with the birds in the sky. This stance toward the world is just the opposite of the Priestly Writer's, which views nature from a divine, cosmic perspective. P's lists always proceed in the other direction, from cosmological space to the inhabited world, from the animals of the distant sky to those that live with humans on the land (1:20–27, 6:20, 7:21, 8:17, 9:10).

This style of thought makes it almost certain that the first phrase of the Yahwist's epic reflects this localized way of looking at the world. When describing creation, the Yahwist places earth before sky: "In the day Yahweh, God, made earth and sky" (2:4b). According to the Priestly Writer, who assumes the position of God above the cosmos, the sky precedes the earth: "When God began to create the sky and the earth" (Gen 1:1, 2:4a). Thus, the first words of each great biblical narrative contain the deliberate expression of two vastly different stances toward nature: the Priestly Writer's cosmic point of view, and the Yahwist's particularistic orientation, the orientation of the farmer eking out a living on the arable land of the Israelite hill country.

The Garden of Eden

The Mediterranean hill country with its mixed agricultural economy of dryland farming and stock raising is portrayed by the Yahwist as the environment in which humans lived during the primeval age before the flood. Yet the Yahwist's epic actually begins in a different environment. This environment is the luxuriant Garden of Eden. Here the world takes shape and the first life comes into being. The ecology of this garden is distinct from the Mediterranean highlands, and this difference must be examined in order to determine the character of the unique landscape represented in the Yahwist's Eden narrative.

The ecology of the garden Two features in particular distinguish the garden in Genesis 2–3 from the highland agricultural environment that was to become the norm for human society. One is its vegetation: the garden is described as a grove of trees, an orchard. Only three kinds of trees are specifically identified, and these primarily because of narrative concerns: the common fig because its large leaves were especially suitable for clothing Adam and Eve (3:7), and the two trees bearing the fruits of knowledge and of eternal life, from one of which the humans eat, and therefore gain knowledge, and from the other of which they do not eat, and thus remain mortal (2:9, 3:22). At the same time the narrator makes it clear that the garden contains many varieties of trees that are both beautiful and fruit-bearing (2:9). Though fruit production is customarily one aspect of the grain-based, diversified agriculture of the hill country, it is not the predominant activity it is pictured to be in this garden.

A second feature distinguishing this garden from agriculture in the hills is its water supply. The garden is dependent not on rainfall (2:5), but on irrigation. Its source of water is a spring, *'ēd,* which rises out of the earth (*'ereṣ;* 2:6).[59] Also referred to as a river (*nāhār;* 2:10), this spring irrigates (*hišqâ*) the arable land (*'ădāmâ*) of the garden. The verb *šqh* (Hiphil: literally "give to drink;"), employed twice by the Yahwist in this narrative (2:6, 10), is the customary term in biblical Hebrew for irrigation agriculture.[60] By contrast, dry farming in the highlands depends entirely on direct rainfall. While the hill country of biblical Israel was dotted with numerous small springs, these are either ephemeral or insufficient to provide water for extensive irrigation over and above the immediate needs of the humans and animals who settled near them.

The Garden of Eden is thus a unique landscape in the epic. This fact, together with the insatiable human interest in the notion of paradise, has led to much speculation and a multitude of proposals for the source of the Yahwist's picture of Eden. One common approach has been to lift Eden out of ordinary time and space and to understand it as a mythical place, to claim, in essence, "that a real locality answering to the description of Eden exists and has existed nowhere on the face of the earth."[61] The garden does in fact exhibit a number of characteristics of a dwelling place more suitable for gods than humans. The Yahwist himself refers to Eden as a divine garden, "the garden of Yahweh" (13:10). Its trees are planted by God, and two bear fruit—the fruit of knowledge and the fruit of life—which upon consumption give one divine attributes (2:9, 3:23). Its spring of subterranean water is the customary location in ancient Near Eastern mythology for divine dwellings, traditionally located at the sources of the deeps.[62] Adding to this "mythical" aura is the fact that the geography of Genesis 2:10–14 is difficult to synchronize with the actual topography of the ancient Near East.

Yet despite its "mythical" aura, Eden's landscape contains many real-world features. It contains springs and rivers, orchards, and people to cultivate, prune, and harvest them. Its waters provide the sources of the great rivers of the ancient Near East, including the Tigris and Euphrates. Because of this, other interpreters have concluded that "the author is obviously trying to locate a definite place"; and they have attempted to identify the actual geographical setting that provided the details for the garden scene.[63] The starting point for this line of interpretation has invariably been the description of the four rivers issuing from Eden in Genesis 2:10–14. Places from India in the East to Spain in the West have been proposed, but the location that has become most popular among scholars in the last century is Mesopotamia.[64] Two primary considerations have led to this view. First, two of the four rivers that originate in the waters of Eden are the great rivers of the Mesopotamian flood plain, the Tigris (*ḥiddeqel*) and the Euphrates (*pĕrāt;* 2:14). Second, the fact that the Yahwist's primeval narrative contains parallels with Babylonian literature—the flood story, for example—and that the Yahwist locates the origin of Israel's ancestors in the Mesopotamian city of Ur (Gen 11:31, 15:7) have suggested the theory that the bulk of these early traditions, including the Eden narrative, were imported from Mesopotamia. Irrigation agriculture like that in the Eden narrative is in fact characteristic of the flood plain of the Tigris and Euphrates in Mesopotamia.

Yet there are difficulties with locating Eden in Mesopotamia. The Yahwist's reference to the headwaters (*rā'šîm;* 2:10) of the Tigris and Euphrates originating in Eden would require a location in Anatolia where these rivers have their sources rather than in the Mesopotamian river valley.[65] Furthermore, the other two rivers that originate from Eden's subterranean waters, the Pîšôn and Gîḥôn, are placed by the Yahwist south of Israel in the area of Arabia and Ethiopia (2:11–13), and have been identified by some as the headwaters of the Nile.[66] No single location for the sources of the Tigris and Euphrates in Anatolia and the sources of the Nile in Ethiopia and central Africa is possible, of course. To make things even more complicated, the second river, Gîḥôn, is the name of the spring in the Kidron Valley that was Jerusalem's major source of water, and it is hard to imagine an Israelite not making this association.[67] To find a location for Eden on the basis of the river geography in Genesis 2:10–14—their exact identification and common source—is hence a confusing and precarious project, as the bewildering array of proposals illustrates.

A more promising approach to understanding the source of the Yahwist's picture of Eden is to follow a clue provided by the Yahwist himself. In his only mention of the garden outside the Eden narrative, J compares it to a setting within his own environs, the Jordan Valley. This comparison is made in one of the early narratives of the postflood era, the story of Abraham and Lot (Gen 13, 18, 19). To explain Lot's attraction to the Jordan Valley where he subsequently moves, the Yahwist provides the following description of it:

> Lot raised his eyes and saw that the whole region of the Jordan, all the way to Zoar, was entirely irrigated like the garden of Yahweh, like the land of Egypt—this was before Yahweh destroyed Sodom and Gomorrah. (Gen 13:10)[68]

The comparison of the Garden of Eden to the Jordan Valley in this statement can only be understood in light of the Yahwist's conception of the natural
history of the Jordan Valley as it is described in this verse and in the
Abraham–Lot narrative as a whole. The great rift valley at the southern end
of the Jordan River and along the Dead Sea is today an arid, desert landscape,
as it was in the biblical period and for thousands of years before.[69] Yet the
Yahwist believed this arid valley ecology had originated in more recent times,
during the lifetime of his own ancestors. According to his description of it in
this verse, the valley Lot saw was an extraordinarily luxuriant scene. As far
south as Zoar, southeast of the Dead Sea, the entire valley floor was irrigated
(*šqh*, Hiphil), presumably by the Jordan River, by the waters of the Dead Sea,
which were still fresh, and by the rich springs at the base of the mountains
on both sides of the valley. As such the Jordan Valley could be compared by
the Yahwist to the "land of Egypt." The Nile Valley, in which 98 percent of
Egypt's people live, is a lush oasis ecosystem. Dependent entirely upon Nile
water delivered through an extensive network of irrigation canals, an intensive and abundant agricultural landscape covers the valley floor right up to
the desert bluffs on either side.[70]

According to the Yahwist, this primitive Jordan Valley environment was
drastically altered in the days of his ancestor Abraham by a single, catastrophic
event, a great firestorm that engulfed the cities of Sodom and Gomorrah
(13:10, 19:24–28). In the description of this event, the Yahwist is concerned
not only to explain the end of these cities and their inhabitants but also to
account for the new valley environment. According to his story, flaming
asphalt (*gōprît*) fell from the skies and struck the entire valley, wiping out its
arable land (*'ădāmâ*) together with its vegetation (*ṣemaḥ*; 19:24, 25). As a
result, the once fertile terrain was turned into a desert marked by deposits of
the same asphalt (*gōprît*) that had fallen from the skies and continued to
smoke (19:24, 28), and by outcroppings of salt, forever to be identified with
the figure of Lot's recalcitrant wife (19:26). This is in fact a precise description of the southern valley of the Jordan and the Dead Sea as the Yahwist
knew it and as it still exists today.[71] The story of Lot thus serves as an etiology not only of the ruins of Sodom and Gomorrah (19:25) and the origins of
Moab and Ammon (19:37–38), but of the desert ecology of the southern rift
valley.

Destruction in the well-watered valley was not total, however. Zoar, the
small settlement where Lot was allowed to take refuge (19:18–23, 30), and
which the Yahwist considered to be the southern limit of the original verdant valley (13:10), was spared. Likely to be identified with one of the south-
ernmost oases of the valley just southeast of the Dead Sea, the oasis of Zoar
was viewed by J as a small, isolated remnant of the rich agricultural environment that had once characterized the entire valley.[72] Presumably the other
oases scattered throughout the southern end of the Jordan Valley and along
the Dead Sea—such as Jericho and En Gedi—were understood to be other
solitary remains of the once luxuriant ecology of the valley as a whole. Considered the only survivors of an earlier environment, these valley oases—

small, fertile outposts in a desert landscape—provide the basis for the Yahwist's image of the ecology of the entire Jordan Valley in its pristine, pre-Lot, state. And since this pristine valley could be compared to the garden of Yahweh (13:10), these same oases, the remnants of that valley, represent the real setting in the Yahwist's own world of a terrain he considered comparable to Eden's ecology. By virtue of the Yahwist's own analogy, these valley oases should be the starting point for an investigation of Eden's environment.[73]

Though they have never been considered for this purpose in any detail, the similarities between an oasis in the Jordan Valley and the Yahwist's description of Eden are quite striking and obvious. Eden, like the valley oasis, is entirely dependent on irrigation rather than rainfall for agricultural production. Because of their southern location and the "rain shadow" cast by the mountains on the west, the valley oases lie in a desert zone that receives less than six inches of rain per year. They exist only by irrigation from rich perennial springs that discharge water from aquifers below the rain-fed mountain ranges on either side of the valley. The Garden of Eden, by comparison, is planted before the advent of rainfall (2:5). It is sustained entirely by irrigation (*šqh*, Hiphil) from a spring (*'ēd*) rising from the ground (2:6). The term "garden"(*gan*) itself is the common designation in biblical Hebrew for irrigation-supported agriculture (e.g., Num 24:6; Deut 11:10).

A second obvious similarity between the Jordan Valley oasis and the Yahwist's garden lies in their characteristic vegetation. Eden, like the valley oasis, is distinguished by its fruit trees. A valley oasis, like modern Jericho, while containing land under grain cultivation, is predominantly known for its production of fruits and vegetables. Its fruit trees, in particular date palms, provide a beautiful visual contrast to its arid environs. These trees today produce fruits from biblical times—e.g., dates, figs, pomegranates—as well as varieties introduced more recently—oranges, grapefruit, bananas, apricots. Due to the tropical climate in the Jordan Valley, crops can be grown year round and marketed in the highlands long after highland harvests have ended. Like Jericho, Eden is characterized by its trees, which were both visually striking and full of edible fruit (2:9). The cultivation of these trees is the agricultural task assigned to the first human being (2:15).

With its perennial water source and bountiful orchards, the valley oasis was a setting in which the major difficulties of hill country agriculture were substantially diminished. For this reason, the valley oasis would have provided an appropriate image for the comfortable existence in Eden that preceded the rigors of dryland farming. For highland agriculture, the essential threat is lack of water. Crops are completely dependent on direct rainfall, which is unpredictable in its timing and amount, and is often insufficient to produce adequate harvests. Drought and famine are constant dangers (12:10; 42:1–2). By contrast, the rich spring at an oasis like Jericho provides a plentiful and stable supply of water year around. Its produce is not at constant risk from the vicissitudes of rainfall.

The character of oasis agriculture moderates other hardships of dryland farming. In the highlands, the terrain itself is an obstacle, its steep hillsides requiring the laborious work of terracing to be cultivable at all. Grain-based agriculture is extremely labor intensive as well, especially during plowing, planting, and harvest. Only a single growing season exists because of the long summer drought. The oasis, by contrast, is on the broad plain of the valley floor. The care of its orchards, once established (Eden's are planted by Yahweh, 2:8), require less work than cereal cultivation.[74] Its perennial water source and temperate climate allow food production year round. This rich and productive agricultural scene is reflected in the name of the garden, "Eden," which must be derived from a West Semitic root, *'dn,* meaning fertility.[75]

The history of human settlement in the Jordan Valley illustrates the attractive character of the favorable ecological conditions of the valley oasis. The mountain range that becomes the heartland of biblical Israel was historically a lightly settled frontier zone. Its formidable obstacles to intensive agriculture inhibited any extensive settlement until the influx of pioneers in the early Iron Age (1200–1000 B.C.E.) who eventually made up the tribes of ancient Israel.[76] Earlier cultures were located primarily in the valleys and along the coastal plain, which flanked the Canaanite highlands, where fertile soil and flat terrain made farming easier. The oasis at Jericho in the Jordan Valley has attracted settlers from earliest times. Its ancient tell contains the remains of a sedentary community that archaeologists have called the oldest city on earth (c. 9000 B.C.E.).[77]

The Yahwist's comparison of this valley oasis ecology to the Garden of Eden (13:10), the obvious similarities between the two, and the appropriateness of the oasis as an image of a more comfortable existence than highland farming suggest that the Jordan Valley oasis may well have provided the concrete model and specific details from which the Yahwist drew for the portrait of Eden. An oasis ecology of this type is therefore the kind of environment most likely represented in the Eden narrative. The Yahwist's parochial perspective, his description of the primeval age in terms of Israel's own agrarian highlands, makes it all the more likely that his portrait of Eden too would have been drawn largely from the local phenomena with which he was familiar.

All of this raises intriguing questions: did the Yahwist think the Garden of Eden was actually located in the Jordan Valley, destroyed perhaps in the great catastrophe of Abraham's day? Was there any tradition of a valley Eden in ancient Israel? These are questions we do not have enough evidence to answer with great certainty. The Yahwist, after all, compares Eden to the Jordan Valley before its catastrophe; he does not equate the two. Yet there are hints of the conception of a valley Eden in J's narrative that deserve mention.

In the first place, the Yahwist represents the primeval age outside of Eden with the local color of the biblical hill country, and therefore it would be in character to represent the garden itself within these same environs. Placing Eden in a distant, foreign terrain would be in some tension with the local, native backdrop of the preflood narrative as a whole. Moreover, details within the narrative may imply that the primeval garden was wiped out in the catastrophe that reduced the valley to a desert. J's description of the valley's demise in Genesis 19, for example, evokes his earlier description of Eden. The terminology used to describe the vegetation destroyed in the catastrophe—*ṣemaḥ hā'ădāmā*, "the growth of the arable land" (19:25)—echoes and reverses the language of the birth of Eden—"Yahweh, God, made grow (*yaṣmaḥ*) from the arable land (*hā'ădāmā*) every tree" (2:9). Only in the Eden narrative and here does the Yahwist employ the root *ṣmḥ* (cf. 2:5, 3:18), until he uses it once more for the trees in the Nile Valley (Exod 10:5). Furthermore, the theme of expulsion is prominent in both narratives, the expulsion of Lot and his wife paralleling that of Adam and Eve. Both couples are forced to leave the comfortable oasis environment (in the valley) and seek refuge in the neighboring hill country with its difficult agricultural demands. One wonders whether these two stories of the transition from valley, oasis agriculture to hill country farming might not reflect in archetypal fashion the actual movement of populations from the old centers of civilization in the plains and valleys to the highland frontiers in the early Iron Age, a population shift that provided the basis for the new Israelite kingdom and for those new neighboring kingdoms in the Transjordanian hills, Ammon, Moab, and Edom.[78]

A Jordan Valley Eden suits the Yahwist's location of the garden "to the east" (*miqqedem*) as does a Mesopotamian Eden, in defense of which this phrase is usually put forward.[79] From the perspective of the heartland of biblical Israel in the hills west of the Jordan, a valley Eden would be properly designated "to the east." Yahweh plants the Garden of Eden to the east (*miqqedem*, 2:8). After Adam and Eve are expelled, presumably to the hills west of the Jordan, Yahweh stations the cherubim to the east near the Garden of Eden (*miqqedem lĕgan-'ēden*, 3:24) to guard the way to it. After murdering his brother, Cain is exiled to a nomadic existence east of Eden (*qidmat-'ēden*, 4:16), presumably the great Arabian desert east of the Jordan and Transjordanian hill country.

The Yahwist's traditions about the ecological transformation of the Jordan Valley are known by other biblical authors as well (e.g., Deut 29:21–22 [Eng vv 22–23]; Zeph 2:9). The most interesting references to this tradition are those in prophetic collections that anticipate, as part of Israel's ultimate redemption, the return of the Jordan Valley to its pristine Edenic state. Apocalyptic supplements to the prophecies of Joel and Zechariah speak of a river rising from the temple mount in Jerusalem, certainly with its source in the Gîḥôn spring (one of Eden's rivers), and flowing eastward to irrigate the Jordan Valley (Joel 4:18; Zech 14:8). Most explicit in this regard is a text from Ezekiel's program of restoration that evokes images of Eden in its picture of the valley's renewal (Ezek 47:1–12). According to Ezekiel's vision of the future, a stream flows eastward from the temple mount and the Gîḥôn spring, becoming deeper and deeper as it descends into the Jordan Valley (vv 1–6). Upon its arrival, it turns the waters of the Dead Sea back into fresh water (vv 8–10), though a few salt areas are preserved for human needs (v 11). Along the banks of the river spring up all varieties of fruit-producing trees just as in Eden (v 12; cf. Gen 2:9). As in the valley oases and the primeval Eden, these trees produce fruit year round, and their fruit bears special healing, life-giving powers (v 12).

Behind these images of renewal may lie the same tradition, of which there are hints in the Yahwist's epic, that life began in a valley Eden. As is common in apocalyptic thought, the time of the end and the time of the beginning coalesce; in the end the world returns to its beginnings. Final restoration and salvation are thus pictured with the archaic imagery of creation. In this case, the ecology of the Jordan Valley, as the home of the primeval garden, will be restored in the day of salvation by the same subterranean waters that first irrigated Eden. The subterranean flow will rise with extraordinary force from one of its four Edenic sources, the Gîḥôn spring at the base of the temple mount in Jerusalem, and return the entire floor of the Jordan Valley to its primeval state.[80]

A Garden of Eden in the Jordan Valley does not, of course, solve the geographical problem of its four rivers (2:10–14), at least in the terms of which this problem has traditionally been posed. Nor will any other location, for that matter, as long as Eden's spring is interpreted as providing a single location on the earth's surface for the source of these four major rivers. At this point it is tempting to excuse the Yahwist from modern concerns with scientific cartography, or to set aside Genesis 2:10–14 as a secondary addition.[81] Aside from inventing an imaginary geography to explain this text, the only explanation for the relationship between such varied watercourses as the Tigris, Euphrates, Gîḥôn, and Pîšôn may lie in the ancient conception of a subterranean sea linking all fresh water sources. According to this view, a deep fresh water current ran below the surface of the earth, and all springs and rivers flowing with fresh water were believed to have their origin in this underground stream.[82] Eden's waters may thus be viewed by the Yahwist not as a single surface waterway dividing into four, but rather as the flow of the same subterranean deep from which the earth's great rivers draw their waters.

This conception of the earth's rivers having a common origin in the same subterranean source of Eden's spring may be reflected in the language of the narrative. The waters that rise out of the earth to irrigate Eden are referred to with the unusual term *ʾēd* (2:6), most likely alluding to the subterranean fresh water deep, for which *nāhār* (2:10) can also be a proper designation.[83] The term *rāʾšîm*, "heads," for the headwaters into which Eden's waters divide (2:10) likely refers (as the Akkadian cognate does) to the springs that represent the sources of Middle Eastern rivers, such as the Tigris and Euphrates (2:14).[84] The names of the two other rivers in the Eden narrative derive, in fact, from Hebrew roots that mean to issue forth, as do the waters of a spring: Pîšôn from pwš, "spring up" (2:11); Gîḥôn, from gwḥ or gyḥ, "burst forth" (2:13).[85]

Locating Eden is, of course, a precarious project. The Yahwist does not provide enough information—perhaps purposely—to place it exactly. J may intend Eden to possess some element of liminality. Yet the suggestions above are intended to call attention at least to several basic traits of the Yahwist's approach to origins. J's treatment of the primeval era is concrete and down-to-earth, drawing its details from ordinary human experience. J is not constructing an otherworldly, "mythic" realm within this narrative. Moreover, the specific earthly setting for this age is not a universal landscape or a foreign terrain, but it is full of the details of the environment of the storyteller, as is further illustrated by the analysis of human life in the garden that follows.

Agriculture in the garden Even in this well-watered place, in the protected and favorable conditions of the oasis ecology of Eden that was the humans' first home, the Yahwist's view of the human as farmer is prominent. The agricultural character of human life is laid out in detail in this narrative, even before the first family is sent out to take up dry farming in the hill country. As has been noted, the first human, *ʾādām,* is made from the particular kind of soil that is cultivable, *ʾādāmâ* (2:7). The task God immediately assigns *ʾādām* in the garden itself is the work of cultivation (*ʿābad*), the same work that is to be his lot outside of Eden (2:15, 3:23). From its very inception, even in Eden, human life is equated with farming.

The Yahwist's account of the creation of the first forms of life in the Eden story is shaped by this agricultural perspective. In his description of the origin of *ʾādām,* of the animals, and of *ḥawwâ,* Eve, the Yahwist draws upon the role each plays in a typical agrarian village. This is so, in the first place, for the first human, *ʾādām,* who is based on the male role in a traditional agricultural family. This interpretation of *ʾādām* as male in the garden narrative, particularly before the first woman is created from him, has been strongly challenged in recent scholarship.[86] Since the Yahwist can employ *ʾādām* as a collective term for the human race (e.g., Gen 6:1), the more general meaning "human being" or "earth creature" (possibly androgynous) has been proposed for its use in Genesis 2. According to this line of interpretation, the Yahwist employs *ʾādām* with the general meaning, "human being," in Genesis 2 before the first woman is created, and then uses *ʾādām* for the man in particular after the woman's creation (e.g., 2:22, 23; 3:8; etc.).

However, the Yahwist's characterization of *ʾādām,* when viewed against the backdrop of common gender roles in traditional agricultural societies, resembles a male from the very beginning of the garden story. In ancient Israel, as in the subsistence agricultural economies of the Mediterranean highlands more generally, the primary work of the male is the cultivation of the family's fields. Such a pattern is present in contemporary villages and is reflected in biblical texts as well. Men plow the fields, sow the seed, harvest the grain, and tend the family's orchards or vineyards. Women, while providing some assistance in the field at peak labor times such as the grain harvest, work primarily in and near the home, raising the children, preparing the food, and growing vegetables in a family garden.[87] Within this picture of the Mediterranean agricultural family, the Yahwist's *ʾādām* is quite clearly the male. The role assigned to *ʾādām,* both inside the garden and outside of it, is cultivation (2:15, 3:23). The very origin and substance of his being reflects his role, cre-

ated as he is out of the cultivable soil he is destined to farm, *'ādām* from *'ădāmâ*
(2:7). Furthermore, the divine decrees that impose the constraints for human
life outside of Eden prescribe for *'ādām* the specific pains that accompany
field cultivation, the painful labor of growing grain from ground prone to
producing thorns and thistles (3:17–19). With its particular masculine meaning in this narrative and its inclusive sense elsewhere (e.g., Gen 6:1), *'ādām*
appears to be used by the Yahwist in the same sense "man" has traditionally
been used in English, to refer to the male and/or the human species as a whole.

   The animals are created to assist *'ādām* in his agricultural tasks. When
the Yahwist describes God's concern that *'ādām* not remain alone (2:18), he
is less concerned with the feeling of loneliness or existential isolation than
with the magnitude of labor involved in subsistence agriculture. J states that
God wished to provide for *'ādām* a "helper" (*'ēzer;* 2:18). Since God has just
made *'ādām* a farmer, this is the obvious task for which *'ādām*'s creator believes
a helper is necessary. Understood in this light, the creation of animals as
helpers is not such a humorous mistake or naive solution to the first man's
isolation as it might first appear.[88] Created from the same cultivable soil,
'ădāmâ, from which the man was made (2:19), and designated with the same
name, *nepeš ḥāyyâ,* "living being," these animals included the domestic species
that played a major role in Mediterranean agriculture. The sense of domes-
ticity among the animals here brought into being is highlighted by *'ādām*'s
naming the animals (2:19–20) and by the Yahwist's mention of *běhēmâ,* "livestock" (2:20; cf. 3:14, 6:7, 7:2–3, 8:20), along with the "animals of the field"
and "birds of the air." By assisting in the most arduous tasks of plowing,
threshing, and carrying loads, cattle and donkeys immeasurably lightened
the burden of farm labor. By providing dairy products for food and wool for
clothing, sheep and goats provided essential products for the subsistence
economy.

   The account of the first woman, like those of the man and the animals,
reflects her particular role in the agricultural family. When the Yahwist says
the man could not find a helper like himself (2:20), the emphasis should be
placed on the term "like himself" (*kěnegdô*) rather than "helper" (*'ēzer*). The
animals just created did contribute to the agrarian economy and were indeed
helpers. But none was sufficiently like the man (*kěnegdô*) to be a suitable
sexual partner. As a consequence, God makes the woman from the substance
of the man himself (2:22, 23). This allows the two to reunite, to become "one
flesh" (2:24), and thereby to establish the family unit that was the basis of
agricultural society. The designation "one flesh" (*bāśār 'eḥad*) refers to both
physical and social aspects of the marriage bond. It designates the sexual
union that produces children and also the contractual establishment of a new
kinship unit within society.[89] With the creation of the woman, the family is
thus brought into being.

   Within this family structure, the first woman's role reflects the female
role in the traditional Mediterranean agricultural family. Her primary activity is the bearing and raising of children. This role is introduced in the narrative of her inception, which focuses on the sexual union of male and female

(2:23–24). The childbearing role is also the basis of her name, ḥawwâ, Eve, which the Yahwist understands to mean "mother of all the living" (3:20).[90] The divine prescriptions for the life of the woman outside Eden focus on this role too. Just as the male work of cultivation is to become painfully laborious for him (ʿṣb; 3:17), so the female role of childbearing is to become painfully laborious for her (ʿṣb; 3:16). As childbearer and fellow worker, the woman takes her place within the family as a helper of her husband. Both, together with their children and animals, are necessary for survival in the life of subsistence agriculture on the highland frontier.[91]

The view that the garden is a royal domain, as some have argued,[92] is not supported by this agricultural portrait of Eden. ʾādām is not presented by the Yahwist as a primeval royal figure but as a cultivator of the ground, as was the typical Israelite farmer. Nor is Eden described as a royal estate. Such a reading of the garden story is overly influenced by Mesopotamian parallels, which do describe the first humans as monarchs, representing as they do a highly urbanized, centralized, royal culture. It may also be influenced by the preceding Priestly account of creation in which the human being is described in decidedly more royal and hierarchical terms.[93] This interpretation does not take seriously enough the thoroughly indigenous nature of the Yahwist's primeval narrative overall, reflecting as it does the life-style of the typical Israelite farmer.

Throughout the primeval era, from the first generation of Adam and Eve to the generation of Noah and his family, the Yahwist describes the world from the point of view of the highland farmer. The landscape of the first human beings is the hill country on the shores of the Mediterranean Sea, the very landscape of biblical Israel and of the Yahwist himself. The Yahwist, just like the epic narrators of neighboring cultures, has in effect created the world in his own image, in the image of the land and culture with which he was familiar. He has envisioned archetypal reality—its world and its people—in terms of his own society and environment. J has thereby founded his own society and environment in the orders brought into being at the creation of the world.

In so doing, the Yahwist has incorporated into his landscape each of the major ecological regions of his world. At the center is the Mediterranean hill country with its dry farming land, its humid climate, and its mixed agrarian economy of cultivation and herding. In this region live all of the Yahwist's primeval heroes—Adam and Eve, Cain and Abel, Lamech, and the flood survivor Noah. Alongside this region is the steppe, with its pasture and sporadic farming land, its semiarid climate, and its specialized economy of seminomadic pastoralism. In such environs live the descendants of Lamech's son Jabal, the tent-dwelling sheep herder (4:20). In the distance lies the desert, with its lack of pasture and arable land, its arid climate, and its inhospitable terrain. It is, for the Yahwist, a hostile and uninhabitable place. To be banished into it, as was Cain, means to assume an existence unbearable for humans and to be expelled from the very presence of God (Gen 4:13–14). Finally, nearby in the Jordan Valley lie the small isolated oases with their

tropical climate and vegetation. Their unusually favorable ecological conditions provide the Yahwist with the nostalgic image of a once existent Eden
in which human life was easier and better than that of his fellow Israelites
struggling to survive on the highland frontier.

The first age of the world and of human culture is thus described by the
Yahwist in terms of his own highland agricultural environment. It is within
the contours of this indigenous setting that the Yahwist's attitudes toward
nature and society in the primeval narrative must be examined.

The Yahwist's Conceptual World: Agriculture and Religion

Agriculture, like all other basic activities, is no merely profane
skill. Because it deals with life, and its object is the marvelous
growth of that life dwelling in seed, furrow, rain, and the spirits
of vegetation, it is therefore first and foremost a ritual. It was so
from the beginning and has remained so in farming communities,
even in the most highly civilized areas of Europe. The husband-
man enters and becomes part of a sphere of abundant holiness.

Mircea Eliade, Patterns in Comparative
Religion

In talking about topsoil, it is hard to avoid the language of
religion.

Wendell Berry, Home Economics

The most important result of the foregoing analysis of the Yahwist's primeval narrative is the discovery that he does not view the world of nature in a
general, universal, or abstract sense. Rather, J writes about the natural world
in terms of a precise, distinctive environment. That environment is the Mediterranean hill country in which the typical family practiced a mixed agricultural economy combining cultivation and herding to meet its subsistence
needs. Only in the context of this concrete setting can the Yahwist's orientation to nature and the human place within it be properly understood.

At the center of the Yahwist's agricultural setting is arable soil, *ădāmâ*.
As such, *ădāmâ* represents the Yahwist's point of orientation, the point from
which the world as a whole is brought into focus, organized, and understood.
It is therefore the most appropriate point to enter the Yahwist's world of
thought and to search for clues to the attitudes and ideology that shape his
stance toward the environment.

Nature

As that from which all life is derived—plant, animal, human—arable soil is
the key to the Yahwist's conception of the structure and essential character
of the natural world. Arable soil provides the organizing principle behind J's

understanding of space, the relationship among nature's various parts, and metaphysics, the nature of being and reality.

The Yahwist's claim that the earth and its various forms of life, including human life, are made of the same stuff reflects the view that they are all in possession of the same essential nature and are thereby part of one, single reality, the essential element of which is arable soil. No terminology in the primeval narrative places any ontological distinction between the forms of life or considers them apart from their physical existence in relation to arable land. The inherent connection between human life and the earth in particular is made by J with special emphasis: the first human shares in his name (*'ādām*) the name of the soil (*'ādāmâ*) and human death is described as a return to the soil. The breath of life (*nišmat ḥayyîm*) that God breathes into this first human to bring him to life does not give him a soul or spiritual being different from other animate beings. The breath *'ādām* receives from God is the physical breath upon which all animate life depends (7:22).[94]

The common lot of humans and animals is a conspicuous feature of the Yahwist's creation narrative. A clear line distinguishing the essential nature of one from the other is difficult to detect. Human and animal alike are called *nepeš ḥayyâ*, "animate creature" (2:7, 19). As with the breath of life, *nepeš ḥayyâ* is used by J for both, and this term also attributes to neither a soul or spiritual being separate from their physical life.[95] This point has been muddled for centuries in English translations by a succession of translators determined to draw a distinction between human beings and animals where none exists in the Hebrew text. In the King James Version (1611), *nepeš ḥayyâ* was rendered "living creature" when used of the animals (2:19), but "living soul" when used of the human being (2:7). While retreating from such an obvious distinction and misuse of the Greek idea of soul, the translators of up-to-date and widely used versions such as that of the Jewish Publication Society (1962) and the New Revised Standard Version (1991) nevertheless preserve the distinction in a subtler fashion. In both translations, *nepeš ḥayyâ* is translated in two different ways: "living creature" for animals (2:19) but "living being" for human life (2:7).

Even such traits as knowledge, acquired by eating the fruit of the tree of knowledge, and language, exercised in naming the animals, do not really set humans apart. It is true that only humans are actually described as eating the fruit of the tree of knowledge, and this act does make them unique in one specific sense. It endows them with the self-consciousness that makes them the only animal uncomfortable with their nakedness (3:7). But animals in J's narrative also possess wisdom and intelligence, as does the snake in the garden, who is distinguished from other animals not because he alone was wise but because he was the wisest of all of them (3:1). Balaam's donkey, at the end of the Yahwist's epic, is another example (Num 22:22–35). The central point of J's narrative about Balaam's donkey is that the donkey had more intelligence than her owner, an acclaimed seer, when she was the first to recognize the messenger of Yahweh in their presence. Both of these animals possess speech as well as knowledge, and both are in a certain respect more cognizant of divine realities than their human companions.[96]

The relationship between J's God and this world, this unified metaphysical realm, is closer and more complex than has been suggested for the God of the Bible by biblical theologians, who have customarily perceived a sharp division between creator and creation. To accommodate a second and separate divine sphere of reality, scholars have attributed to ancient cosmologies the conception of a two- or three-tiered universe. According to the former, the world can be divided between heaven and earth, the divine and human realms.[97] According to the latter, the earth is flanked above and below with other realms, both usually associated especially with divine power.[98]

There are suggestions in the Yahwist's narrative of just such a layered view of reality. It is characteristic of J to describe God as "descending" (*yārad*) to investigate affairs on earth or to make contact with human beings (e.g., Gen 11:5, 18:21; Exod 3:8, 34:5). Moreover, the mountaintop and the tree, both symbols of contact between earth and sky, are typical points of revelation in the Yahwist's narrative (e.g., Gen 12:6–7; Exod 19:20). Even symbols of a subterranean realm, such as the spring welling up in Eden, mark sacred space in J.

But the most striking characteristic of J's cosmology is the insignificance of these other spheres and the significance of the terrestrial sphere as the realm of divine activity. J provides no details at all about a heavenly realm, nor does he describe any activity in this realm, of God or of God's messengers who frequently meet Israel's ancestors on earth. When J begins his epic with the phrase, "In the day Yahweh made earth and sky . . . ," he is more likely referring to the sky as a part of the terrestrial realm than designating two distinct spheres of reality. Nor does J talk about the underworld. When people die they go not to Sheol nor to any realm of the dead but back to the soil. That is all J tells us.

In fact, when God is described by J, God is pictured as a participant in the terrestrial sphere. It is the Yahwist's concrete, agricultural terrain that J's deity inhabits and in which he appears to be largely at home. J's God, a strongly anthropomorphic figure, lives a very earthly life. He plants the Garden of Eden, walks in it, and talks to its residents whom he has fashioned from the ground. He meets Cain in the field, closes the door of the ark behind Noah, smells the fragrance of his offering, and eats dinner with Abraham. The line between divine and human beings is so indistinct at points that divine beings appear wholly human (e.g., Gen 18:2, 32:24).

Knowledge and immortality might be thought of as setting the creator apart from creation, since these are divine qualities that God places off-limits to humans in the garden. But even these qualities are not part of another order of being for J. They are understood in terms of this same physical world, where they are in fact available to humans in the actual substance of the fruit of two of Eden's trees. When the first couple eats the fruit of the tree of knowledge, the two of them actually acquire divine knowledge and become like God (3:22, 23). For divinity and humanity alike, this knowledge was bounded by the parameters of time and space in the physical world. God, like people, had to investigate events for which he was not present (3:9–11, 11:5–6, 18:21).

Immortality is the key quality, according to the Eden narrative, that sets God off from humans. One might in fact read the Eden narrative as an explanation of the ways in which humans are like God and different from God. Humans are like God in that they possess knowledge. Humans are unlike God in that they are mortal. But even immortality was not located by J in another metaphysical order. It too was available to the humans for the eating. To keep it from humans, in fact, God had to expel them from the garden where the tree of life was located, and God had to place guards to protect it (3:22–24). Had humans attained it, immortality would have consisted of ongoing life in J's own concrete world, not life in another.[99]

In summary, J views the world of nature as a single metaphysical reality, the central and defining feature of which is *ădāmā*, arable land. Nature's constituent parts, the earth and soil and its various forms of life—plant, animal, human—are distinct features of the same organic system, sharing a common essence derived from the soil. Even the character and activity of J's deity are narrated largely in terms of this same metaphysical realm. However one might wish to define or explain the ontological difference between God and humanity in J's epic, it can hardly be put in the categorical terms of the absolute transcendence of nature customarily employed for the Bible's God. J's deity is primarily a participant in the same agrarian realm inhabited by all other life.

The Yahwist's unitary view of reality does not mean that all of its parts were granted the same status, that none was valued over others, or that no sense of hierarchy is to be found in J's epic. It does mean, however, that whatever special valuation or hierarchy does exist among created life derives not from a conception of different orders of being or inhere in different innate natures. The values placed on different natural phenomena and the sense of hierarchy among nature's constituent parts derive rather from the simple realities of subsistence agriculture. Arable soil, with its humid climate where dry farming is possible, is home for humans and other forms of life and thus the standard in relation to which other types of environmental regimes are evaluated. The neighboring deserts, for example, are abhorred. With their uncultivable soil and meager rainfall, they were hostile to the forms of life that typified Mediterranean agriculture and were thus viewed with considerable horror and fear. For J the desert is a wasteland, unsuitable terrain for human and divine beings alike (Gen 4:13–14). By contrast, the ecology of the oasis—with its stable source of water, temperate climate, and tropical vegetation—is viewed in a truly nostalgic light. Life in such a setting is pictured by J, as the Eden story illustrates, as the first human environment unaffected by most of the risks and rigors of dryland farming in the Israelite hills.

Within inhabitable space, the arable soil, as the basis for all life, holds a kind of fundamental and indispensable position in the order of things. A sense of this vital power of the land over its creatures is almost certainly reflected in the language J employs for the human cultivation of it. The term for cultivation in J is *'ābad,* the customary verb in biblical Hebrew to express servitude. It is used by J, for example, to describe the servitude of a servant to his master (Gen 12:16) or of one people to another (Gen 27:40; Exod 5:9). It is also used for Israel's service to God in its worship (e.g., Exod 4:23; 7:16, 26). While *'ābad* may have acquired a technical connotation somewhat removed from its root meaning—as for example, the English "cultivation" does not always call to mind its linguistic connection with "cult" and "culture"—there can be no doubt that at some level the use of *'ābad,* "serve," for "cultivate" represents the Israelite sense of the dependence of human life on the land. Cultivation was an act of service to that which held absolute power over one's survival and destiny.

Among the forms of life dependent upon *'ădāmâ,* their relationships reflect their roles in an agricultural society. Plant life is described in terms of those domestic varieties cultivated by highland farmers for food: grain (2:5, 3:18), fruit trees (2:9, 16; 3:1, 7; 8:11), and vines (9:20). Animals are considered the farmer's "helpers," the purpose for which J believes they were created (2:18). As such the animal kingdom is viewed primarily in terms of the domestic species that played such a large role in the mixed economy of Mediterranean agriculture as sources of food and goods and as work animals in the fields. These animals, of course, take orders from the farmer. Thus it is appropriate for the human, who trains, harnesses, and cares for these animals, also to name them. But J's Eden narrative says little beyond this about the relative superiority of human beings, since naming does not in and of itself represent the act of one in a superior position.[100]

Human beings, while granted no special status by virtue of a unique innate nature, are nevertheless the center of J's interest. The environment, the land and its various forms of life, is described according to the needs of the subsistence farmer. Furthermore, the human drama determines the shape of the epic narrative from beginning to end. J's creation story illustrates this pattern well. The formation of human life is the first divine act in the epic, preceding even the creation of plants and animals on the earth (2:7). The climax of the creation account is the elaborate formation of a second human being, the woman, and with her creation the establishment of human procreation, marriage, and kinship structures (2:21–24).[101]

One could certainly call this perspective on nature anthropocentric, since it views and values nature from the experience of the human farmer. Yet J's anthropocentrism is an extremely humble kind, bounded strictly as it is by the realities of subsistence farming. It lacks any exalted view of human beings, since they possess no unique essence that sets them apart from and above other creatures. Furthermore, humans are regarded as subservient to the soil upon which their survival depends. The human being is viewed more as an ordinary member of the community of life than as a privileged being set apart from it.

The position assumed by God in J's "hierarchy" is, together with *'ădāmâ,* certainly a premier one. Both are "served" (*'ābad*) by human beings. And to God belongs the ultimate power to produce and sustain life. Human existence thus depends upon the presence and favor of God. Yet J's deity is cast in the shape of his human heroes and stands very close to them. In a real sense, God is the divine farmer. His place is on the 'ădāmâ (2:7, 8; 4:14). He plants the garden on it (2:8), puts humans to work on it (2:8, 15), inspects their work (3:8), meets Cain in the fields (4:8–9), and above all controls the productivity of arable soil (3:17–19, 4:11, 8:21–22). His activity is seen in the success and failure of the agricultural enterprise. Like J's human farmers, J's deity is a limited figure whose human qualities have long been recognized as a hallmark of J's theology.

The distinctiveness of these conceptions of J may be highlighted by contrasting them with the perspective of the Priestly Writer. While P also subscribes to the view that the world is a single metaphysical reality defined by physical existence on earth, he regards this scene in quite different terms. In the first place, P's view of the world is much broader than J's. While J describes life and its beginnings entirely within the context of a highland farm on arable soil, P assumes a more cosmic stance in his creation account, dividing the universe carefully into three distinct regions: sky, sea, and earth ('ereṣ; 1:6–10). Forms of life do not all originate from 'ădāmâ as in J's account, but have their origin in the specific environment to which each is distinctive: plants and land animals on the earth ('ereṣ; 1:11–12, 24–25), sea creatures in the waters, and birds in the sky (1:20–23). For the Priestly Writer, this precise tripartite structure of the universe and its life forms at creation appear to explain and legitimate certain features of the distinction between clean and unclean animals that underlie the dietary and sacrificial regulations over which priests preside.[102] Thus, whereas J's conceptions of the environment and its forms of life reflect the experience of the farmer, P's representation of the world reflects the interests and concerns of a priestly party.

The Priestly concern for categories of life and the hierarchical relationships among them is particularly clear in relation to human life. Whereas J's first human shares an origin in the soil with all of the other forms of life, P's first humans have a more distinctive beginning and a more powerful position in the world. For other forms of life, the region of the globe to which each life form is related is commissioned to produce it: in other words, "Let the earth produce vegetation . . . " (1:11–12; cf. 1:20, 24). This is not the case with humans. Instead, God alone creates them in the divine image (1:26). Simultaneously, humans are commissioned to rule (rādâ) over all other creatures, and to subdue (kābaš) the earth ('ereṣ; vv 26, 28). Behind the Priestly conception of humans ruling over nature in God's image appears to be the setting of kingship and royalty with which Israel's priesthood was closely allied.[103]

As is the case with J, P's deity shares many of the characteristics of his human heroes. Like P's humans, P's deity assumes a particularly exalted stance in the natural hierarchy, a stance reminiscent of the elite position of priest or king whose images and interests are so apparent in P's creation narrative. P's deity's place is in the sky above the earth, as his creative acts indicate. They proceed from the sky (1:3–8, 14–19), to the waters (1:9–10, 20–23), and then to the earth (1:11–13, 24–25). Within this universe, he establishes the boundaries by which the priest may distinguish clean from unclean. P's God creates by royal decree: orders are issued and carried out. He exercises dominion over the cosmos as humans do on earth. P's deity thus shares the royal and priestly traits of P's first human beings.

From two biblical authors, sharing the same basic landscape and metaphysical worldview, come two distinctive portraits of the arrangement and relationship of nature's constituent parts. And these different images appear to be closely related to two distinct social situations within ancient Israel, the role of the priest presiding over Israel's religious institutions and practices and the role of the typical Israelite farmer battling the odds of subsistence agriculture.

Culture

It has been customary to treat J's primeval narrative as an account of the growth of sin in the earth, so that, after the first act of disobedience, each episode of the narrative escalates the human capacity for evil until God is forced to wipe out the human race with the flood. This record of human failure in the primeval age, including also the attempt to build a city and tower after the flood (Gen 11:1–9), are then regarded as the backdrop against which God moves to select Abraham and his descendants for a special covenant relationship. Illustrative of this traditional approach is Gerhard von Rad's assertion that "the one basic notion which the writer has here taken for his theme [is] the growing power of sin in the world."[104] Claus Westermann, to cite just one other example, finds in J's primeval narrative a motif of "crime and punishment" designed to document the human revolt against God.[105] The effect of such interpretations of the primeval narrative has been an almost exclusive interest in the divine-human relationship in these stories and the attention to human society in isolation from its natural surroundings.

Largely left out of—or at least of only secondary interest in—this "growing power of sin" approach to the primeval age is an important motif that appears in each of the major episodes of this age: the curse on arable soil. The motif of the soil's curse is in actuality neither a minor nor an ancillary concern of the narrator's. It occurs prominently at the narrative climax of each of the individual episodes, and these appearances together provide narrative and thematic cohesion for the primeval narrative as a whole. The soil's curse is an element around which narrative tension is built, and it is the only issue ultimately resolved by the flood. The Yahwist's primeval narrative might be described, without exaggeration, as a drama of the soil, a narrative designed to explain and define the relationship between arable land and its farmers.

Just how this is so can be seen by a brief review of the theme of the soil in the primeval narrative's primary episodes. It should be recalled, in the first place, that the first sentence of the Eden story—and of the primeval narrative itself—focuses the composition that follows on arable soil. The precreation state, spelled out in the sentence's opening subordinant clauses, is described in terms of arable land, that is, its unproductive character due to the lack of rain and of a farmer to till it. And the first act of creation, described in the sentence's main clause, is the shaping of a farmer from the soil who will be able to till it. The Eden narrative itself, builds through a divine command and human disobedience toward a set of divine pronouncements (3:14–19), which are at once the consequence of human disobedience and the prescription for life outside of the garden.[106] The lengthiest of these pronouncements, and their climax, given as much attention itself as the preceding ones regarding the snake and the woman combined, places a curse on the soil. This curse introduces a theme that is to become the leitmotif of the primeval narrative, the relationship between human morality and the soil's productivity. From this point on, the primary consequence of immorality will be the soil's sterility and the disruption of the relationship between farmer and land.

The story of Cain and Abel moves toward the same climax. This account, too, builds through a divine command and a human act of disobedience toward a divine pronouncement at the culmination of the narrative. And the pronouncement on Cain mirrors the preceding one delivered to his father in the Eden narrative. As it was for the first man, the consequence of Cain's immorality is the soil's sterility, and this sterility is expressed in the same language of curse introduced in the garden. In Cain's case the relationship between farmer and arable land is severed completely, so that should Cain till the soil it would not produce at all (literally, "no longer provide its power," (lō'-tōsēp tēt kōḥāh; 4:12). For his crime, Cain is banished from arable land into the arid desert, a fate he considers comparable to death (4:13–14).

The relationship between human morality and the soil's productivity is brought to a final climax and a new resolution in the flood story, the last episode of the primeval narrative. The ultimate result of the immorality–sterility equation that has operated throughout the primeval era is the complete severance of the primal link established at creation between farmers and arable soil, between 'ādām and 'ādāmâ. On account of the pervasive immorality of the entire human race, God strikes the land with a deluge that destroys all of its life, returning it to its lifeless state before creation (6:5–7; 7:4, 22–23).

Having come to an end in the flood, the relationship between farmer and land is placed on a new footing through Noah the flood hero, who, with his family and the animals on the ark, survives the deluge. That Noah was to restore the farmer–land relationship was announced at his birth, when his life's mission was described as providing "relief from our work, from the painful labor of our hands, from the arable land (ʾādāmâ) that Yahweh has cursed" (5:29). Following the flood, Noah completes this mission with two acts. First, he builds the first altar mentioned in the Yahwist's epic and presents an offering, in response to which God promises to lift the curse on arable soil and guarantee, in the postflood era, the soil's productivity and its annual harvests (8:20–22). Second, Noah plants a vineyard on arable land (9:20), now freed from its primeval curse, thereby reenacting creation when God planted a garden in soil free from the curse.

Thus Noah is instrumental in reestablishing the relationship between farmer and arable soil and also in placing this relationship on a new foundation in the postdiluvian age. This new foundation established by God, through lifting the curse and promising regular seasons and harvests, does not eliminate the rigors of dry farming in the Mediterranean highlands nor the occasional failure of their annual harvests, on account of which Israel's postdiluvian ancestors are forced to find grain in Egypt or Philistia (12:10; 26:1; 42:2, 4–5). But the relationship between the farmer and the soil has taken on a new character in two respects. In the first place, the productivity of the land is set on its own footing; it is no longer linked absolutely and irrevocably to human morality. God acknowledges that sin is part of the human condition and that, if the human race is to survive, the fertility of arable soil on which it depends must be exempted from the consequences of its sin. "I will no longer curse arable land on account of human beings," God tells Noah, "since the thoughts of the human heart are evil from childhood; and I will never again destroy every living thing I have made" (8:21). The occasional famines with which Israel's ancestors must deal in the postflood era are in fact not linked by the narrator to human sin.

A second way in which the farmer–land relationship takes on a new shape in the postflood era lies in the moral character of the Yahwist's heroes. In contrast to the prediluvian heroes Adam and Cain, who disobey God's commands, J's postdiluvian heroes, Noah and Abraham in particular, obey God's commands and find favor in God's eyes. Noah is in fact the first hero to be called "righteous" by J (7:1). Unlike Adam and Cain before him, he does everything God commands (7:5). Abraham, like Noah, is righteous and obedient (12:4, 15:6, 18:19, 26:5), and both are blessed with agricultural wealth (9:20–21, 13:2, 24:34).

The relationship between arable soil and its human farmers is thus stabilized in the new age. This is accomplished on the one hand by granting the land an autonomy by which it would maintain its productive powers even in the face of human immorality. It is accomplished on the other hand by the appearance of righteous heroes whose obedience brings agricultural blessings to themselves and their descendants.

A brief survey of other ancient Near Eastern traditions about the primeval age—that is, the time before the flood—will be useful to illustrate the distinctive character of J's agricultural focus in the primeval narrative as well as the fact that prediluvian traditions are commonly aimed, as are J's, at describing the development of selected key traits of the culture that produced them. Sumerian traditions, for example, of which the Sumerian flood story and the first section of the King List are the primary examples, have as their central concern the description of the origins of Sumer's major political and social institutions, its first cities, irrigation canals, and kings. The aim of these traditions is described succinctly by Jacobsen: "The myth thus celebrates—reflecting quite accurately and realistically the economic possibilities of Southern Mesopotamia—the potential of irrigation agriculture and the dependence of the latter on strong governmental organization for its success. It is accordingly—if we would wish to use Malinowski's term—a 'charter' for the state, specifically for the city state."[107] Thus the Sumerians, as does J, claim their own social and economic way of life to have been founded within the events of the primeval era. For the Sumerian traditions, this was the establishment of the city state with its irrigation agriculture. For J, this was the rural dryland farming characteristic of Israelite society.

The Old Babylonian account of the primeval age, preserved in the Atrahasis Epic, reflects a different cultural interest. This primeval narrative focuses not on the development of dryland agriculture nor on the development of the city state and its irrigation agriculture, but on the issue of human reproduction.[108] Its drama is found in the unrestrained growth of human beings, made originally by the gods to do their farming for them. The gods respond to the outlandish numbers and noise of the human race by destroying it in a flood (with a single family surviving) and by instituting a series of new measures for the postdiluvian age that will control human reproduction and keep it within limits. These new measures—for example, barren women, female cultic personnel who do not marry, demons who snatch babies at birth—explain various factors in the author's own world that inhibit human procreation.[109] In Atrahasis and J alike, a basic cultural issue is highlighted within a narrative drama of the preflood age. In both, original problems encountered during the preflood age are resolved by the establishment of a new order instituted for the postflood age. In Atrahasis this issue is human reproduction, in J's epic it is agricultural production.

The theme of human procreation is certainly not absent in J's primeval narrative. Human fertility actually represents a clear parallel to the land's fertility. J's creation narrative first establishes the production of the soil, with the creation of the farmer and the garden (2:7–17), and then goes on to bring into being the reproduction of the human species, with the creation of the first woman (2:18–25). Just as the fecund ground and womb are brought into existence in Genesis 2, so they are both imperiled by human disobedience in Genesis 3. Reproduction of offspring just as production of crops will be possible henceforth only through painful labor, 'iṣṣābôn, the characterization of childbirth and cultivation alike (3:16, 17). Later references to the theme of human fertility include Eve's naming of the first human child to emphasize the marvel of human (pro)creation (4:1) and the brief reference to the multiplication of the human race and the limitation of the individual's lifespan before the flood (6:1,3). Taken together, these references to human reproduction may represent for J something of the same etiological aim of the Atrahasis epic to explain the limitations that have been placed by God on human procreation and population growth. But they do not represent for J the central problem of the primeval age. Though a concern to J, the issue of human fertility is not developed in the consistent and central way in which the issue of the land's fertility is.

Those parts of the primeval narrative that derive from the Priestly Writer share the interest in human procreation present in the Atrahasis epic. Yet in contrast to Atrahasis, procreation and population growth are viewed by P as positive phenomena without restraints, both before and after the flood. The God of P commands procreation as a human responsibility: it is the first command delivered to the human couple at creation (1:28), and the first one delivered to Noah and his sons after the flood (9:1). It remains the mandate for P's heroes throughout the postdiluvian era (e.g., Gen 17:2, 35:9, 47:27; Exod 1:7).[110]

When viewed against the background of these comparative primeval traditions, the Yahwist's unique interest in agricultural production stands out with particular clarity. For J, the chief cultural issue around which the primeval narrative is shaped is the nature of the relationship between human society and the arable soil, which provides the basis for its agrarian economy. It is this human–soil relationship that is stabilized with the new measures instituted by God after the flood. In light of its serious interest in the dynamics of the relationship between people and land, J's primeval narrative cannot be characterized as an "historical" account concerned about humans alone or about the divine-human relationship in particular. The agricultural setting of this drama is not a mere stage upon which the events of the divine-human relationship unfold. It is rather the theme of the drama itself, providing the terms by which culture is defined and the relationship between humanity and God is played out in the world.

Religion

Just as the Yahwist conceived of society in terms of the agrarian landscape on which it depended, so God also is understood in terms of this agricultural environment. Divine activity in J's epic is associated particularly closely with the two natural phenomena most crucial to agricultural production, rainfall and fertile soil.

The paradigmatic illustration of God's association with rain occurs in the primeval narrative's opening sentence.

> Before any pasturage was on the earth,
> And before any field crops had sprung up;
> Since Yahweh, God, had not made it rain on the earth,
> And there was no man to cultivate the arable soil. (2:5)

The connection of God with rain here stands in parallel relationship to the connection of man with cultivation, thus suggesting that rain defines God's activity in the same basic way that cultivation defines man's activity. Furthermore, these statements about God and man appear among a series of phrases listing the most fundamental facts of existence, the absence of which signify the state of the world before creation. The connection between God and rain is thus just as foundational to the Yahwist's view of the world as the connection between man and cultivation.

The Yahwist's conception of the Mediterranean rainstorm as a manifestation of God's activity in the world may be illustrated with several further examples. As commentators have noted, the rainstorm is a unique aspect of

J's version of the flood story.[111] The Priestly writer by contrast describes the flood as the complete disintegration of the cosmic orders established in his account of creation (Gen 1:1–2:4a), with the earth's boundaries collapsing and the waters above and below them engulfing the land (Gen 7:11, 8:1–2a) and returning the universe to its watery, precreation status (1:2). But for J, the flood is the result of torrential Mediterranean rains delivered by God (Gen 7:4, 12; 8:2b). In the final, third movement of the epic, J's association of God with the Mediterranean rainstorm is particularly apparent in the rain and hail storm that devastates the Egyptians (Exod 9:13–34), in the storm that destroys Pharaoh's armies at the sea (13:20–22; 14:19–20, 24–25), and in the great storm theophany at Mt. Sinai (19:9–15, 18, 20–25).

In this regard, J's God shares many of the essential characteristics of the ancient Near Eastern storm god. The closest comparison is with the Canaanite storm god, Baal, whose manifestation in the thunderstorm and whose control of rain and fertility are celebrated in the mythic literature from Ugarit.[112] The prominence of the storm god, Baal, in the Canaanite pantheon and J's characterization of Israel's deity as a storm god are neither coincidental nor unrelated to the dryland farming on which the agricultural economies of both societies were dependant. More will be said about J's deity as a storm god in the analysis of the southern narratives of Egypt and the desert (chapter 4), where the ancient Near Eastern motif of the battle between storm god and sea is employed as a fundamental structural scheme.

Just as rain is considered a manifestation of divine power, so is the germination of seeds in fertile soil. The paradigmatic illustration of God's association with arable land is a text in the story of Cain and Abel, in which Cain laments his banishment from the family estate.

> You have driven me today from the face of the arable soil (*pĕnê hā'ădāmâ*),
> And from your face (*pānekā*) I will be hidden. (4:14; cf. v 16)

The close association between arable land and the presence of God is emphasized in Cain's complaint by the parallel placement of land in the first phase and God in the second, and by the use of the word *face* for both. In this play on the word *face*, referring to "surface" or "landscape" in the first phrase and to "presence" in the second, the Yahwist has identified God directly with arable land.

This association of God and arable soil is, of course, frequently made in the primeval narrative. At creation, God produces from it the trees of the garden and the animate species, animal and human alike, that live upon it. Throughout the narrative, God controls the soil's fertility, restricting it in response to the deeds of Adam and Cain, but calling it forth at creation and at the beginning of the postdiluvian age. The divine promise that begins the postdiluvian age guarantees the soil's capacity to produce the regular harvests of the Yahwist's landscape (8:22).

On the basis of the close association between J's deity and both rain and the soil, it would be entirely proper to describe nature as the realm within which God's activity is observed and God's presence is made known in the world. God is also revealed, of course, within the boundaries of human society in direct encounters with human beings, so that the realm we refer to as culture or history can be described as the realm of God's activity as well. But, it would be improper to separate these realms distinctly or to assign them different values as modes of God's revelation. Of course, God is not to be equated with the rain or the soil, any more than God is to be equated with a human being. But by functioning as the media of divine presence and activity, nature and history alike assume the sacred status that contact with the divine bestows.

The conception of nature as a sacred sphere, full of divine activity and presence, is enhanced by the Yahwist's depiction of it as the realm within which the worship and service of God is performed. The prime illustration of this is the first ritual act of the primeval narrative, in which Cain and Abel present offerings to the deity (4:3–4). The content of their offerings is the first and finest produce of the mixed agricultural economy in which they are involved: Cain presents the produce of the soil, while Abel presents the first-born of the flock. Religious ritual is therefore based in the agricultural life-style of the first human family.

The significance of Cain's and Abel's religious ritual lies not in the divine-human relationship alone, but in its effect on the success of agriculture as well. This ritual presentation appears to represent the recognition on the part of the farmer that the land's productivity is a sacred phenomenon bestowed by divine power, and the belief that a gift of the produce will dispose the deity favorably to insuring fertility in the future.[113] The term by which J designates Cain's and Abel's offerings is *minḥâ,* "gift," (Gen 4:3–4). When employed elsewhere by J in noncultic contexts, *minḥâ* designates a present delivered to a superior to gain his favor (e.g., Gen 32:14, 19; 43:11, 15).[114] Thus the religious ritual in the story of Cain and Abel reflects at once the human gratitude for the produce of their agricultural economy and a plea for healthy harvests in the future. It is a ritual whose source and purpose derive from the dependence of society on the land's productivity.

Not far behind the Yahwist's description of the first farmers and their religious ritual lies a common ancient Near Eastern tradition, present in Sumerian and Babylonian literature alike, that the human race was created to farm for the gods and to feed them with the results of their harvests.[115] Such an explanation for the creation of humans and for their offerings of agricultural produce is not explicitly made by J, nor for that matter denied or criticized. But it is echoed in certain details of J's narrative. God plants a garden with trees bearing divine fruits, in which he likes to walk; then God makes the first human to cultivate and care for it. Furthermore, the image of God inhaling (*wayyāraḥ;* 8:21) the soothing odors of Noah's offering is, as commentators have noted, vividly reminiscent of the gods gathering to dine on the offering of the Babylonian flood hero, Atrahasis.[116] Since the Yahwist neither affirms nor denies this old understanding of human agriculture, it is impossible to decide conclusively whether he assumed it to be the case, or whether he no longer thought in quite these terms.[117] Whatever position one takes, one cannot deny the formative role Israel's agricultural economy played in the shaping of its ritual and of its understanding of religious devotion.

The Biblical View of Beginnings

The Yahwist's account of the beginning of the world in his primeval narrative, as it has been described here, challenges the two most influential modes of thought for the understanding of nature in the Bible. One is that nomadic pastoralism and sedentary agriculture were practically distinct styles of life in antiquity and that Israel conceived of its origins in terms of the former. The other is that nature and history were separate spheres in biblical thought and that Israel valued the latter and devalued the former, even in its conception of the creation of the world. Both of these traditional modes of thought have been fully characterized in chapter 1. The challenges J's primeval narrative represents for them may be summarized here.

The Desert versus the Sown

According to J's primeval narrative, the world's first humans are not easily classified in terms of the traditional dichotomy between pastoralism and agriculture, shepherds and farmers. Rather, their livelihood derived from a way of life in which herding and cultivation were both essential components. The first human is created from arable soil to cultivate it and is provided with domestic animals as "helpers" in his agricultural pursuits. The sons of the first couple are engaged in the same mixed agricultural economy, cultivating the ground and herding sheep. The flood hero begins the new era involved both in viticulture and the care of domestic animals, some of which he offers to God as his first act of worship after the flood. Only Jabal, one of Lamech's sons who represent different specializations within this archetypal mixed agrarian economy, may be described as a specialized pastoralist.

The emphasis actually falls on cultivation rather than herding in J's primeval economy. Arable soil, *ădāmâ,* provides the focal point of J's primeval landscape. J's major figures, Adam, Cain, and Noah, are specifically described as cultivators, a fact directly founded in the creation of the first human from cultivable soil, *ādām* from *ădāmâ.* Throughout the primeval period, the productive capacity of arable land is a major concern, resolved finally by Yahweh's promise of agricultural stability in the postflood era. A. M. Khazanov, in his monumental work on nomadic pastoralism, saw this more clearly than most biblical scholars have: "In this connection I must point out that the Bible gives chronological priority not to pastoralism, and certainly not to pastoral nomadism, but to agriculture (cf. Genesis 4.2 and, particularly, 4.20). Neither Cain, nor even his younger brother Abel, 'a keeper of sheep', but only 'Jabal: he was the father of such as dwell in tents and of such as have cattle.'"[118] In sum, J does not describe beginnings from the perspective of a nomadic pastoralist. His primeval society reflects the diversified rural economy typical of the Mediterranean hill country from ancient to modern times, in which grain-based agriculture is combined with sheep and goat herding to meet subsistence needs and reduce the risks inherent in this environment.

History versus Nature

J's primeval narrative also challenges the traditional notion that, even in its conception of creation, biblical thought distinguished clearly between nature and history, and in the process devalued nature and raised history to the level of ultimate concern. This view, which has attracted many articulate supporters over the last century of biblical scholarship, is already found in classical form in the writings of Julius Wellhausen. In spite of his unusually deep appreciation for J's interest in, and closeness to, the natural world, he had this to say about J's primeval narrative: "It is true that the Jehovist also placed these ethnic legends at the entrance to his sacred legend, and perhaps selected them with a view to their forming an introduction to it; for they are all ethical and historical in their nature, and bear on the problems of the world of man, and not the world of nature."[119]

To isolate the "world of man" from the "world of nature" in this way and to emphasize the "historical" character of these stories runs counter to J's mode of thinking. Human life and the earth itself are part of a single sphere of reality for J and may be severed from one another only by doing violence to the Yahwist's conception of the world. To begin with, 'ādām, the first human, and 'ādāmâ, the ground, are composed of the same substance, as their names make clear. They share a single metaphysical reality, the concrete world of the hill country in which physical survival and well-being were the fundamental challenges. The common distinctions in Western thought between matter and spirit, body and soul, material and supernatural, and this world and the next, by which human life is given a distinctive essence and separated off from the rest of nature, were not part of J's conceptual universe.

Furthermore, human activity is primarily oriented toward nature in the primeval age. Made from arable land, the first human is given the archetypal vocation of cultivating it. Religious ritual consists of offering to the deity the results of one's agricultural labors, the first fruits of the harvest, and the first born of the flock. All human behavior in fact reverberates in the natural world. The primary consequences of Adam's and Cain's disobedience lie in the threat posed to the connection between farmer and soil. And the result of Noah's obedience was the divine promise of agricultural stability. Primeval society is understood fundamentally in terms of its agricultural character and its dependence on the productivity of arable soil.

Finally, J's images of God reflect this close bond between nature and society. Yahweh is not assigned to the sphere of nature or of society alone, but is pictured in terms of both. Yahweh is described by J, as is commonly noted, in clear anthropomorphic language: he breathes, plants trees, speaks Hebrew, walks in the garden, changes his mind, and perhaps even consumes the food offered to him. He is imagined, in fact, according to the human society with which J was familiar, as a divine farmer. At the same time,

Yahweh's activity and presence in the world is expressed in terms of natural phenomena: rainfall and the processes of fertility in particular. The realm of agriculture was a sacred sphere full of divine presence and power.

Nature and society are thus conceived by J as part of a single reality, and they can hardly be discussed meaningfully apart from one another. Nor can they be played off of one another according to their relative value. To argue for the primacy of one over the other, of the farmer over arable soil or of arable soil over the farmer, would certainly have been a puzzling proposition for J. Their inherent bond, their absolute interdependence, is a foundational fact of the order established at the origin of the world. J, of course, looks at the world entirely from the perspective of a human being engaged in highland agriculture, and his epic may thus be called anthropocentric or seen as preoccupied with human experience. But J's perception of the human is so completely grounded in its physical setting that the human cannot be understood apart from it. Arable land is not just a stage for the human drama, but the very source of human life. The drama of the primeval age is not at all merely human. It involves the delicate interplay and eventual resolution of the relationship between human behavior and productive soil, between culture and nature.

The Universal versus the Particular

The interpretation of J's primeval narrative presented here, while aimed at working out in systematic fashion J's orientation to his natural environment, challenges several other modes of thought that have become axiomatic in understanding the biblical conception of origins. One of these is the designation of the primeval age as an era of universal history, to be distinguished from the following age as an era of national history depicting Israel's past in particular. According to this point of view, the episodes in J's preflood narrative are to be read as stories about humanity as a whole. Wellhausen, for example, believed that "the materials of the narratives in question have not an Israelite, but a universal ethnic origin;" and Gunkel spoke of "their locality being remote and their sphere of interest the whole world."[120] Of more recent commentators, George Coats's remarks are representative: "The first major unit of the OT contains a narrative description of events from long ago and far away. The principles in the narratives thus have no immediate contact with the culture or times of historical Israel. They are the subjects of world history in a primeval period."[121] This description of the beginning of Genesis is so common that it has become a truism in biblical scholarship.[122]

Yet the preceding analysis of J's primeval narrative presents quite a different picture. The setting for these stories is the distinctive and particular environment of biblical Israel, not some general setting or distant terrain. And its major characters are the kind of hill country farmers typical of the majority of the population of biblical Israel. They are not generic representations of the human race. Furthermore, the natural environment and the social world of J's primeval era is essentially the same as that in the ancestral narratives that take place in the biblical hill country after the flood. J has thus described creation not in terms of the world as a whole and of humanity in general but in terms of the precise environment and culture of which he was a part. As far as J was concerned, ʾādām was the first Israelite farmer and lived on hill country soil. To describe the primeval period in J's narrative as concerned with universal human issues, as is the rule, takes no account of the particularity of the narrative and represents a misleading picture of J's view of origins.

In his rendition of the antediluvian age as the beginning of his own world and culture, J reflects the normal practice in ancient Near Eastern treatments of origins. Each tradition is designed to provide a foundation narrative for its own culture and the local realities with which its audience is familiar. The Sumerian creation tradition documents the founding before the flood of irrigation agriculture, the city state, and its royal government. The Atrahasis epic explains the pattern of human reproduction and the particular social limitations upon it with which Babylonians were familiar. With just such an indigenous perspective, J describes in his primeval narrative the origins of his own highland agricultural setting, its distinctive environment, and its kinship-based agrarian society. In this regard, the primeval age is just as "national" in character as the events that follow it.

This sense of the integrity and distinctiveness of each origin tradition has often been lost on account of the enthusiasm for the parallels between them. J's flood story in particular has many points of contact with its Mesopotamian counterparts, and this has led to the view that Israel "borrowed" these traditions from its neighbors.[123] Consequently, the accounts of the flood and other primeval events have customarily been considered non-Israelite, a fact that has played into the notion that Israel's origin narrative reflected a broader sweep of ancient culture than Israel itself and was more universal in tenor. These traditions, including the interest in creation itself, have even been considered extraneous to Israel's own theology and a late and somewhat peripheral addition to J's epic literature. Such was the influential view of Gerhard von Rad. He held the view that J's primeval traditions "derive from a totally different sphere of culture and religion" than the rest of J's epic, and he proposed in his ground-breaking essay on the development of hexateuchal traditions that J's primeval material was the last to be added to Israel's epic narrative.[124] When Martin Noth composed his monumental *History of Pentateuchal Traditions* he did not even include the primeval narrative among the major themes of pentateuchal literature. Such views of the universal or nonindigenous character of the biblical account of the creation of the world and the origin of human society cannot be sustained in the face of the thoroughly Israelite character of J's primeval narrative brought to light in the foregoing analysis.

Myth versus History

Another traditional approach to biblical origin narratives that is challenged by this interpretation of J's primeval traditions is the characterization of them as myth. According to traditional views, the primeval narrative is considered distinctively mythical, to be distinguished in this regard from the following material—the traditions about the ancestors, Egypt, and the desert. Hermann Gunkel, who set out the parameters for twentieth-century discussions of myth in the Hebrew Bible, separated the stories of the primeval era from the legends of the patriarchs because he saw in them "a more decidedly 'mythical' character."[125] Since Gunkel, the term *myth* has been widely used in one sense or another to attribute to the Bible's origin narratives a special status.[126] This is a rather complicated issue to evaluate because the term *myth* has taken on so many different meanings. Yet in none of its major senses is it a useful category for attributing to J's primeval stories a distinctive character that would set them apart from the stories which follow. Two examples should serve to illustrate this.

According to one traditional definition, which is primarily philosophical and literary in character, and which was employed by Gunkel in his work, myth is a story about gods.[127] In the primeval stories, according to Gunkel, the divinity is the leading actor, while in the legends of the patriarchs, humans are the real actors. Though he recognized this distinction as a relative one, Gunkel's views can hardly be maintained on the basis of the picture of J's primeval narrative presented here. J's major characters, Adam and Eve, Cain and Abel, and Noah and his family, are real individuals and actors. They play the same roles in the world and in society that are played by their immediate descendants in J's epic itself, and that would have been played by the members of Israelite society at the time of J. Moreover, God relates to them in the same way in which he relates to human beings after the flood. The roles assumed by humans and by God in the primeval narrative are typical of, rather than different from, their roles in J's epic as a whole and in his own society. It is therefore misleading to label J's account of origins as myth in this sense.

According to a more phenomenological definition common in the comparative study of religion, a myth is a narrative of origins. It has a foundational function, recounting founding events that explain the origins of things in the world and in society.[128] There can be no doubt that this is exactly the function of J's primeval narratives. They explain and establish the realities of Israel's environment and its agrarian society down to its smallest details. At the same time, this function does not set these stories apart from the following ones in J's epic that play the very same role. Like the primeval narratives, the stories of Israel's postdiluvian ancestors describe foundational events that bring into being the natural realities, for example, the desertification of the Jordan Valley in the Lot stories, and the social realities, for example, the power balances between Israel's tribes in the Jacob and Joseph stories, which are part of J's own world. On the basis of this understanding of myth, J's entire epic must be identified as myth, or another designation must be discovered for it. The primeval narrative cannot be distinguished from its larger setting in J's work in this regard.

One dimension of this second phenomenological understanding of myth that appears at first to distinguish J's primeval narrative from what follows is the concept that myths describe primordial time, a time before all history.

They occur *in illo tempore,* to use the designation of Mircea Eliade.[129] In the sense that J's primeval events take place before the flood that ends the first age and necessitates a new beginning, these happenings are set off from the era that follows and in which J and his audience live. At the same time, it would be incorrect to identify J's primeval events as timeless, as loosened from history and sequence, or as occurring in a time other than that of everyday reality. Adam and Eve begin a sequence of generations that, through Noah, continue throughout the remainder of the epic. The character of time for J's primeval heroes, their position in the historical flow of human culture, in every way corresponds with the character of the epic as a whole. While the flood divides the eras, it does not alter in any basic way the character of time and the flow of events that comprise human history.

This rejection of the concept of myth as an adequate definition for J's narrative of origins in the antediluvian period is in no sense a claim that J has "demythologized" older myth or that J's narratives represent "broken myth."[130] In the manner in which J presents the interaction between divine and human in the primeval age, in his conception of time, and of the foundational character of antediluvian events, J is no more or less "mythical" or "historical" than the ancient Near Eastern traditions most comparable to J's preflood narrative that have been previously discussed. If we have to choose between myth and history as designations for J's narrative as a whole, it is most appropriate to call J an historian, as John Van Seters has characterized him, and to refer to the genre of his narrative as historiography.[131] Yet historiography in our age is quite a different phenomenon from what J's narrative represents.

The most useful approach may be to use terminology that avoids the ambiguity of myth and the modern connotations of history in order to describe the character of J's narrative as a whole including its primeval opening. I prefer the term "epic," which has been widely employed for the great narratives of antiquity that chronicle the deeds of gods and heroes who gave shape to national cultures. This is the terminology that Frank Cross has defended for some time as particularly appropriate for Israelite literature and its early narrative traditions, J and E in particular. J's primeval narrative, as J's entire epic, fits well Cross's understanding of epic as "a traditional narrative cycle of an age conceived as 'normative,' the events of which give meaning, self-understanding to a people or nation," a cycle in which the divine and the human are both participants.[132]

The End of the Primeval Age

Finally, the interpretation presented here challenges the scholarly custom of including in the primeval era everything in Genesis 1–11 until the call of Abraham in Genesis 12:1.[133] According to J, the primeval age actually ends with the flood. Noah, his sons and their descendants, the tower of Babel, and Terah's journey from Ur to Haran all belong to the same postdiluvian era inhabited by Abraham, Isaac, and Jacob. It will be useful here in conclusion to pull together the evidence already noted that points in this direction.

The key datum is the ʾădāmā, the focal point of J's primeval landscape. In the antediluvian period, as a consequence of the behavior of J's primeval citizens, it lies under the curse. The growing threat of this curse provides the leitmotif and drama of the primeval age. The power of the curse reaches its climax in the catastrophe of the flood and is resolved immediately afterward by God's decision to lift the curse and promise to ensure the land's productivity in the postflood era. J never again refers to the curse on arable soil.

Immediately following the flood, the theme of divine blessing, a central concern of J, is introduced for the first time. It is bestowed upon Noah's son Shem (9:26), as it will be upon his descendants Abraham (12:2), Isaac (26:3), and Jacob (28:14, 32:30 [Eng v 29]). The blessing includes in its purview the land on which Israel's agricultural economy flourished (e.g., 12:2, 7; 26:3), a large population (e.g., 22:17), and the political hegemony of Israel over its neighbors (e.g., 9:26–27, 12:2–3, 27:28–29). The divine curse, when it reappears in the postflood era, has only this latter political intention, placing under its power those peoples who threaten Israel's security (e.g., 12:3, 27:29).

The distinct political orientation of both blessing and curse following the flood highlights the fact that it is with the descendants of Noah in the postdiluvian age that J initiates the genealogical etiologies that explain the national identities and their balances of power that make up the political landscape of J's own day. These begin with the blessing of Shem's line (9:26), from whom Israel's ancestors descend, and the cursing of Canaan's line (9:26), whose land Israel's ancestors are granted (e.g., 12:6–7) and whose practices they are prohibited from following (Exod 34:11–16). Such political concerns and etiologies are not a part of the antediluvian age.[134]

A second key datum pointing to the flood as the end of J's primeval age is the behavior of J's heroes, which precipitated the curse on ʾădāmā on the one hand and led to its resolution on the other. J's major antediluvian figures, Adam and Cain, are disobedient, acting against explicit divine commands (2:17, 4:7), as are their descendants whose behavior leads to the flood (6:5–7). Noah by contrast is J's first obedient hero, doing everything Yahweh commands (7:5). He "finds favor in the eyes of Yahweh" (6:8) and is called righteous (ṣaddîq, 7:1), the first to be so characterized by these typical J phrases. His descendants among Israel's ancestors will exhibit these same traits. Abraham too is obedient to God's commands (12:4), finds favor in God's eyes (18:3), and is called righteous (15:6).

Noah's behavior is thus contrasted with that of J's antediluvian characters, who represent a negative image of human living, and presented as paradigmatic of Israel's ancestors in the postdiluvian era. His first two acts in the new age only underline his role as the initiator of a new era. Upon disembarking from the ark he builds the first altar to God (8:20), an act to be repeated by Abraham (12:7, 8; 13:18) and Isaac (26:25). Next, Noah plants a vineyard (9:20), reenacting Yahweh's planting of the garden at creation and reestablishing highland agriculture as the fundamental pursuit of Israel's ancestors who descend from him.

J's understanding of the flood as the division between the first and second eras of Israel's history has to commend it the common-sense recognition that the destruction of all life necessitates the beginning of a new age. This was in fact the view of Mesopotamian traditions of the flood. In the Sumerian King List, for example, the flood represents the point at which the institution of kingship, founded first at the beginning of the antediluvian era, must be lowered from heaven a second time to reconstitute human society.[135] In the Atrahasis epic, to cite another case, the pattern of reproduction and the social constraints to it with which its audience was familiar, were instituted first immediately after the flood, which brought to an end the imbalances present in the primeval era.[136]

On this basis, J's antediluvian narrative should be viewed as a distinct and unified section within his epic of Israel's origins as a whole. It should be read as a unified literary complex describing creation, early history, and flood, the kind of literary complex represented in other ancient Near Eastern primeval traditions.[137] What is distinctive about J's primeval narrative is the way it founds, at the origin of time, the natural landscape and social structures typical of the agricultural society of biblical Israel.

3

The Ancestors in Canaan

They themselves emerge from the antique gloom of consecrated
tradition with forms molded by generations of recital. . . . They
are full of incident and character; and they are firmly rooted in
the soil.

J. Estlin Carpenter, *The Hexateuch*

The second major section of the Yahwist's epic begins in Genesis 9 with the family of Noah, the only human survivors of the flood, and concludes with the emigration of Jacob's family to Egypt in Genesis 45–50. Its narratives are dominated by stories of Israel's ancestors residing in the Canaanite hill country that made up the heartland of biblical Israel. Of these ancestors, the families of Abraham, Isaac, and Jacob are given by far the most attention. The stories of these three families in the hills of Canaan reveal most about the Yahwist's environment and his attitudes toward it in this part of the epic.

This one section of the Yahwist's epic accounts for more than half of its total length, and by the simple virtue of size it dominates the epic as a whole. Some, including the father of the documentary study of the Pentateuch, Julius Wellhausen, have considered it the very heart of J's narrative. "The story of the Patriarchs, which belongs to this document almost entirely, is what best marks its character; that story is not here dealt with merely as a summary introduction to something of greater importance which is to follow, but as a subject of primary importance, deserving the fullest treatment possible."[1] The same conclusion has been reached in a recent study of J by the literary critic Harold Bloom, who considers these stories of Israel's ancestors the "narra-tive center" of the epic, framed by the primeval and exodus stories that take their significance from these ancestral narratives.[2] Peter Ellis, while believing that the Yahwist's epic reaches its climax with the Sinai covenant, recognized the dominant place of the ancestral narratives. "Structurally viewed the saga bulges in the center. Even if there had been an account of the conquest joined to the Exodus and Numbers sections of the national history, the 800 verses given to the patriarchal history would still seem long. Any analysis of the saga as a whole, therefore, must take this imbalance into account."[3]

Yet no such central significance has been attributed to the accounts of Israel's ancestors in this part of J's epic by most biblical scholars over the past century. The prevailing view has been, in fact, to regard the ancestral narrative as an introduction or prologue to a more important event to follow. That event has by most been identified as the exodus from Egypt. This point of view was put into classical form for the last generation of biblical scholars by Gerhard von Rad. According to von Rad, the ancestral narratives are for J in no sense crucial in themselves; they are only significant as they point toward the exodus and settlement traditions that follow. In J's hands, "the whole patriarchal period has ceased to be regarded as significant in itself; it is now no more than a time of promise pointing to a fulfillment outside itself. . . . In this way the whole relationship between God and the patriarchs is presented as a preparatory stage, which reached its fulfillment only in the divine revelation, and in the appropriation of it by the community descended from the patriarchs."[4] This judgment that the center of J's interests lies outside the ancestral narratives and that the ancestral narratives are preparatory in character is reflected in Martin Noth's influential study of Pentateuchal traditions, Claus Westermann's monumental Genesis commentary, and by most who have recently taken up the study of J in particular, including Peter Ellis, Robert Coote, and John Van Seters.[5]

In spite of this more recent tradition of scholarship, Wellhausen's early sense of the strategic importance of the ancestral narratives in J's ideology still has much in its favor. In the first place, the heavy reliance of the "preparatory" school on external literary models for assessing the structure and focus of J's epic should be pointed out. This is particularly true for von Rad and the many who have been influenced by him. Rather than starting with J's epic itself, von Rad read and analyzed it through the lens of a set of "historical creeds"—especially Deuteronomy 26:5b–9, and 6:20–24, and Joshua 24:2b–13—which he believed to be older than, and the sources of, J's traditions, both problematic presumptions.[6] Since these creedal texts highlight the exodus and settlement motifs, von Rad took these events to be central for the Yahwist as well.

A second external literary lens through which J has been interpreted is the later Priestly Writer, who aimed through a series of additions to J to reorient the perspective of the old traditions. P's major reorientation of the older Yahwistic traditions was to shift their focus to Mt. Sinai, where the cult was instituted, a reorientation P accomplished by the insertion into the narratives of a series of covenants (Gen 9:1–17, 17:1–27, Exod 31:12–17) culminating at Sinai, and by the incorporation into the Sinai narrative of a massive corpus of cultic and social law. While there can be no doubt that the center of the Priestly Work into which J was incorporated lies at Mt. Sinai, the question must be raised whether P's perspective is also J's.

When the Yahwist's epic is considered on its own merits, a number of its features point to the central position of the ancestral narratives. First, of course, is the sheer size of the ancestral materials when compared to the rest of J's narratives. One does not expect the longest and central movement of the epic narrative to be devoted entirely to preparatory matters. Second is the manner in which the ancestral narratives provide the focal point for the narratives that precede and follow them. The primeval narrative is the prologue to the ancestral narratives, founding in the first age of world history the environmental and social realities that will be the basis for the ancestral stories which follow. And the Egypt, desert, and Sinai experiences are presented as a temporary exile from the hill country in which the ancestral narratives take place. J's southern narratives in Exodus and Numbers are constantly and thoroughly oriented toward the Canaanite hill country, a fact that will be addressed in detail in chapter 4.

Furthermore, the Yahwist's interest in explaining Israel's place in the world, its relation to its land and its neighbors, is worked out more fully here than in any other section of the epic. The manner in which this is accomplished is in large part the aim of the following analysis. At the outset of this analysis of the ancestral narratives, it is important not to dismiss them as possessing a merely preparatory or subsidiary character. The view of the land and the relationship of people to it in these stories is in no way a secondary concern to J. J's views disclosed in the ancestral narratives lie at the very heart of his sense of place and theology of nature.

The Environment of the Ancestral Age: Israelite Highland Agriculture

The lives and movements of Israel's ancestors in the book of Genesis have been taken to provide some of the strongest evidence for the Bible's pastoralist orientation. The herds and tents of Abraham, Isaac, and Jacob have suggested a nomadic existence for these patriarchs and their families, a suggestion only strengthened by their frequent migrations across the countryside. In its classical form, shaped substantially by Albrecht Alt, this approach connected Israel's ancestors with a kind of pure pastoral nomadism, which originated in the desert away from settled areas and maintained a distinct economy and set of social norms, until it slowly evolved with sedentarization into the agricultural life characteristic of biblical Israel.[7]

As has been noted in chapter 1, such a pure form of autonomous desert pastoral nomadism—based as it is on outdated views of the ecological setting, social structure, and history of societies in the biblical environs and time frame—can no longer be used as a model for understanding Israelite origins or its social organization.[8] Yet the image of Israel's ancestors as pastoral nomads, completely distinct in their economy and customs from sedentary Canaanite farmers, has been in the past century the most common lens for reading the ancestral narratives. Both Gerhard von Rad and Martin Noth relied heavily on Albrecht Alt's reconstruction of patriarchal origins and life-styles.[9] And many readers before and since would not quarrel with Julius Wellhausen's image of the patriarchal families: "They are all peace-loving shepherds, inclined to live quietly beside their tents."[10]

Because of the serious problems new scholarship has raised about the kind of pure, desert-based pastoral nomadism posited for Israel's ancestors by most scholars in the first half of the twentieth century, several modified pictures of Israel's ancestors have been proposed. An early one, argued in one form or another by both W. F. Albright and C. H. Gordon, explained the ancestors' nomadic activity as linked to their occupation as traders and to the donkey caravans they employed in this pursuit.[11] Such mercantile nomadism was seen as the explanation for the frequent movement of Israel's ancestors in Canaan and for their contacts with Syria and Egypt as well.

A more recent modification of the traditional understanding of Israel's ancestors as pastoral nomads is developed by Robert Coote and David Ord in their study of the Yahwist.[12] According to Coote and Ord, J's society was made up almost entirely of "peasants," small farmers in the Canaanite hill country, yet J portrayed their ancestors as nomadic pastoralists, as Bedouin such as inhabited the southern deserts in the Negev and the Sinai Peninsula. This was done, according to Coote, not because nomadic pastoralism represented the origin of the majority of Israel's population or because it was still preserved in the customs or ideology of sedentary Israelites, but primarily for a strategic reason. David needed the loyalty of the southern Bedouin as a buffer to protect his state from Egyptian threats. The Yahwist, David's court historian, therefore wrote his epic for the ears of the Bedouin sheikh in attendance at David's court, casting the history of Israel in terms of his culture to invite and solidify Bedouin support for David's kingdom. In this case, the ancestors are in fact interpreted as pastoral nomads just as in traditional scholarship. But the purpose of this portrayal has been radically revised.

A third modification of the traditional view has exerted by far the greatest influence on recent understandings of the economy of Israel's ancestors. This modification springs largely from recent investigations undertaken by M. B. Rowton, J. T. Luke, and V. H. Matthews into the relationships between pastoralist and urban populations at the Syrian site of Mari during the early second millennium B.C.E.[13] According to these studies, pastoralism in the Levant, including that practiced by Israel's ancestors, needs to be reconceived as "seminomadic" or "enclosed" (Rowton) pastoralism. In this type of herding, pastoralists are involved in a symbiotic relationship with sedentary areas as part of a "dimorphic" (Rowton) society. They are neither isolated from urban areas nor self-sufficient. They dwell rather in semiarid zones contiguous with their sedentary neighbors and rely on the trade of pastoral for agricultural goods. They may even practice some cultivation themselves to supplement their herding economy. Their mobility is transhumant, following a rather regular movement from pasture to pasture dictated by the seasonal year.

Such an economy of seminomadic pastoralism has now been taken over widely as a model for understanding the ecological orientation of the ancestral narratives. It has been employed by Rowton, Luke, and Matthews themselves to illuminate the stories of Genesis.[14] And it is being adopted by biblical scholars as well. William Dever, for example, employs it in his reconstruction of the patriarchal period of Israelite history, as does Claus Westermann in his commentary on the patriarchal narratives.[15]

The new understanding of Israel's ancestors as specialized, seminomadic pastoralists interacting with their sedentary neighbors in a dimorphic society has many advantages over the older view of them as isolated desert pastoralists. Yet even here a rather sharp distinction between nomadic pastoralism and sedentary agriculture is maintained that does not deal precisely enough with all of the details in J's portrait of his ancestors. Some details in the ancestral narratives identify them as residents of the arable land itself who are involved in its cultivation. Moreover, certain features of these stories often connected with nomadism, especially herds and movements, may not in the end reflect nomadism at all. As was the case with the Yahwist's primeval narrative, his ancestral narrative must be carefully reexamined to discover the ecological setting it assumes before the Yahwist's attitudes toward the environment in this section of the epic can be properly understood.[16]

Sedentary Agriculture in the Ancestral Narratives

The Yahwist's portrait of Israel's ancestors contains numerous details that associate them directly with sedentary agriculture and point to this setting as the perspective from which their stories are told. One of the most important of these is the divine gift of land to Israel's ancestors and their descendants, a distinctively prominent theme in J and one that provides a key unifying motif to the epic's entire postflood era.[17] According to J, Abraham is the primary recipient of the promises of the land. The first promise is delivered to him at Shechem (Gen 12:6–7), the second in the vicinity of Bethel and Ai (13:14–17), and the third at Hebron and its environs (13:18, 15:7–21). To Abraham's grandson Jacob the promise of land is repeated at Bethel (28:13–16), and to his son Isaac it is delivered in the area of Beersheba and Gerar (26:2–5, 23–25, 32–33).

The crucial fact that emerges from this series of land grants is that they cede to Abraham and his descendants the agricultural heartland of biblical Israel. Shechem, Bethel, and Hebron are the old centers—in the north, center, and south—of the Canaanite hill country. They mark out a line along the top of this mountain range, where the humid climate is conducive to intensive agriculture and where the choicest arable tracts in these highlands are located. The ancestors are thus linked, not to the semiarid zones to the east and south of this territory that were conducive to specialized pastoralism and in which the modern Bedouin still reside, but rather with the richest agricultural land of the Israelite highlands, traditionally inhabited by sedentary farmers. Ownership of land, a fixed asset, is characteristic of sedentary societies, but less so of nomads, whose primary capital rests in their mobile herds.

The residents of the semiarid and arid zones close to the hill country are not Israel's ancestors but the ancestors of Israel's neighbors. Ishmael, father of the Ishmaelites, is the best example. Banished from Abraham's household into the semiarid or arid territory (*midbār*) south of Hebron, his mother Hagar receives there an announcement of Ishmael's birth that destines him to reside in this area, moving across it like the wild ass (*pere'*) and living in tension with his sedentary neighbors (16:7–12). The only exception to this pattern that links Israel's ancestors with the humid highlands lies in the grant of land between Beersheba and Gerar to Abraham's son Isaac. While cultivation is practiced in these areas, their semiarid climate makes them more conducive to an emphasis on stock raising within the mix of cultivation and herding that characterizes Mediterranean agriculture. The sites of Beersheba and Gerar will be taken up in more detail when the pastoral aspects of ancestral farming are examined.

In all of these accounts of Yahweh's gift of the land, J consistently uses the general term *'ereṣ* instead of the more particular *'ādāmâ*, arable soil. There appear to be two reasons for this. First, the land in the Canaanite highlands promised to Abraham and his descendants was in J's time composed not only of arable tracts but also of grazing and forested areas that made up a considerable portion of these hillsides. For such terrain with diverse land uses, the general *'ereṣ* is a more adequate and inclusive designation.[18] Second, one of J's interests in the postdiluvian period is to describe the origins of the actual political units that comprised his world and thereby to explain and legitimate their relationships and the balances of power between them. For this purpose the term *'ereṣ*, employed characteristically by J to designate a country or political territory, is the appropriate one.[19]

Not only are Israel's ancestors granted possession of the hill country with its prime arable land, they are also pictured as residents at home in it. One of the ways in which J achieves this is through a precise use of the vocabulary for residential status. An expression J consistently avoids using for Israel's ancestors as residents of the hill country is the word *gēr*, "resident alien," an individual who lived outside of his own landed property and outside the protection of his own kinship structures.[20] J reserves this term only for those instances when Israel's ancestors travel outside the hill country and take up temporary residence away from home: in Egypt (Gen 12:10, 15:13, 47:4), Philistia (Gen 21:34, 26:3), or Syria (Gen 32:5). For their residence in the hill country, J employs the verb *yāšab*, "live, dwell" (e.g., Gen 13:7, 18; 22:9; 24:3; 34:10). Thus J does not present his ancestors in the highlands as an unlanded, transient folk, whether foreign immigrants or nomadic pastoralists. For J, they are firmly rooted in the hill country and are temporary, alien residents only when outside of it. This point of view is reinforced by the naming of the hill country as Jacob's own land (Gen 30:25, 32:10) or the land of his ancestors (Gen 31:3), when he is temporarily residing in Syria. Furthermore, J's ancestors purchase no property from others in the hill country as they are pictured as doing by the Elohistic (Gen 33:19–20) and Priestly writers (Gen 23:1–20).

J's perspective contrasts clearly with the Priestly Writer's in this regard. According to P, Israel's ancestors are *gērîm*, resident aliens, in the hill country itself. In fact, one of P's characteristic expressions for the hill country, the heartland of biblical Israel, is *'ereṣ mĕgūrêhem*, "the land of their sojourning/alien residence" (Gen 17:8, 28:4, 36:7, 37:1; Exod 6:4; cf. Gen 23:4, 35:27). P's terminology may have less to do with an understanding of his ancestors as seminomadic pastoralists residing temporarily among their native, sedentary neighbors than with his interest in distinguishing sharply between the stages of Israelite history. The promise alone was delivered to the ancestors, according to P, and the actual possession of the land was not accomplished until a later period. These two aspects of the ancestors' alien status in the hill country may not be unrelated. In any event, they provide a clear contrast to the view of J on this matter.

J's portrait of Israel's ancestors as landed people at home in the Israelite highlands appears to be challenged by the occasional reference to them living in tents, because such are characteristic of nomadic populations in the surrounding semiarid zones. Yet J describes the kinds of homes inhabited by Israel's ancestors in a variety of ways. In some cases, they are pictured living in houses (*bāttîm*; Gen 27:14, 29:13, 33:17) rather than in tents (*'ohālîm*). Moreover, the common Hebrew idiom for the extended family, *bêt 'āb*, "house (hold) of the father," which is related to the Israelite multiple-family village compound, is employed by J for ancestral households (e.g., Gen 7:1, 12:1, 15:3, 18:19, 30:30, 38:11, 46:31).[21] In certain instances, when tents are mentioned, the contexts rule out nomadic life-styles. Noah, a tender of vineyards (Gen 9:20), which demand long-term sedentary farming, lies down in his tent (*'ōhel*; 9:21). In other instances, references to tents carry idiomatic rather than literal meanings. For example, when Jacob is contrasted to his brother Esau, a man of the field (*'îš śādeh*), as one sitting in tents (*yōšēb 'ohālîm*), the phrase likely carries the simple sense of "staying at home," a homebody (25:27).[22]

The occasional references to tents in J's ancestral narratives thus do not necessarily depict Israel's ancestors as seminomadic pastoralists.[23] Two explanations for their mention appear most likely. First, tents may be employed for specialized tasks within the mixed agricultural economy typical of biblical Israel. For example, they may be used in the field during peak work periods such as the harvest or by members of the family watching the household's flocks some distance from home. Second, many of J's references to tents occur in the course of his account of Abraham's initial journey through Canaan from north to south (12:8; 13:3, 18; 18:1), a journey that has as its purpose the granting of land to Abraham and his descendents and his laying claim to it, and does not reflect the patterns of transhumant pastoralism typical in the environs of the Israelite hill country. The nature of such ancestral travels will be taken up in more detail later in the discussion of pastoralist aspects of ancestral narratives.

The sedentary character of J's ancestors is also illustrated by their close association with the urban areas of the hill country. Of course, pastoralists may have close and repeated contact with urban populations, as is characteristic of the societies in Mari and its environs.[24] But the behavior of J's ancestors goes somewhat beyond this. Abraham builds altars at Shechem (Gen 12:6–7), Bethel (12:8, 13:3–4), and Hebron (13:18), which are certainly understood by J to legitimate Israel's worship at these cities in his own day. Isaac builds an altar in the city of Beersheba, thus founding its sanctuary (Gen 26:23–25). In this case, by the digging of a new well, Isaac even founds the city itself, or at least provides it with a new name (26:25, 32–33). Such activity hardly suggests a pastoral orientation for Israel's ancestors or for the Yahwist who placed their narratives at the heart of Israel's epic.

Descriptions of Israel's ancestors actually cultivating their land adds further evidence to J's portrait of them as sedentary farmers. Taken together, these descriptions outline the same kind of grain-based, dryland farming founded in the primeval age as the typical pursuit of human society. One of the clearest portrayals of this agricultural setting is found in Isaac's patrimonial blessing of his son Jacob, granting him the family's inheritance:

> Oh, the scent of my son
>   like the scent of the field
>   which Yahweh has blessed.
>
> May God grant to you
>   the dew of the skies
>   and the plenty of the earth,
>   an abundance of grain and wine. (Gen 27:27–28) [25]

Such a blessing requests for Jacob the same divine powers associated with Yahweh in the primeval age: the production of rain in the skies and fertility in the earth. First and foremost, it bestows the hope for an abundance of grain (cf. 27:37).[26]

A grain-based agricultural economy such as this is reflected in the practice of Isaac himself, who is described as sowing grain (*wayyizra'*) and reaping an abundant harvest (Gen 26:12). It can be seen as well in the story of Joseph, whose brothers travel to Egypt for the express purpose of buying grain, their supplies having been exhausted because of a lack of rainfall in the hill country causing drought and crop failure (Gen 43:1–2, 44:1–2). Vignettes of cereal cultivation can also be seen in the Elohist's work, a document with an ecological orientation similar to the Yahwist's, when Reuben returns from the wheat harvest (*qĕṣîr ḥiṭṭîm;* 30:14) and Joseph dreams of his brothers binding sheaves in the field (37:5–8). It may be that the Yahwist's distinctive image for the ancestors' multitude of descendants, *ka'ăpar hā'āreṣ* "like the soil of the earth" (Gen 13:16, 28:14), was intended to recall the creation of the farmer from the soil he was destined to farm (Gen 2:7, 3:19).

The diet of Israel's ancestors illustrates this reliance on cereal production. In the meals of Israel's ancestors, of Abraham (18:5–6) and Lot (19:3), of Isaac (27:17) and his sons Jacob and Esau (25:34), and of Jacob's sons (37:25), bread is the staple.[27] In fact, bread (*leḥem*) is so basic to the ancestral diet that, in J's diction, bread becomes almost synonymous with "food" (e.g., 47:12, 15) and "eating bread" synonymous with partaking of a meal (e.g., 37:25; 43:25, 32). The ancestral diet also included lentils ('*ădāšîm*), the primary ingredient of the stew Jacob prepares for Esau, thereby attributing the cultivation of legumes along with grain to Israel's ancestors.[28]

As was typical of agriculture in biblical Israel and has been typical throughout the Mediterranean highlands until today, grain production was combined by Israel's ancestors with horticulture and viticulture, the growing of trees and vines for their fruit. For the Yahwist, this aspect of ancestral agriculture is described primarily in terms of the cultivation of vineyards and the production from them of wine. Vineyards are mentioned specifically in relation to Noah, the first farmer after the flood (9:20–21), to Isaac and Jacob in Isaac's patrimonial blessing (27:27–28), and finally, to Judah in the blessing of Jacob (49:11–12) that concludes the ancestral narratives.[29] Wine is a typical beverage at ancestral meals (9:21, 19:32–34, 27:25). While cereal cultivation can be practiced as a supplemental activity by seminomadic pastoralists, as it is by the modern Bedouin, tending vineyards is a sedentary occupation, demanding a long-term investment in the land before its fruits can be harvested.[30] This aspect of ancestral farming, together with the rest of the data surveyed above, points to the conclusion that J pictured his ancestors engaged in the sedentary agriculture typical of biblical Israel in his day.

Pastoralism within a Mixed Agrarian Economy

According to the Yahwist, Israel's ancestors were pastoralists. They raised and owned livestock, an activity that plays a major role in a number of J's narratives. It is this occupation that is noticed first by most readers of these stories and, as has been noted, has come to define the economy of Israel's ancestors in an exclusive sense. Given the evidence for the ancestors' involvement in sedentary agriculture just described, their herding of livestock must be looked at anew and reevaluated. When this is attempted, key features of the ancestors' pastoralism may be recognized as fitting best into the mixed agrarian economy typical of biblical Israel, in which the raising of animals was one aspect of sedentary village agriculture based on the cultivation of grains and fruits.

The ancestors' livestock The kinds of animals owned by J's ancestors is one important factor that points in this direction. The animals J attributes to the ancestors—sheep and goats (*ṣōʾn*), cattle (*bāqār*), donkeys (*ḥămōrîm/'ătōnōt*), and camels (*gĕmallîm*)—are the same domestic species characteristic of sedentary sites from the biblical period for which archaeologists have analyzed faunal remains. At Iron Age sites in the hill country and its immediate environs, based on numbers of bones found, sheep and goats were the most numerous, making up on average about two-thirds of the animal population; cattle were next, normally at a third or less of the population; and donkeys and camels accounted for much smaller percentages.[31] This population pattern in the livestock of sedentary agriculturalists is reflected exactly in the order by which Israel's ancestors' animals are listed. Sheep and goats always precede cattle in J's lists of animals, and these two types of animals are often mentioned alone without reference to other species (e.g., Gen 12:16, 26:14, 50:8).[32] When donkeys and camels are included in J's enumerations, they regularly follow flocks and herds (e.g., Gen 12:16, 24:35, 32:6).[33] Thus, in the kinds of animals J attributes to Israel's ancestors, as well as in the order in which they are enumerated, the ancestral livestock mirror the domestic animal populations known to have made up the pastoral component of sedentary agricultural towns and villages in the Iron Age, the period of biblical Israel.

Particular attention must be directed to the place of cattle in J's ancestral narratives. Not only are they regularly listed with sheep and goats among the ancestors' possessions, they occur at other important points in the narrative as well. A heifer ('eglâ) is one of the animals ritually killed in the covenant ceremony God initiates with Abraham (15:9–10). And a calf (ben-bāqār) is slaughtered for a meal Abraham provides for a party of guests who visit him at Hebron (18:7–8). Of all of the animals attributed to Israel's ancestors, cattle are the clearest indicator of a sedentary society. They are primarily raised in the hill country as draft animals, being used to plow the fields for the production of grain. Thus their high profile among the ancestors' possessions most likely reflects an economy involved in intensive cultivation.[34]

The sheep and goats owned by Israel's ancestors are not directly involved with cultivation. Just the opposite: they are raised as a supplement to the growing of crops in order to diversify the economy and thereby limit the risk of subsistence farming. They supplement the agrarian diet with dairy products and, to a lesser extent, meat and they provide wool for clothing. Through their supplementation of the diet and their exploitation of pasture lands, a different environmental niche than arable land for crops, they give the subsistence farmer a broader, more stable base for survival.[35] As such, sheep and goats represent one part of a mixed agricultural economy.

One indicator that sheep and goats play this complementary role in a sedentary agricultural economy is J's reference to the herdsmen of Israel's ancestors. Both Abraham and Lot have shepherds (rō'îm) working for them (13:7–8), as do Isaac and Abimelech, king of Gerar (26:20). Specialized herdsmen such as these are typical of agrarian societies in which the care of a family's or village's flocks are entrusted to professional shepherds who make up a minority of the population. Such professionals may graze their employers' herds near the village or take them to distant pastures for extended periods. By contrast, specialized herdsmen are uncharacteristic of nomadic societies in which the majority of the population is involved in the maintenance of the herds and in the periodic mobility demanded by seasonal changes in pasturage.[36] In both the Abraham–Lot and the Isaac–Abimelech narratives, quarrels and conflict are initiated by the shepherds, a narrative detail that likely arises from the low estimation of such specialized herdsmen in settled agrarian societies.[37]

In this context, Joseph's presentation of his family to Pharaoh deserves consideration (Gen 46:28–34, 47:1–6), because it appears to contradict the picture that has just been described. When introducing his brothers to the king of Egypt, Joseph instructs his brothers to tell Pharaoh they have all been shepherds since their youth, and not only themselves but their ancestors as well (46:34). This would appear to define all of the ancestors exclusively as specialized pastoralists, rather than as farmers involved in a mixed agricultural economy. Such in fact is the interpretation commonly derived from this account.[38]

Yet the details of the story suggest just the opposite. In the first place, Joseph's need to instruct his brothers carefully about their occupation as specialized pastoralists would hardly have been necessary if this in fact is what they were (46:34). His emphasis on this occupation—"from our youth until now, and not only we but our ancestors as well" (46:34, 47:3)—is suspect in the same sense. Such precise and overly stated instructions are best understood if such a profession had not been theirs, or if this were only one aspect of a mixed agricultural economy in which they were involved.[39] In the second place, Joseph's instructions are presented not as an identification of the traditional occupation of his family but as a strategy for their settlement in foreign territory: "Say, 'your servants are herders of livestock' . . . in order that (ba'ăbûr) you may live in the land of Goshen" (46:34). Because shepherds were regarded with disdain by the Egyptians, Israel's ancestors would not in such an occupation threaten their Egyptian hosts, and they would be allowed to exploit a specialized and undesirable economic niche (46:34). In fact, the Pharaoh even places his own livestock in Jacob's care (47:6).

One final point deserves mention regarding J's presentation of the livestock of Israel's ancestors. Because of J's special interest in the southern tribe of Judah and because his narratives place Israel's ancestors for the most part in the south, in Hebron and Beersheba and their environs, J has customarily been thought of as a southerner. Due to poorer soil and less rainfall, the southern hill country does not have the quantity of choice arable land found in the north. Conversely, the south has a greater quantity of grazing land, more suitable for raising livestock than intensive cultivation. As a result, the pastoral aspects of the mixed economy of Mediterranean farming have generally been given greater emphasis in the south.[40] If J's models for Israel's ancestors were the wealthy southern farmers with whom he was familiar, it is not surprising that J would take special delight in extolling their wealth by listing the herds they possessed (e.g., 12:16, 24:35, 32:15). Such a practice may reflect the balance of herding to cultivation in the south rather than any exclusive pursuit of a pastoralist economy.[41]

Indeed, it is misleading when speaking of the Israelite hill country and its environs to separate herding from cultivation. It is better to think in terms of a continuum between them. The question is not which one is practiced but in what combination and with what balance in the economy. For J, Israel's ancestors were wealthy southern farmers, with an economy based in the sedentary cultivation of grains and fruits, and supplemented with the extensive herding possible on the pastures of the southern hill country.

The ancestors' journeys One further aspect of the ancestral narratives deserves specific attention because it has played such a major role in the assessment of J's ancestors as pastoral nomads. That is their mobility, their movement from place to place, a feature of their life-style that has been almost automatically identified with nomadism.[42] Indeed, J's ancestral narratives are full of migrations. Following the flood, Noah's descendants move east into the Mesopotamian river valley (Gen 11:1–2). From here, Abraham's family moves west via Syria to the Canaanite hill country (11:28–30; 12:1–4a, 6). After taking up residence in these highlands, the ancestors take trips to Egypt twice, once by Abraham (12:10–20) and once by Jacob (46:28–34), to Philistia (by Isaac, 26:1–33), and to Syria (by Jacob, 27:41–45). In addition, they move within the hill country itself, locating at its major towns, Shechem, Bethel, and Hebron, as does Abraham upon his initial arrival (Gen 12:6–9, 13:18).

The key question that must be asked in order to determine the significance of these movements is the purpose for which they were undertaken. Jacob's trip to Syria, for example, was motivated by his brother's plot to kill him, not by any pastoralist demands. In fact, the pattern of movement described in the ancestral narratives bears little resemblance to the kind of transhumance or regular seasonal migration practiced by specialized pastoralists in the vicinity of the Canaanite highlands. Such transhumant pastoralists in general exploit the semiarid grazing lands in the eastern hills, the Negev to the south, and the Judean Desert. Their movement in these areas between the rainy and dry seasons normally covers a range of only thirty-seven miles in the Negev and twelve in the Judean Desert, and then in a rather regular annual pattern.[43] Regular transhumance in these areas and over these distances does not characterize the ancestors, who instead travel between different countries and within the humid agricultural zones in the heart of the biblical hill country.

The real purpose of the movements of Israel's ancestors in J's narratives has to do with the basic etiological aim of the epic. In this regard, the major characters function as eponymous ancestors; they represent the national groups of J's own world whose names they carry. Their interactions with one another are narrated to explain and legitimate relationships and balances of power, ideal or real, which J wished to validate. Their activities are described primarily in order to show the origins of and to legitimate circumstances with which J's audience was familiar.[44] In this sense, J's ancestral narratives carry forward the etiological goals already encountered in the primeval narrative.

It is within this context that the ancestors' movements in J must be primarily understood. In regard to the ancestors' travels within Canaan itself, Wellhausen understood this very well: "The patriarchal journeys up and down in JE are not designed to represent them as wandering nomads, but serve to bring them in contact with all the sacred places with which they had special associations."[45] Such is exactly J's intent in narrating the stops of Abraham at Shechem, Bethel, and Hebron. J uses this itinerary for two purposes. At each site Abraham and his ancestors are granted the land and its environs, thus establishing possession of the entire hill country; and at each site Abraham builds an altar, thus founding and legitimating the Yahwistic sanctuaries at the hill country's major urban centers. It is first and foremost to claim the land and to establish its major sanctuaries that J's Abraham moves from place to place, not to respond to the demands of transhumant pastoralism.

When the ancestors travel outside the hill country, into the territories of other ancient Near Eastern governments, the ultimate etiological goal of these travelogues in J's epic is to define the nature of the relationship between the Israelite descendants of its ancestors and the descendants of these neighboring peoples. Jacob's trip to Haran, for example, provides a historical explanation for features of the Israelite–Aramean relationship in J's day. Jacob's marriage to Laban's daughters signifies the ancient connections Israel believed to exist between itself and the Arameans (29:1–30), and the treaty between Jacob and Laban establishes the border between the lands of these two peoples (31:49).[46] A story such as this is not about pastoral nomadism but about political alliances. Even at the surface level of the narrative, pastoral nomadism is not an obvious feature. While Jacob does herd sheep and goats as a youth (25:27, 30:25–43), his travels are not related to this. He goes to Laban to escape his brother's rage and save his life (27:41–45), moving in the process from one town to another (26:33, 27:1, 29:4).

By far the most significant relocation of Israel's ancestors outside of the hill country occurs at the end of Genesis when Jacob's family moves down to Egypt. This important journey is prefigured in an earlier story about Abraham's trip to Egypt (12:10–20), a narrative that has many parallels to the subsequent account of Jacob and his family.[47] In the case of Jacob's family, the initial trip to Egypt is undertaken not as part of a regular pattern of seasonal transhumance but as a result of extraordinary climatic conditions that produced a serious drought. Moreover, the trip is motivated not by decreasing pasturage but by a dwindling supply of grain and increasingly severe famine conditions (42:5, 43:1–2). On the initial trip, the entire family is not involved. Only the sons are sent to purchase grain while the household head, Jacob, remains at his residence in the hill country. The final move is a major relocation, requiring numerous wagons and pack animals (45:16–28). These details are less characteristic of a seminomadic society whose entire population is involved in a regular pattern of transhumance to maintain their herds than they are of an agricultural family in the southern hill country whose crops have suffered repeated failure and who have become refugees emigrating in the hope of survival. Such is the portrait of J's ancestors at the surface level of the narrative.

At the etiological level, the ancestral move to Egypt is designed by J to explain and define the relations between Egypt and Israel in his own day. These relations, in light of J's treatment of them, are unusually complex and paradoxical. On the one hand, Egypt is a haven preserving the lives of Israel's ancestors. On the other hand, by enslaving its ancestors (Exod 1:8–12) and nearly wiping them out at the sea (Exodus 14–15), it represents the greatest threat to Israel's existence. The character of this complex relationship will be analyzed in greater detail in chapter 4. Even this brief survey should make it clear, however, that the movement of Israel's ancestors to Egypt in J's epic is narrated not in the context of seminomadic pastoralism but with the aim of defining the relationship between two agricultural societies.

Isaac's journey to Gerar in the land of the Philistines (Gen 26) is, of all the ancestral movements in J, the one that might best be explained in terms of seminomadic pastoralism and seasonal transhumance.[48] It takes place within the semiarid zone south of the hill country that was particularly conducive to such an economy and it involves disputes over water sources for Isaac's herds. Yet as the conclusion of the narrative clearly indicates, its ultimate purpose is to bring Isaac into contact with the Philistines in order to establish the city of Beersheba and its water supply as ancient Israelite property (vv 23–25, 32–33), to lay claim to various water sources between Beersheba and Gerar (vv 17–22), and to validate those claims through a treaty agreed to by Isaac and the king of Gerar (vv 26–31). Territorial claims such as these, all characteristic of a landed kingdom such as the Israel of J's time, lie behind this story and the movements of Isaac depicted in it. Even in its narrative details, some of which have already been referred to, Isaac is pictured as a southern farmer, cultivating grain (v 12) and having in his household specialized herdsmen (v 20), just as does Abimelech of Gerar.

One other ancestral journey deserves attention, Abraham's move from Ur in the Mesopotamian river valley to the Canaanite hill country (11:28–30, 12:1–4a, cf. 15:7). According to one influential school of thought, which held that Israel's ancestors could be located historically at the beginning of the second millennium, at least a thousand years before J's epic, Abraham's migration was associated with the movements of the Amorites, an important group at this time believed to be nomads from the desert fringes.[49] However, in the face of serious challenges to the early second millennium dating of the patriarchs and to the traditional interpretation of the Amorites, such a nomadic background for Abraham's journey can no longer be defended.[50] In fact, according to J, Abraham leaves an urban area, Ur, and immediately locates in other urban areas, Shechem, Bethel, and Hebron. For J, Abraham's travels have nothing to do with nomadic behavior. J's interest in locating Israel's ancestry outside of the hill country is likely associated, as Kyle McCarter has suggested, with a process of ethnic boundary marking by which the Israelite community of J defined itself over against the local Canaanites.[51] In fact, the sharp difference between Israel's ancestors and those of the Canaanites is one of the most elemental concerns of the Yahwist throughout the epic.[52]

Thus the movements of Israel's ancestors are employed by J to explain the origin and current legitimacy of the territorial, political, and cultic realities of his day. These are travels shaped primarily by the etiological and ideological concerns in the service of which the narratives are told. Norman Gottwald, in his critique of the traditional nomadic interpretation of ancestral travels, refers to their ideological tenor as the motif of "migrations as preparations for religious destiny."[53] Such concerns, rather than a conception of his ancestors as seminomadic pastoralists, lie behind J's narration of their travels. Indeed, when the details of these travel narratives, together with those of the ancestral narratives as a whole, are closely examined, they reflect a view of Israel's ancestors as hill country farmers practicing the diversified agricultural economy typical of the Israelite populace.

The environmental setting of the Yahwist's ancestral narratives is therefore the same setting presumed in his primeval narratives. Israel's ancestors following the flood are involved in the same agricultural economy established at creation in the primeval age as the lot of humankind, and reestablished by Noah after the flood. They practice the mixed farming that has been typical of the Mediterranean highlands for millennia, in which grain-based cultivation is supplemented with fruit crops and animal husbandry to meet the demands and to limit the risks of subsistence agriculture. This is the setting within which the Yahwist's views of nature, of the human place within it, and of its relationship to the divine in the ancestral narratives have been shaped. Only by examining the Yahwist's thought within the context of this environment can it properly be understood.

The Place of Nature in the Ancestral Narratives

The modern dichotomy between nature and history has affected twentieth-century interpretation of the ancestral traditions in significant ways. Perhaps the most important consequence of such dualistic thinking has been the sharp distinction commonly drawn between the primeval and patriarchal ages, linking the former to nature and the latter to history. According to this approach, the primeval narrative concerns itself with creation. Its horizon is the world (of nature), its character mythic, and its treatment of humanity abstract and universal. By contrast, the ancestral narrative concerns itself with human culture. Its focus narrows to follow the affairs of an actual people, a single, distinct family whose experiences inaugurate a particular history, the national history of the people of Israel. In the ancestral narrative, the biblical narrator thus leaves behind the realm of nature and myth and enters the world of history proper.

Many statements from recent scholarship could be gathered to show the broad influence of this stance toward the ancestral traditions. A few representative comments may be mentioned by way of illustration. A good example to begin with comes from the most detailed modern commentary on Genesis. Its author, Claus Westermann, speaks of the Yahwist "setting the story of primeval events before the historical section proper," by which he means the stories of Israel's ancestors and their descendants in Genesis 12–50 and Exodus. These patriarchal stories "present the history of Israel" while the primeval narrative possesses "a far wider horizon," presenting "what Israel has to say about God the creator."[54]

Remarks from two other recent commentaries on Genesis provide further illustrations. E. A. Speiser argues that the break between the primeval and patriarchal stories "is sharper than is immediately apparent." The call of Abraham in Genesis 12:1–3 signals

> the beginning of the integral history of a particular group as opposed to background episodes in the prehistory of the race as a whole. The story commences with one individual, and extends gradually to his family, then to a people and later still to a nation. Yet it is not to be a tale of individuals or a family or a people as such. Rather it is to be the story of a society in quest of an ideal. Abraham's call, in short, marks the very beginning of the biblical process.[55]

A similar tone is set by Walter Brueggemann in his introduction to the ancestral narratives: "The one who calls the world into being now makes a second call. This call is specific. Its object is identifiable in history. . . . The God who forms the world is the same God who creates Israel."[56] These views are compatible with, if not in some sense directly dependent on, the view that biblical literature can best be described as *Heilsgeschichte,* or "salvation history," one of whose most eloquent spokesmen was Gerhard von Rad.[57] According to von Rad, the history of redemption began with Abraham. His call in Genesis 12:1–3 was "the opening of redemptive history with its promise of a blessing for Israel and, through Israel, for all the races on earth."[58] Abraham thus represents not only the beginning of history proper but the beginning of the history of human redemption as well.

A consequence of this assessment of the ancestral narratives as especially historical in character, when compared to the primeval story, has been a major effort in the last century to establish the historicity of the ancestors.[59] On the basis of emerging archaeological data from the second millennium B.C.E., various proposals have been constructed to locate the patriarchs in specific settings, ranging from the Middle Bronze Age at the beginning of the second millennium to the Early Iron Age at its end. No commentary of Genesis nor introduction to the Hebrew Bible is complete without an extended treatment of this debate on the historical veracity and context of Israel's ancestors.

The treatment of the ancestral narratives as history proper and the special interest in their social and political character that have characterized biblical scholarship have led to the neglect of those aspects of these stories that ground them in specific environmental contexts, even though these contexts are more often than not determinative for the structure and aim of the narrative. Such an approach has contributed substantially to the sharpening of the dichotomy between nature and history and to the theological judgment that nature is subordinate to history in biblical thought.

Nature and Society

A major problem the Yahwist's epic poses for this common assessment of the ancestral narratives as distinctively historical when compared to the primeval story has already been addressed in the interpretation of the primeval traditions in chapter 2. There it was pointed out that by whatever standard one wishes to differentiate history from myth—whether by the balance of divine and human agency, or by the conception of real or mythic time, or by the "founding" intent of the narrative—no clear line can be drawn between the primeval and ancestral periods within J's epic.[60] The narratives of both ages are designed to explain the origin of the natural and cultural realities that defined Israelite society at the time of the Yahwist.

A second problem the Yahwist poses for a narrowly historical appraisal of the ancestral age arises more directly from the character of these narratives themselves. As was the case in the primeval story, human culture in the ancestral narrative is largely defined in relation to its environmental context. No individual, family, or clan is of interest to J apart from its specific, concrete environmental milieu. And no event is narrated by J that is not motivated by, or does not have a major impact upon, the natural settings in which its main characters live.

The interrelationship between culture and nature in these narratives has already been illustrated in detail in the first part of this chapter. In the stories of Israel's ancestors, as in the primeval narrative, land plays a crucial and foundational role. And, as in the primeval narrative, the land at the center of the ancestral landscape is the arable terrain in the heartland of the Israelite hill country. It is this land on which Noah, first patriarch of the new era, reestablishes agriculture as the archetypal human vocation in the postflood age (9:20). And it is this land that is ceded to Israel through Abraham, the next great patriarch of this era and its archetypal figure for J (12:1–4a, 6–9; 13:14–17; 15:7–21).

The culture of Israel's ancestors, as it is described at the beginning of this chapter, is in substantial respects shaped by their adaptation to this environment. Their way of life is rural and agrarian, their livelihood dependent on a mixed agricultural economy based on dryland cultivation of grains and supplemented with fruit crops and the herding of sheep and goats. The character of ancestral society thus represents a direct continuation of the archetypal agricultural nature of human existence established with the creation of Adam and reestablished by Noah after the flood. Their work, their residence, their migrations, and as will be seen, their social conflicts and religious rituals, all reflect the realities—the demands and challenges—of this highland agricultural economy.

Two further observations may be made about the role of the land in J's particular treatment of the ancestral age. The first regards the prominence of land within J's theology of promise. The promise motif, with its divine blessing, represents the unifying theme in J's presentation of the ancestral era, in much the same way that the curse on arable land was the unifying concept in the primeval era. The theme of promise, as Kurt Galling once put it, is "the red thread through the whole work."[61] Expressed in formulaic language to each of Israel's ancestors, the promise includes the divine gifts of land, descendants, nationhood, and blessing.[62]

Particularly conspicuous within J's theology of promise is the gift of the land. In each of its occurrences in the promise formula, land stands first in the list of divine gifts (12:1–3, 7; 13:14–17; 26:2–5; 28:13–15). Furthermore, the promise of land is singled out as the special focus of the covenant between God and Abraham; it is the single promise guaranteed within this crucial covenant ceremony (Gen 15:7–21). In addition, land alone, of all of the elements of the divine promise, is retained by J in the narratives of Egypt and the desert as a leitmotif running through these stories and uniting them with the great body of ancestral legends at the heart of J's epic (Exod 3:8, 16–17; 13:5, 11; 33:1–3a; Num 11:12; 14:23).

Here, as in the primeval narrative, J's preoccupation with the land as the primary context for understanding human society takes thematic precedence over the ancient primal concern for human procreation itself. Procreation is, of course, a major theme in J's ancestral narratives, especially highlighted by the continual threat of the barrenness of Israel's matriarchs (11:30, 16:1–2, 25:21, 29:31), by God's repeated response in the granting of heirs (18:10, 25:21, 29:31), and by the inclusion of descendants in J's promise theology (e.g., 13:16, 22:17). Yet within J's promise formula, whenever the promises of land and descendants occur together, land always takes precedence. The distinctive emphasis on land in J's development of the promise theology may be brought into clearer focus by contrasting it with the Priestly perspective. The Priestly Writer, in the spirit of his theology in the primeval narratives, focuses primarily on procreation in the ancestral age, presenting descendants as the foremost blessing bestowed on Israel's ancestors (17:1–8, 35:11–12, 48:3–4; cf. 1:28, 9:1). Offspring are always the first element in the divine promise in Priestly texts.

A second observation about the role of land in J's ancestral narrative regards its political significance. Not only does the particular land Israel's ancestors inhabit play a defining role in their agricultural way of life, it also provides the territorial base for their ethnic and national identity. Together with land in J's promise theology is the guarantee of nationhood (12:2; cf. 18:17–19, 25:23).[63] Abraham resides and establishes religious sanctuaries at major urban centers—Shechem, Bethel, and Hebron—of the Israelite nation (12:6–8, 13:18). And in the promise of land expressed in the Abrahamic covenant, God defines the land of Abraham's descendants according to the ideal boundaries of the Davidic Kingdom (15:18–21).[64]

In J's ancestral narratives, as in his primeval narrative, the arable land of the Israelite highlands plays a foundational role in his understanding of human society and history. It defines the contours of the agricultural economy of Israel's ancestors and prescribes the territorial base for the nation of Israel composed of their descendants. The close link within J's theology between these meanings of land is expressed well in the view of land held by the current inhabitants of Baytin, a contemporary village at the site of ancient Bethel. "As in all landed societies, there is a strong attachment between the villager and the land he owns," writes Abdulla Lutfiyya in his anthropological study of Baytin. "The land is much more than just a source of income: it is a status symbol. The land is also a sacred border that links the villager with the past and the future. He inherits the land from his ancestors and expects to pass it on to his own children. Land ownership signifies a mystical relationship connecting the individual with the nation state. From this new interpretation (sic) has sprung the widely quoted saying '*man lā arda lah la watana lah*,' or 'he who possesses no land, has no fatherland.'"[65]

Just as the Yahwist's understanding of the origins of Israel is influenced in major ways by Israel's own specific environment, so are his views of the origins of Israel's neighbors. Together with his account of Israel's beginnings through the line of Shem, Abraham, Isaac, and Jacob, the Yahwist narrates the beginnings of Israel's closest neighbors—the Ishmaelites, Moabites, Ammonites, and Edomites—through stories of their first ancestors. In these etiological narratives, as in those of Israel's origins, the environment plays a prominent role in J's perception of culture.

One of the clearest examples is J's description of the origin of the Ishmaelites, Israel's neighbor on the desert fringes (Gen 16:7–14). The scene in which Ishmael's birth is announced is designed primarily to explain the association of the Ishmaelites with the desert through which their trading caravans passed (37:25, 28b; 39:1). The annunciation of Ishmael's birth takes place, not within the household of Abraham in the hill country at Hebron where Isaac's birth is announced (18:1, 10), but in the desert (*midbār*) to the south where his mother Hagar was driven by Isaac's mother Sarah. This desert setting is highlighted by the literary framework of the narrative, which twice specifies (vv 7, 14) the exact desert oasis in the western Negev at which these events occur.[66] The birth announcement itself focuses particularly on Ishmael's desert habitat.

> He will be a wild ass of a man;
> His hand will be against everyone, and everyone's hand against him,
> And in front of all of his brothers he will encamp. (16:12)

This announcement describes Ishmael as a wild ass (*pere*; v 12), a migratory species that inhabits the arid regions in which the narrative is set. With this animal metaphor, J evokes a number of characteristics of Ishmaelite culture: its desert environs, its trading economy (for which the domesticated donkey, along with the camel, was a primary beast of burden), and its—to the mind of the sedentary farmer—"uncivilized" temperament. This uncultured portrait of the Ishmaelites, typical of the attitude of sedentary societies toward the more transient populations at their margins, is continued in the following lines, which describe Ishmael (and thus his descendants) living outside the settled zone and as more prone to violence than his sedentary neighbors (v 12).[67] J's account of Ishmael's origins thus has been largely shaped, in its narrative form and in its oracular content, by geographical considerations, which J thought essential for understanding Ishmaelite culture.[68]

J's account of the origin of the Moabites and Ammonites in the Transjordanian hills is just as strongly influenced by environmental factors. In fact, the story of their origins is inseparable from a narrative once characterized by Hermann Gunkel in his taxonomy of legends as a "geological legend," a legend undertaken to explain the origin of a locality.[69] This is the narrative of the devastation of the southern Jordan Valley in Genesis 19, which has already been discussed at length in the analysis of the Garden of Eden in chapter 2. From its beginning, the story of Lot, father of Moab and Ben-ammi, is driven by environmental contingencies. Lot moves out of the hill country west of the Jordan because of a dispute between his and Abraham's shepherds over grazing land (13:7–11a). Settling in the verdant Jordan Valley, he is forced to move again to escape the natural disaster that reduced the valley floor to a desert (19:24–28). This time he settles in the hills to the east. Like Israel's first ancestors, Adam and Eve, who were forced from the oasis ecology of the Jordan Valley into highland farming in the Israelite hill country west of the Jordan, so Moab's and Ammon's first ancestor Lot, together with his daughters, is driven out of this valley ecology to the hill country east of the Jordan. In these highlands, in the heartland of the nations of Moab and Ammon, Moab, "the father of Moab to this day," and Ben-ammi, "the father of the Ammonites to this day," were conceived and born (19:30–38). Again their natural setting is seen by J to have played a defining role in the cultures of Moab and Ammon.

A third example of J's propensity for thinking of cultures in terms of their natural settings is his etiological narratives of the Edomites, descendants of Jacob's brother Esau, who inhabited the highlands southeast of the Dead Sea in the biblical period. Two motifs, characteristic of Edom's first ancestor and of its land, are introduced at Esau's birth and run through the narratives about him. They are the motifs of redness ('dm) and hairiness (ś'r), both traits possessed by Esau at his birth. He emerges from the womb a ruddy, reddish color ('admônî; 25:25), the same color ('ādōm) of the lentil stew for which he later sells his birthright (25:30–31). On this account, he receives the name Edom ('ĕdôm, v 30), "red." The choice of redness as a motif in these stories—for Esau's complexion at birth and the stew by which he loses his social status as firstborn—is certainly to be seen as J's etiological embellishment of the geographical and political designation Edom, deriving ultimately from the reddish color of the Nubian sandstone characteristic of the mountains of Edom east of the Arabah.[70]

Esau is also born with a thick mantle of hair ('adderet śē'ār; 25:25). This feature, too, becomes crucial in Esau's disenfranchisement. Considered by his blind father Isaac as the key to his identity (27:21), Esau's hairy physique is "usurped" by Jacob when he covers his skin with sheep's wool to pass himself off as his brother (27:11–17, 21–23). On account of this hairy appearance, he receives the name Esau ('ēśāw; 25:25), a name not linguistically related to śē'ār, "hair," but close enough in sound for J to connect the two by his typical penchant for folk etymologies. śē'ār, "hair," is actually related to the alternate name J employs for Edomite territory, Seir (śē'îr; 32:4), a name likely originating from the wooded ("bushy") mountains of Edom.[71] The two central motifs employed by J to describe the appearance of Esau and the loss of his familial status are thus etiological elaborations on two natural features that typified the land of the Edomite people.

J's understanding of the Edomites in terms of their environment is no-where more clearly illustrated than in Isaac's blessing, the climax of the narratives in Genesis 25 and 27 about Jacob and Esau as youths. In Isaac's blessings of both sons, productive land is the prime concern. To Jacob (and his descendants) is granted the inheritance of the firstborn, the fruitful soil of the Israelite hill country, blessed by Yahweh, where abundant rainfall supports grain farming and vineyards (27:27–28). To Esau (and his descendants) is granted by contrast the Edomite plateau where less productive land and less rainfall place greater demands on subsistence economies (27:39).[72] It is here that Esau is residing when Jacob returns with his family and possessions from Haran and is reconciled to his brother (32:4; 33:14, 16).

Esau's hunting, as one might expect, is the story's detail that has elicited from commentators most remarks in an environmental vein. In this case, too, outmoded dichotomies are painfully apparent, in particular the nineteenth-century "tripartite theory" that separated hunting, herding, and agriculture and saw civilization advancing from one to the other.[73] According to this scheme, Jacob represents the shepherds who supersede the hunters represented by Esau. To Westermann, for example, the story of the lentils (25:29–34) "is originally a 'civilization' myth about the shepherd who gained supremacy over the hunter, and could well have had its origin in the Transjordan where the conditions existed for such a transition."[74] This view of social development, however, is no longer accepted by anthropologists, nor was it J's way of thought, which considered highland agriculture to have been instituted as the lot of humankind at creation. Faunal remains document the fact that hunting was a common practice of the sedentary villages in the Canaanite and Israelite hill country.[75] The story of Jacob and Esau thus fits properly into the subsistence agricultural environment that characterizes J's primeval and ancestral narratives overall. The extent to which J wished to evoke an element of uncouthness among the Edomites by portraying their ancestor as a hunter, as has been suggested, is difficult to say.[76] While the hunter can be viewed as somewhat uncivilized because of the time he spends in the wild, it is just this talent of Esau's that his father Isaac particularly admires (25:28). At the same time, Isaac's reference to Esau's living by the sword in the "blessing" he delivers (27:40), together with the characterization of him as a hunter, may signal J's conception of the Edomites as potentially violent, a view not dissimilar to his portrait of the Ishmaelites.

The Philistines, Israel's neighbor in the coastal plain to the southwest, are not derived by J from the line of Shem, Abraham, Isaac, and Jacob, as are the Ishmaelites, Moabites, Ammonites, and Edomites. They are rather the descendants of Ham, Egypt, and Caphtor, a genealogical placement reflecting their origin outside of Palestine, in the Aegean, and their associations with Egypt to the south.[77] While the origin of the Philistines is not described within a narrative as are the origins of Israel's other close neighbors, J's account of them in the story of Isaac and of their king, Abimelech, in Genesis 26 is as absorbed with the relationship between a society and its environs as are his ethnological etiologies. The story of Isaac and Abimelech is basically about natural resources: land claims and water rights in the semiarid zone in the environs of Beersheba, southwest of the hill country. The aim of the narrative is to legitimate, through the agreement reached by Isaac and Abimelech, Israel's claim to Beersheba and to certain lands and wells to the west, and the Philistines' claims to Gerar and the lands and wells in its vicinity (26:1–5, 17–33). Here again J's account of his own society, as well as that of his neighbor, is motivated and shaped by the realities of the natural environments that defined not only the subsistence economies of these societies but their national identities and the political relationships between them.

Nature and Religion

In the treatment of the patriarchs the interest of J plays largely
around the scenes of their life, their family relations, and the
localities hallowed by their worship. . . . its conceptions of the
early cultus cannot be ignored, for in them is partly to be sought
the real clue to its origin.

J. Estlin Carpenter, *The Hexateuch*

What is of importance is the theophany in and for itself, its
occurrence on that particular place. It must not be regarded as an
isolated fact, but rather as the striking commencement of an
intercourse between God and man which is destined to be
continued at this spot, and also as the first and strongest expres-
sion of the sanctity of the soil.

Julius Wellhausen, *Prolegomena to*
the History of Ancient Israel

The religion of Israel's ancestors, as the Yahwist describes it in these narratives, is infused with the same outlook that is present in the Yahwist's conception of the origins of his and his neighbor's societies: a people and its history cannot be understood apart from its physical context, apart from the environment that plays such a major role in defining its economy, its political status, and its way of life. In fact, J's accounts of divine appearances to his ancestors and of the ancestors' religious behavior serve primarily to demonstrate that the bond between Israel's ancestors and the land they inhabit and farm is not a profane relationship but one that possesses a deep and sacred character. In the ancestral narratives, as in the primeval story, the arable land of the Israelite hill country stands at the center of J's landscape and at the core of his theology.

Traditional approaches This portrait of ancestral religion as grounded in the land presents a different perspective from the one that has dominated the discussion of ancestral religion within scholarly circles for the last generation. Initiated by Albrecht Alt's influential article "The God of the Fathers," this discussion has been predicated on the sharp dichotomy between pastoral nomadism and sedentary agriculture, which provided the context for Alt's reconstruction of ancestral religion.[78] According to Alt, two distinct types of deities, and the religions related to them, are to be discerned behind the Yahwist's ancestral narratives, where they later came to coexist in a less than harmonious relationship. One of these was the religion of sedentary Canaanite farmers. It involved the worship of local numina, anonymous deities (*'ēlîm*) whose only important characteristics were their associations with particular holy places in the land of Canaan. Thus, *'ēl bêt-'ēl* was worshiped in Bethel, *'ēl 'ôlām* in Beersheba, and *'ēl rŏ'î* in a desert sanctuary in the Negev.[79]

The other religion, according to Alt, arose outside the sphere of civilization in the nomadic life of the desert. It involved the worship of the "god of the father," a deity who had no connection with a specific sanctuary but who entered into a relationship with a particular person, an individual after whom the god was named and who was considered the originator of that deity's cult. Such a deity, the God of Abraham, for example, was not the *numen* of a place but the patron of a family or a social group, moving with it on its journeys.

In this reconstruction of ancestral religion two dichotomies join and mutually reinforce one another. On the one hand are the sedentary farmers with their stationary deities linked to nature, to specific sacred sites in their environment. On the other hand are the nomadic pastoralists with their mobile deities associated with the historical process, with a society as it moves through space and time. The sharp distinction between natural and historical religions to which such thinking leads is particularly apparent in Alt's comments about the origin of this second type of religion:

> The seeds of a completely different development from that of local and nature gods were implanted at the very inception of the cult: the god was not tied to a greater or lesser piece of earth, but to human lives, first that of an individual, and then through him to those of a whole group. . . . The gods of this type of religion show a concern with social and historical events which most other primitive numina either lack altogether or possess only to a much more limited degree. This makes it even more appropriate to the way of life of nomadic tribes, and explains why their migration and settlement did not involve its rapid disappearance.[80]

Alt considered this second, historical type of religion the genuine religion of Israel's own ancestors, whom he assumed were nomadic tribespeople from the desert. Even when this desert religion later came to be combined, according to his view, first with the Canaanite gods of the local sanctuaries when Israel's ancestors settled down, and then with Yahwism when the Israelite nation was formed, this religion of history left its characteristic stamp on Israelite religious thought and on the epic narratives of J and E. The historical orientation, present in the desert deities of Israel's nomadic ancestors, thus became the defining feature of Israel's religious consciousness. To Alt, the religion of the God of the fathers was "a religion which had one essential mark of the later religion of Yahweh. For it stressed above all the relationship between God and man, and between God and whole groups of men, without any fixed association with one place. . . . The idea that Yahweh rules over the nation as a whole and over its history, is clear and precise from the beginning, and is the most distinctive characteristic of the religion of Israel."[81]

Alt's assessment of the religion of Israel's ancestors has exerted a major impact on subsequent scholarship. Both Gerhard von Rad and Martin Noth, in their influential studies on the Pentateuch, believed Alt had said "what is essential concerning the origin and nature of the patriarchal tradition" and had thereby laid the foundation for further study.[82] In his recent work on Genesis and its ancestral traditions, Claus Westermann has adapted Alt's model for his presentation of ancestral religion. He, too, sees two strains in ancestral religion, a religion associated with the social group arising out of the seminomadic, pastoralist way of life practiced by Israel's ancestors, and a religion associated with the local shrines of sedentary Canaanites with whom these ancestors later came into contact.[83]

A fundamental problem with this dualistic reconstruction of ancestral religion, potentially fatal in its own right for Alt's hypothesis, is the implausibility of the underlying environmental scenario. As has been noted in chapter 1, sheep and goat pastoralists cannot exist as desert nomads but only as seminomads within the semiarid zones contiguous with sedentary agricultural society. Nor can they exist in such splendid isolation from their neighbors as Alt assumed; they can only specialize in pastoralism to the extent that they are integrated into a larger sedentary economy. Thus the very conditions necessary for Alt's reconstruction cannot have existed in the biblical period, or in any period of ancient Near Eastern history.[84]

A second problem for Alt's hypothesis lies in the inscriptional evidence he presents to support his distinction between divine titles related to people, in other words, gods of the fathers, and those related to places, the local numina (*'ēlîm*). Frank Cross has reexamined the inscriptional data and shown that neither in the Nabatean sources, upon which Alt argued, nor in other comparative data, are *'ēl* designations, which Alt connected with local shrines, and "the god of the father," which Alt connected with nomadic tribes, mutually exclusive or distinct.[85] In the inscriptional corpus, as in the Bible—for instance, *'ēl 'ĕlōhê yiśrā'ēl*, "El, God of (the patriarch) Israel" (Gen 33:20, E)— the two are identified from earliest times.

A third problem is presented by the biblical text itself and by the J epic in particular, the pentateuchal source that carries the bulk of Israel's ancestral traditions. J's narratives do not present in their portrait of Israel's ancestors the data for the kind of reconstruction of ancestral religion Alt attempted. As has already been demonstrated, the Yahwist considers Israel's ancestors to be hill country farmers, practicing the same kind of mixed agricultural economy instituted for humankind at creation. The pastoralism practiced by the ancestors was one aspect of an economy based on cereal cultivation in the arable highlands. Nothing in J's narratives of these families can be construed as the remnants of, or used to reconstruct, an archaic stage of autonomous nomadic pastoralism practiced by desert tribes.

J's primary concern in the ancestral narratives, in fact, is to show how Israel's ancestors are united with the hill country, the heartland of biblical Israel, and to explain their relationships with their neighbors, each linked to their own environs in distinctive ways. Thus in J's political conception of Israelite society, as in his depiction of its basic agricultural economy, the Israelite hill country plays a central and definitive role.

Theophany When the overtly religious aspects of J's ancestral narratives are examined, a picture emerges that is in complete harmony with this portrait of the relationship between the ancestors of Israel and the arable zones of the Israelite highlands they inhabit. J's accounts of divine appearances, of the sanctuaries of Israel's ancestors, and of the ancestors' ritual behavior are focused primarily on the interrelationship between the ancestors and the land in which they live. This can be best illustrated by a survey of the appearances of Yahweh in J's ancestral narrative and the ritual behavior of Israel's ancestors that accompanies these theophanies.

The key divine encounters in the Yahwist's ancestral narratives involve Abraham, J's archetypal patriarch, and follow a clear pattern encompassing four regular elements brought together to define the event. God's appearance to Abraham at Shechem, described in Genesis 12:6–7, is the first of these divine encounters in the hill country, and as it is also the briefest, provides a good point to introduce J's formulaic narratives of these special sacred encounters. Upon his arrival in the Israelite highlands, the first experience Abraham has is a theophany of Yahweh (12:6–7). God's appearance is described with a reflexive form of the verb *rā'â*, "see"—"he made himself visible," or "he appeared" to Abraham (v 7)—J's customary manner of describing divine manifestations (Gen 18:1; 26:2, 24; cf. 46:29 with a human subject).[86] The theophany takes place at a site marked by a natural feature, in this case a particular oak tree, located at an important hill country city, Shechem (v 6). The point of the theophany is the divine gift of the land in Shechem's environs to Abraham and his descendants (v 7). Abraham's response is to construct an altar (*mizbēaḥ*) to commemorate the deity's appearance and to identify the site at which that appearance occurred as a sacred place (v 7).

These four elements of J's divine encounters—the theophany, a feature of the landscape, a divine land grant, and the construction of an altar—characterize the experience of Abraham at his next residence, Bethel (12:8–9; 13:1–5, 7–11a, 12b–18). Here, too, Abraham builds an altar at a site marked by a natural feature, in this case a mountain located near the city of Bethel (12:8). At this site, God appears to Abraham, granting him and his descendants once again the land in all directions as far as his eyes can see (13:14–17). The Yahwist twice describes Abraham's worship at this site with the formula he employs throughout the epic to describe the worship of God: "There Abraham called on the name of Yahweh" (12:8, 13:4; cf. 4:26, 21:33, 26:25; Exod 33:19, 34:5–6).

At Hebron, Abraham's third and primary residence in the hill country, the same fourfold pattern characterizes his encounter with the deity. At a grove of oak trees in Hebron, Abraham constructs an altar to God (13:18; cf. 18:1). To this sacred site J relates a series of divine appearances. Two concern the promise of heirs (15:1–6, 18:1–5) and one the fate of the citizens of Sodom and Gomorrah (18:16–33). But the most elaborate theophany, and the only one in which a covenant is forged between God and one of Israel's ancestors in this section of J's epic, occurs to validate the bond between Abraham and this land (15:7–21).

One other divine encounter conforms to this pattern established in the narratives about Abraham at Shechem, Bethel, and Hebron. This is Isaac's experience at Beersheba (Gen 26), located at the southern edge of the Judean foothills where they meet the semiarid Negev. Here God appears to Isaac (reflexive of *rā 'â*; vv 2, 24), and in response Isaac builds an altar and calls on the name of Yahweh (26:25). The site of this theophany and Isaac's altar is marked by a tamarisk tree, planted by Isaac's father Abraham (21:33), and by a well dug by Isaac's servants (26:25, 32–33). The divine address that accompanies the theophany grants Isaac both this land on which it occurs and a multitude of descendants (26:2–5, 24).

Two other vivid theophanies occur in J's ancestral narratives, Jacob's night encounter at the Jabbok (Gen 32:23–33) and Hagar's encounter at the desert oasis on the road to Shur (Gen 16:7–14). Both occur at the margins of the Israelite hill country, and in neither instance is an altar built or a divine promise about the land made. At the Jabbok, Jacob's name is changed to Israel; at the desert oasis, Hagar's son is named and his destiny defined. Both stories relate the appearance of God to specific natural features, a river in one case and a spring in the other, and thereby mark these sites as sacred. Yet their peripheral locations, their lack of altars, and the absence of a divine promise of land place these encounters at the margin of J's sacred landscape.

In association with the four major theophanies and their land grants, Israel's ancestors construct an altar (*mizbēaḥ*) at Shechem, Bethel, Hebron, and Beersheba. These sites are thus rendered sacred not only by the appearance of the deity, but also by the ritual installations with which the ancestors construct a sacred space. As scholars have long recognized, these accounts of altar building are etiologies for the religious sanctuaries in these towns where the worship of Yahweh was conducted on a regular basis in the day of the Yahwist.[87] Such stories serve to legitimate Israel's worship at these places by connecting them with a primitive appearance of God and by attributing the altars in their sacred precincts to Israel's first ancestors. J's conception of these sites as active sanctuaries is disclosed not only by their altars, but also by his use of the term *māqôm,* which here must carry its technical sense of "shrine, sanctuary" (12:6; 13:3, 4, 14; 28:16), and by his reference to Israel's ancestors as "calling on the name of Yahweh" in worship (12:8, 13:4, 21:33,

26:25).[88] There is no reason to suppose, as is common among interpreters, that these altars were temporary installations built outside these towns by pastoral nomads camping in their vicinity.[89] The oak of Moreh where Yahweh appears and Abraham builds an altar is in the sanctuary of Shechem (*měqôm šěkem*; 12:6), just as the sacred oaks at which Abraham builds his third altar are located in Hebron proper (*běhebrôn*; 13:18).[90]

The only other theophany that accompanies the construction of an altar in the Yahwist's ancestral narratives occurs immediately after the flood at the very beginning of the second age of world history. After disembarking from the ark, apparently on the highlands of Canaan in J's traditions, Noah constructs the first altar in the epic. In the theophany to Noah, God promises the land's productivity in the new era. Thus the first divine appearance after the flood and Noah's altar itself are archetypal for the experiences of revelation and for the altars constructed later by Abraham and Isaac. All serve to establish the enduring relationship between the descendants of the Yahwist's heroes and the arable lands they inhabit.

A most remarkable fact about these divine revelations in J's ancestral narrative is that they occur in association with a concrete feature of the natural landscape, a feature the Yahwist is concerned to identify precisely.[91] At both Shechem and Hebron, the oak tree (*ʾēlôn*) marks the site of the divine appearance (12:6, 13:18, 18:1).[92] The most stately and impressive of the trees that provided natural forest cover in the Israelite highlands, some oak species reach a height of twenty-five meters and a crown circumference of twenty meters, attaining an age of several hundred years. The majestic oak is revered by biblical writers as a symbol of power and longevity (cf. Amos 2:9, Isa 2:13), and is associated with the presence of divinity (Gen 35:8 [E]; Judg 9:6, 37; Hos 4:13).[93] Its name, *ʾēlôn*, appears to be related to the Hebrew word, *ʾēl*, "deity."[94] The oak at Shechem is called by J *ʾēlôn môrěh*, a designation with two possible meanings. As it stands, the term *môrěh* is a participle of the verb *yārā*, "teach, instruct," and this points to a literal translation, "the oak that instructs," that is, the oracular oak, or the oak at which divine oracles are received. At the same time, J's use of the verb *rāʾâ*, "see," twice in the next verse to describe God's appearance at the oak suggests that J may have been playing on the similarity in sound between the oak's title *môrěh* and the verb *rāʾâ*, in order to signify the tree as the oak of revelation.[95] In either case, the oak is viewed by J as a medium for the appearance and communication of Yahweh. In addition to his appearance at oaks in Shechem and Hebron, Yahweh's appearance at Beersheba is marked by the tamarisk tree (*ʾēšel*; Gen 21:33, 26:23–25), a tree adapted to the sandy soil and more arid conditions of the Beersheba area.[96]

The revelation of God at Bethel is marked by another natural feature, the mountain (*har*; 12:8; 13:3–4, 14–17). Since this location, on which Abraham builds an altar, is identified by J as a precise site between Bethel and Ai, *har* is more appropriately translated "mountain" than the general "hill country" preferred by most translators (e.g., NRSV, JPSV, NEB). From this particular height, Abraham is able to view in all directions the land God grants to him (13:14–15). The mountain, as the tree, is associated with the self-disclosure of God in ancient Israel. It is in fact the predominant natural feature marking the presence and communication of Israel's God, as the importance of Mount Sinai and Mount Zion in the biblical record illustrates.[97] As will be seen in the next chapter, the Yahwist's narrative of Egypt and the desert in the third and final part of the epic is structured around two crucial revelations at Sinai, the southern mountain (Exod 3:2–4a, 5, 7–8, 15–22; 19:7–15, 18, 20–25).[98]

To Isaac, Jacob, and Hagar, God appears at sites marked by water sources. These are the well (bĕʾēr) at Beersheba (26:25); the Jabbok, a stream (naḥal; 32:23–24 [Eng vv 22–23]) flowing into the Jordan from the Transjordanian highlands; and the spring (ʿayin) and well (bĕʾēr) at Beer (bĕʾēr)-lahai-roi on the road to Shur (16:7, 14).[99] The point at which fresh subterranean waters make contact with the earth's surface is thus also viewed as especially conducive to divine encounters. The spring marking Eden's location has already been discussed in such a sacral context.[100]

Mircea Eliade has described these natural features—the tree, the mountain, the water source—as traditional symbols of a cosmic or world axis (axis mundi), which breaks the plane of ordinary earthly space allowing the penetration of divine presence and power from above or below. The tree's branches reach into the heavens, its roots into the underworld. The mountain likewise rises into the sky and is founded deep in the earth. The spring issues from subterranean regions. At such points of intersection, these apertures in the world, the divine powers behind the cosmos break through ordinary space in a special and decisive fashion. Such places are thus sacred locations, points where communication between divine and human is particularly and permanently possible.[101]

Behind the Yahwist's association of divine revelation with such specific features of the natural landscape lies the recognition of a close bond between divinity and the natural world. In these major ancestral theophanies, divine communication is mediated directly through natural phenomena. Nature therefore cannot accurately be described as desacralized, inert, or profane in the Yahwist's epic. It is the realm through and within which God becomes present in the world. And the sites of divine appearances—with their symbols of the world axis and their ancestral altars—assume a particular sacredness within the natural landscape.

Thus it is misleading to speak too exclusively of human history as the realm of divine revelation and activity in the Yahwist's narrative. God is, of course, described in form and in speech with human images (18:1–2, 32:25 [Eng. v 24]). And God can appear to Israel's ancestors anywhere, even outside the boundaries of the hill country (12:1, 31:3), without any specific natural feature to mediate the revelation. Yet in the primary theophanies in which the promise theology of J is articulated, natural phenomena represent an authentic means of divine self-disclosure. For J, the phenomenal world plays as signficiant a role as the medium of divine revelation as does the historical event.

The close association between nature and revelation in these ancestral theophanies is only strengthened by the importance of land in the divine communication itself (12:7, 13:14–17, 26:2–5). The aim of the ancestral covenant in J's account, ratified by the ritual ceremony in which God and Abraham—J's archetypal ancestor—are both participants, is to establish the bond between Abraham, Abraham's descendants, and the land of biblical Israel (Gen 15:7–21). The encounters between God and Israel's ancestors are thus not exclusively focused on bringing into being a new divine-human relationship but are also intended to establish a social union between a people and the environment within which they live.[102]

Sacred geography The relationship between nature and the divine in the Yahwist's worldview can be illustrated further by considering the way in which divine appearances order the spatial world of the ancestral narrative. As has been noted above, four of the theophanies to Israel's ancestors are invested with particular significance by J, because they are commemorated by the construction of an altar, which establishes the site as a religious sanctuary. These theophanies occur at Shechem, Bethel, Hebron, and Beersheba.

Each theophany, as the preceding analysis has shown, is associated with a traditional symbol of the *axis mundi,* or cosmic axis: the oak tree at Shechem and Hebron, the mountain at Bethel, and the tamarisk tree and well at Beersheba. The cosmic axis is not just a point within ordinary space conducive to divine revelation, but a center around which the cosmos itself is organized, to employ once more Eliade's language of sacred space. Such a center marks the point of divine manifestation and the location around which the inhabited world is ordered and organized. Outside this familiar space is a dangerous realm, the desert or the world of the foreigner where life is precarious.[103]

The cities of Shechem, Bethel, and Hebron, in fact, lie along the central spine of the biblical hill country that makes up the Yahwist's landscape. Shechem in the north, Bethel midway from north to south, and Hebron in the south were social, economic, political, and religious centers around which Israelite society in these areas of the hill country was oriented throughout the biblical period. Only Beersheba to the southwest, at the border between hill country and Negev, does not hold such a central position within J's landscape. The only sanctuary established by Isaac, rather than Abraham, it is no doubt included among this elite group because of its function as the southern boundary of the Yahwist's Israel and because of its significance for the southern population from which the Yahwist undoubtedly came.[104]

The manner in which these sanctuaries function as sacred centers can be seen in the Yahwist's epic itself not only by the ancestors' close relationship to them but also by the role they play in the movements of Israel's ancestors. These sanctuaries function as sacred portals for the journeys of Israel's ancestors outside the land, and thus anchor even these migrations to the hill country itself. Abraham enters the land through the sanctuary at Shechem (12:6–7). The sanctuary at Bethel provides the point of departure and point of return for Abraham's trip to Egypt. This is clear in the Yahwist's itinerary of the trip, and is particularly emphasized by J's repeated reference to the sanctuary (*māqôm*) at Bethel to which Abraham returned as the same from which he had departed (12:8–9, 13:1–4). The hill country sanctuary as portal is also illustrated by Jacob's trip to Syria, where again Bethel provides the point of departure and return. At the Bethel sanctuary, on Jacob's way to Syria, God appears to Jacob, renewing the promise of land, descendants, and blessing, and promising to protect him and return him to the very spot of this divine encounter (Gen 28:13–16).[105]

When God does appear to Israel's ancestors outside of a sanctuary at the sacral center of J's landscape, it is invariably to direct them toward it. This is the case for Jacob in Syria, where God encounters him to urge him to return to his homeland (31:3). It is the case for Abraham, when God first speaks to him in Syria, directing him to the Israelite hill country (12:1–3). In the final section of J's epic this is characteristic of God's appearances to Moses and Israel in Egypt and the desert, where theophanies focus primarily on Israel's return to the land of its ancestors (e.g., Exod 3:7–8, 33:1–3).

The archetypal religious events in J's ancestral narrative, the theophanies in the center of the Israelite hill country and the altars constructed by Israel's ancestors to commemorate them, serve primarily to bestow a sacred character upon the interrelationship between Israelite society and its particular terrestrial setting. The appearances of God are mediated through concrete phenomena typical of J's landscape, and they are motivated by the divine word linking Israel's ancestors to the arable zones at the heart of the Israelite highlands. The altars built by Israel's ancestors insure the permanent sanctity of these sites and order J's landscape around these sacred centers. Even the movements of the ancestors are governed by this sacred geography centered in the hill country of biblical Israel. Such a religious consciousness cannot be labeled as narrowly historical but must be recognized as possessing a profound sense of the intimate and defining relationship between people and land. It is a consciousness that considers space, as well as time, as a sacred category.

Ancestral Traditions in Biblical Thought

Most of Israel's traditions about its ancestors have been preserved in the Yahwist's epic. Of the ancestral narratives in Genesis 9–50, J's account encompasses more than the Elohistic and Priestly works combined. The Elohist's traditions are considerably fewer, making up only a fourth of the whole, while the Priestly Writer's additions represent merely a sixth of the entire ancestral story. Aside from the Abrahamic covenant in Genesis 17 and the purchase of Machpelah in Genesis 23, the Priestly Writer is primarily responsible for genealogical supplements and occasional chronological notices. Our image of Israel's ancestors is thus derived primarily from the Yahwist's epic.

This image, in the first place, is not well served by the traditional dichotomy between nomadic pastoralism and sedentary agriculture nor by the designation of Israel's ancestors as nomadic pastoralists on the fringes of Canaanite agricultural society. Israel's ancestors, in J's narrative, are granted the arable land in the heart of the Israelite highlands and are described as residents of it, establishing Yahwistic shrines at its major population centers. Within this land they practice the mixed agricultural economy typical of biblical Israel. In addition to the cultivation of grain, they grow vines and orchards, crops that demand a long-term investment in the land. Judged by the mix of animals they own and by their use of specialized herdsmen, the pastoralist activities of the ancestors are best understood as part of a mixed agricultural economy practiced by sedentary hill country farmers. The journeys of these figures are not typical of nomadic or seminomadic pastoralists in the semiarid zones in the vicinity of the highlands but are employed by J to lay claim to Israelite land, to validate its sacred spaces, and to explain and legitimate Israel's relationships with its neighbors. Furthermore these trips are all framed by the sacred centers of Israel's own terrain. Just as in the primeval narrative, so here in the postflood age, J presents the ancestors of Israel as archetypal Israelites, putting into effect and practicing the agricultural economy and agrarian way of life typical of the Israelite society that comprised J's audience.

J's image of Israel's ancestors is also not well served by the traditional dichotomy between nature and history that has come to define the interpretation of the family narratives in this part of the biblical story. What is distinctive about these traditions is neither a new historical consciousness nor a specific, selective interest in human society that marginalizes the value and significance of the natural environment. What is especially characteristic about these narratives is the interplay between societies and their environments. The etiological aim that underlies these family narratives is not historical in a narrow sense, the explanation of the political world of J's era and the interrelationships between its societies. Rather J aims to demonstrate the origin and nature of the relationship between these societies and their environmental settings. Whether for Israel in the highlands west of the Jordan, for Edom in the mountains to the southeast, or for the Ishmaelites in the desert fringes, the Yahwist conceives of a society's origin and character in terms of its precise geographical setting. Just as Israel's own agricultural way of life is founded in creation itself and practiced by its ancestors, Noah, Abraham, Isaac, and Jacob after the flood, so are the transient lives of the Ishmaelites grounded in their desert origins, and so are the mixed economies of Moab, Ammon, and Edom derived from their highland settings east of the Jordan.

In light of J's understanding of human experience as shaped by its environment, the common claim that the ancestral narratives initiate a new departure in historical literature and the historical consciousness must be questioned. This claim has usually been made in terms of a narrowing of the biblical horizon: the world of creation in the primeval age gives way to the experience of a single family and its particular and distinctive historical journey. Thus Israel's interest in history and backgrounding of nature become even more prominent in these stories of Abraham, Isaac, and Jacob.

There can be no doubt that the political shape of J's world is a major, even distinctive, concern in the postflood portion of the epic. Only after the flood does J commence his etiological accounts of the actual political landscape of his day. By means of the segmentary genealogies beginning with Noah's sons, J maps out the relationships between the cultures of Egypt, Mesopotamia, and Syria-Palestine (from Noah's descendants in Gen 9–11), and finally, the relationships among the tribal elements within Israel itself (from Jacob's sons in Gen 29–50). The establishment of such political entities and their relationships are not the concern of the primeval narrative.

The special political character of the postflood age can also be seen in J's description of the origins of Israel itself. Only after the flood, beginning with the curse on Canaan and blessing on Shem (9:20–27), and continuing with the promise of nationhood, land, and descendants to Abraham (e.g., 12:1–3), are Israel's ancestors described in terms of a political entity. While such a national identity is presupposed for Israel's first ancestors in the primeval age, it does not become an explicit part of J's narrative until the postflood age. In the primeval narrative, the arable land in the hill country west of the Jordan functions primarily as the basis for the agricultural economy and way of life of Israel's antediluvian ancestors. In the ancestral narrative, this same land, the focal point also of J's postflood landscape, now also is regarded as the territorial base for the Israelite state composed of the descendants of these ancestral figures.

This new political orientation in J's ancestral narratives of the postflood era is undeniable, yet it does not support the traditional view that with these narratives the horizon of the biblical story has been narrowed from the realm of creation to the realm of Israelite history proper. On the contrary, J's ancestral narratives represent a broadening of narrative scope. Whereas the primeval narrative focuses exclusively on Israel's ancestors in the hills between the Jordan and the Mediterranean Sea,[106] the ancestral narratives of the postflood era expand their purview to encompass the peoples and lands in the larger ancient Near Eastern world, primarily those closest to Israel—for instance, the Moabites, Ammonites, and Edomites in the highlands east of the Jordan—but also the more distant cultures of Egypt and Mesopotamia. And whereas the primeval narrative focuses on the relationship between land and people in terms of the agricultural realities of subsistence agriculture for the village family, the ancestral narrative enlarges the perspective to include within this relationship the concept of land as the basis for the territorial state. Properly speaking, J's ancestral narratives represent an expansion, both in the meaning of land for Israel itself and in the spatial sweep of ancient Near Eastern geography brought into the epic vision.

In the context of this widening perspective, J's sense of the vital bond between a culture and its environment is nowhere eroded. The peoples of the ancestral age—the forebears of Israel and its neighbors—are thought of only in concrete contexts. Their characteristics—their ways of life, the shape of their economies, their wealth or poverty, the relations with one another—are considered by J to be inseparably linked to their distinctive environs. Such an understanding of human societies as grounded in natural contexts, while expressed from the human point of view and thus of course "anthropocentric," is predicated upon a sense of the profound connection between culture and nature. No dichotomy between nature and history, such as biblical scholars have become comfortable with, can be extracted from J's epic or the conceptual world that underlies it.

The religion of Israel's ancestors, in J's understanding of it, functions above all to give sacral significance to the affiliation between the ancestors and the land in which they live. The major divine revelations are mediated through sacral elements of the landscape itself—tree, mountain, well—and are concerned in the first place to signify the hill country as a sacred trust bestowed upon Israel's ancestors and their descendants. The sacred spaces the ancestors construct in response to these revelations provide permanent centers in which this sacred bond between people and land can be renewed and reenacted. Such a religious consciousness is so thoroughly grounded in the Israelite hill country that to reconstruct a different origin for Israel's religion, which eschews this sense of place, as have Albrecht Alt and others, involves speculation that runs directly counter to the character of Israelite religion as it is described in the texts we now possess.

Throughout the ancestral narrative, as in the primeval narrative, land looms as a major theme in the theology of J, a much larger and more important theme than has often been acknowledged by biblical theologians preoccupied with the divine-human relationship. There have always been those to remind us how crucial land is in biblical thought, among them Walter Brueggemann in a recent "Overture to Biblical Theology" entitled *The Land*.[107] This useful study illustrates at once the inadequacies of biblical theologies that have omitted this theme and the amount of reconceptualization that is still required of us to understand the biblical point of view. At the outset of his study, Brueggemann makes the claim that "land is a central, if not *the central theme* of biblical faith" (Brueggemann's emphasis).[108] He goes on to say that "it will no longer do to talk about Yahweh and his people but we must speak about Yahweh and his people *and his land*. Preoccupation with existentialist *decisions* and transforming *events* has distracted us from seeing that this God is committed to this land and that his promise for his people is always his land"(Brueggemann's emphasis).[109]

Yet in the title of the chapter in which these sentences occur, "Land as Promise and as Problem," Brueggemann expresses his uneasiness with the concept of biblical society's real rootedness in the land. Israel is most Israel, so to speak, when it is on the move: "Israel's faith is essentially a journeying in and out of land, and its faith can be organized around these focuses . . . Israel is a landless people when we meet it earliest and most often in biblical faith. . . . Israel is embodied in Abraham, Isaac, and Jacob in the earliest presentations as *sojourners* on the way to a land whose name it does not know" (Brueggemann's emphasis).[110] Behind such a presentation of land is an enduring belief in the especially historical character of biblical faith, a faith not so much nourished by the spaces in which it grows as by its restless movement into the future. While exile from the land is certainly a crucial aspect of biblical experience, as the Yahwist's own epic attests, the arable land of the Israelite hill country is the starting point for biblical thought. At least this is the case for J, whose ancestors are not sojourners but sedentary Israelite farmers with a religious faith grounded in the sacred sites of the hill country in which they live.

The high profile of land in J's ancestral narrative becomes all the more significant in light of the fact that this narrative represents the main body and theological center of the epic as a whole. The connection developed here between Israel's ancestors and the land and the establishment of its sacred centers focus the entire epic on the arable soil of the Israelite highlands. This is the context from which the creation of the world in the primeval age is narrated. And it is the context as well for narratives of Egypt and the southern deserts, with which J's epic concludes, and to which we now turn.

4

The Southern Narratives

The Yahwist's ancestral narrative concludes with the resettlement of the family of Jacob in the Egyptian delta, to which it had moved in response to a severe famine that struck broad areas of the ancient Near East (Gen 37–50). After a hiatus, in which the descendants of Jacob had become numerous and their cordial relations with Egyptian authorities had cooled (Exod 1:8–12), the narrative is resumed by J. Three significant events dominate the remainder of the Yahwist's epic and bring it to a close: the escape from Egypt, the encounter with God at Mt. Sinai, and the journey through the southern desert toward the homeland of their ancestors in the Israelite hill country.

It is with events in this final part of J's epic that the climax of the entire narrative has generally been associated. No one has been more influential in this respect than Gerhard von Rad, who, in his 1938 article, "The Form-Critical Problem of the Hexateuch," argued that the core around which J constructed his epic was to be found in the exodus of the Israelites from Egypt and their settlement in Canaan. In this he was influenced strongly by several "creedal" statements elsewhere in the Bible that focus on these two events (Deut 26:5b–9, 6:20–24; Josh 24:2b–13), each of which he judged to be an archaic, archetypal summary of Israel's formative experiences, "a Hexateuch in miniature" as it were.[1]

In one form or another, many have followed this tradition and have been strongly influenced, as was von Rad, by these "creeds." In his analysis of the development of pentateuchal tradition, Martin Noth came to the conclusion that the theme "Guidance out of Egypt" was "the kernel of the whole subsequent Pentateuchal tradition. ... The narrative of the deliverance from Egypt," he wrote, "constitutes the point of crystallization of the great Pentateuchal narrative in its entirety."[2] Such a position is now taken commonly.[3] Claus Westermann's remarks are typical: "The central part of the Pentateuch tells the story of the rescue at the Reed Sea, Ex 1–18. This event was the basis of the history of a people. It gave both parts of the book of Genesis the character of an introduction."[4] In their study of the Yahwist, Robert Coote and David Ord take a similar position. For them, the exodus is the event in terms of which the entire epic must be viewed.

> The one story in J that has the most bearing on all others is the story of the revolt and escape of a bond of disenfranchised, oppressed laborers from Egypt. If J represents the cardiovascular system of the Pentateuch, then this episode, often referred to as the exodus, represents its heart. It is this which gives vitality and meaning to the rest of J and to which we must repeatedly return if we are to keep the whole of J in perspective. Every story in J, insofar as it is a part of a larger whole, must be understood as it relates directly to this pivotal event.[5]

An alternative view, that the theophany and covenant at Sinai are the highpoint of the pentateuchal story, is represented by Peter Ellis. In his study of the Yahwist, he concludes that "the Sinai covenant may rightly be termed the climax of the Yahwist's saga."[6] In this opinion, Ellis appears to be too strongly influenced by the Priestly point of view. Such a judgment must certainly be defended for the Priestly Writer whose work and interests are reflected in the final shape of this material. According to P, the revelation at Mt. Sinai was the definitive event in Israel's history. Through a series of covenants—through Noah (Gen 9:1–17), Abraham (Gen 17), and Moses (Exod 31:12–17)—P orders Israelite history to reach its defining moment at Mt. Sinai. By the positioning at this point in the narrative of the great body of priestly legal traditions (Exod 25–31, 35–40; Leviticus; Num 1:1–10:28), the Priestly Writer has firmly established Sinai as the culmination of Israel's ancestral traditions. From Sinai came all of the regulations that were to govern the life of Israel as a sacral community centered in its cultic institutions, the priesthood and the tabernacle.

Whether the covenant at Mt. Sinai, or the exodus from Egypt, may be seen as the center of the older Yahwistic epic is another matter, especially when this final section of the epic is viewed in light of the extensive ancestral narrative that precedes it. From the perspective of the preceding ancestral narrative, J's southern stories assume a peripheral position within the structure of the epic as a whole. One indication of this is the relative brevity of these narratives. No story in its own right—the exodus, the revelation at Sinai, or the desert journey—takes up more than a third of the narrative space J devoted to Israel's ancestors' lives in the Israelite hill country. Combined, these narratives are only 70 percent of the length of the ancestral narrative and just over a third of the epic's entire length. For the Egyptian sojourn, a period of four generations according to J (Gen 15:16), no details at all are provided. Peter Ellis, while maintaining the Sinai event as the climax of the epic, recognized this narrative "imbalance" and asserted that any analysis of the saga as a whole must take it into account.

Narrative magnitude alone does not of course determine the literary or theological center and periphery of a work. Yet there are other features of J's epic that subordinate these southern narratives to the more substantial ancestral narrative which precedes them. One of these features is J's presentation of the Egyptian sojourn as an ancestral journey. As has been shown in the preceding chapter, ancestral migrations outside of the hill country are viewed by J as movements away from the center. Such trips outside the highlands are motivated only by extraordinary environmental or social threats, as when Abraham traveled to Egypt because of famine, or when Jacob fled for Syria because of conflict with his brother. During their temporary residence in these foreign locations, J refers to the ancestors as *gērîm*, resident aliens. Each journey is anchored in the hill country by locating its point of departure and return at one of the sacred centers within this terrain. In the theophanies experienced at these geographical portals, the permanent union between the ancestors and the hill country is reaffirmed in the face of the temporary separation effected by the journey.

These characteristics of the earlier ancestral journeys are all a part of the journey to Egypt initiated by Jacob at the end of Genesis and completed by his descendants in the narratives of Exodus and Numbers in the final section of J's epic. The journey outside the hill country in this final section of the epic is thus not a new story, as far as J is concerned, but an elaborate narrative expansion of a common theme in the postflood era, the temporary dislocation of the ancestors from the sacred center of their landscape, the arable highlands west of the Jordan.

The extent to which the southern narrative conforms to J's formula of the ancestral journey can be seen by comparing it to Abraham's trip to Egypt in Genesis 12:10–20.[7] Both journeys are motivated by a severe famine (Gen 12:10, 43:1, 47:4) and result in the temporary relocation of the ancestors in foreign territory as *gērîm*, resident aliens (12:10, 47:4). As aliens on foreign soil, death is a serious threat (Gen 12:11–13; Exod 1:22). After God intervenes with a series of plagues (*ngʿ*; Gen 12:17; Exod 11:1), Israel's ancestors depart for their homeland with great possessions (Gen 12:16, 13:2; Exod 12:35–36). Abraham departs from Bethel and returns to it by stages through the Negev (12:8–9, 13:1–4), and Jacob leaves Hebron and his descendants return to it by stages through the Negev (Gen 37:14; Num 13:17, 22–24).

The more elaborate travel narrative describing the Egyptian and desert sojourns is viewed by J, just as the earlier ancestral journeys were viewed, as a movement away from the center and into the periphery of J's landscape. The epic's concluding narrative, therefore, does not shift the focus or recenter the epic. This can be illustrated further by considering the theophanies at the southern mountain. As J describes these appearances, they are primarily concerned to recall and renew God's prior promise of the Israelite hill country to Israel's ancestors. In them, Yahweh is identified as the God of Abraham, Isaac, and Jacob and commits himself to reuniting their descendants with the land he gave to them (Exod 3:7–8, 16–17; 33:1–3a; 34:11). These divine revelations themselves thus point back to the ancestral narratives that precede them.

This treatment of the Mosaic period is distinctly different from the later Priestly Writer's, who located in this era the origins of true and proper Israelite worship. According to P, Moses was the first to learn of the divine name Yahweh (Exod 6:2–9), and Moses mediated the cultic and social law that was to govern Israelite life. According to the Yahwist, by contrast, the origins of Yahwism go back to the beginning of time, when the divine name Yahweh was known and when Israel's ancestors called upon it (2:4b, 4:26). Proper worship was initiated with the flood hero, Noah, the first obedient ancestor and the builder of the first altar in the Yahwist's epic. It was established for Israel by the archetypal ancestor Abraham, whose obedience brought blessing to his descendants and whose altars marked out the sacred centers of the Israelite hill country.

When considered in light of this evidence, the southern narratives that conclude J's epic are decidedly peripheral, not because they are unimportant or of little consequence, but because they do not represent the focal point of the Yahwist's landscape or theology. The stance from which the southern narrative is composed and from which its events are viewed and interpreted is the arable land of the Israelite hill country, which marks the focal point of J's landscape in the primeval and ancestral narratives. It is in the mountains inhabited by Israel's ancestors that the center of J's sacred geography and the sources of his theology are to be found, rather than in the temporary and peripheral sojourn in the south. This point is substantially reinforced by a reexamination of the environmental context presupposed in the narratives of this third and final part of the Yahwist's epic.

The Environmental Perspective in the Southern Narratives

Perhaps nothing has contributed more to the image of Israel as a nomadic, pastoralist society in origin than the narratives of Israel's ancestors wandering through the desert on the way to the promised land. In these narratives, found today in the books of Exodus and Numbers, the Israelites spend an entire generation, according to J (Num 14:20–25), living in the great desert of the Sinai Peninsula south of the Israelite hill country after their departure from Egypt and before their settlement in the highlands of Canaan. The simple narrative logic of such an account suggests that before the Israelites became Canaanite farmers they were desert nomads and that these nomadic origins must have placed an indelible mark on the Israelite psyche.

Such a view is only enhanced by the story, found within these narratives, of the remarkable encounter between God and Israel at Mt. Sinai, traditionally located deep in the Sinai Desert.[8] This vivid theophany, together with the claims of the Elohist and the Priestly Writer that the divine name Yahweh was first revealed to Israel at this time, have suggested a peculiar and special relationship between Israel's deity and the desert.[9] Israel appears to meet its God in the desert and acquire thereby a religion with desert origins.

These plain facts of the desert narrative have led to the conception that the Bible possesses a nomadic or desert ideal. According to this viewpoint, initiated by K. Budde and reaching a high point in the works of John W. Flight and Samuel Nyström, biblical writers held the wilderness in particularly high regard, considering it the matrix for the formation of Israelite society and the setting in which was born Israel's distinctive religious genius.[10] Such an orientation was perceived not only in the pentateuchal narratives but in the preexilic prophets and in other biblical authors as well.[11] This view that Israelite theology is shaped in a foundational way by the desert is a major component of the work of H. and H. A. Frankfort referred to in chapter 1, from which a few sentences may be repeated by way of illustration. "The bond between Yahweh and his chosen people had been finally established during the Exodus," write the Frankforts. "The Hebrews considered the forty years in the desert the decisive phase in their development. And we, too, may understand the originality and the coherence of their speculations if we relate them to their experience in the desert . . . the desert as a metaphysical experience loomed very large for the Hebrews and coloured all their valuations."[12] More general treatments of Western religious and cultural values, such as George Williams's *Wilderness and Paradise in Christian Thought,* Herbert Schneidau's *Sacred Discontent: The Bible and Western Tradition,* and Max Oelschlaeger's *The Idea of Wilderness,* have disseminated to a wider audience this belief among biblical scholars that the Bible presents its readers with a nomadic or desert ideal.[13]

While there have always been skeptics about this emphasis on the desert as a formative influence on Israelite thought, the most substantial critique has been delivered by Shemaryahu Talmon in a work entitled "The 'Desert Motif' in the Bible and in Qumran Literature."[14] In his analysis of the stories of the desert in the Pentateuch and of references to it in other biblical literature and in texts from Qumran, Talmon challenges the theory of a desert or nomadic ideal among biblical writers on two counts: that biblical sources do not present desert life as a social ideal or the desert period as the ideal era of Israelite history, and that the existence in biblical society of a reform movement that advocated a return to a nomadic ideal is based on questionable historical and sociological judgments.

The Desert

The Yahwist, by providing the earliest extensive treatment of the desert journey from Egypt to Canaan, represents a particularly crucial piece of evidence for the consideration of the arguments in this debate. When the Yahwist's southern narratives are examined as a whole, they reveal themselves to be no more partial to the desert nor shaped by its environment than are J's earlier narratives of the primeval and ancestral ages. Like these earlier portions of the epic, the southern narratives reflect the orientation of the sedentary farmer in the Canaanite highlands. Though they describe Israel's ancestors passing through the desert, they reflect a narrator who is not at home in the desert but in the farming villages in which lived the majority of the population of biblical Israel.[15]

Numerous details of J's desert stories, indeed their whole atmosphere, illustrate the sedentary agricultural perspective from which they have been composed. To begin with, Israel is represented by J not as residing in the desert but as journeying through it from one sedentary agricultural area to another, from the Nile Valley to the Canaanite highlands. The goal of the exodus journey from the beginning is the cultivable land granted to and inhabited by Israel's ancestors Abraham, Isaac, and Jacob (Exod 3:8, 17; 33:1; 34:11–12; Num 10:29, 14:15–16). God says of Israel when he first appears to Moses, "I will come down to deliver them from the hand of the Egyptians and to bring them up from that land to a good and broad land, to a land flowing with milk and honey, to the place of the Canaanites, Hittites, Amorites, Perizzites, Hivites, and Jebusites" (Exod 3:8). J's characteristic use of the verb *'ālā*, "to go up," to describe the departure of Israel from Egypt points toward the culmination of the journey as an ascent into the hill country of biblical Israel. Israel's journey through the desert is thus presented by J as a relocation of a sedentary people, not as a movement typical of the seasonal migration or regular transhumance of the seminomad. This relocation would have involved a direct, straightforward trip through the inhospitable Sinai, according to J, had it not been for the Israelite fear of the hill country's inhabitants upon their arrival. Only as a result of divine punishment, when they refuse to go forward into the hills, are they banished to the desert until the unfaithful generation dies there (Num 13:27–31, 33; 14:1b, 4, 20–25).

J's description of the Canaanite hill country, in the narrative of the Israelites' arrival at it, bears the perspective not of a desert nomad who is a stranger to it but of a farmer at home in it. Moses' instructions to the spies reflect the concerns of the hill country farmer: he tells them to determine whether the land is rich or poor and whether it has orchards, and he asks them to bring back some of its fruit (Num 13:17–20). They return with a single cluster of grapes so large it is carried on a pole by two men, and with some pomegranates and figs (13:23). This special interest in vineyards and orchards reflects a particularly sedentary perspective. While grain can be cultivated by seminomadic pastoralists on an annual basis on marginal land, vineyards and orchards are a strictly sedentary enterprise, demanding good land, plentiful rainfall, years of investment in the land, and thereby the permanent settlement of their cultivators. Indeed, this little story is situated in the agricultural year of the sedentary farmer by a detail familiar to those who practice viticulture: it occurred at just the time when the grapes first ripen (13:20). At one level, the tale actually serves as an etiology for the name of a valley near Hebron, the Wadi Eshcol (*'eškōl*, "cluster of grapes"), known to the sedentary Israelites living in the area for its production of grapes (13:23–24). None of these features of the narrative would be of natural interest to the nomadic pastoralist whose investment is not in land and long-term cultivation but in mobile herds. They are rather characteristic of the Israelite agricultural society who made up the audience of J's epic.[16]

Just as J's depiction of the Israelite hill country in these desert narratives reflects the stance of someone at home there, so his depiction of the desert reflects the stance of one for whom the desert is alien and hostile terrain. For Moses, after he kills the Egyptian taskmaster, as for Israel, when it flees from Egyptian control, the desert is not a home but a place of temporary refuge, a place of escape only when life in sedentary society becomes unbearable. The desert is a last resort. In this regard, the desert in these narratives plays the role it plays in the story of Hagar (Gen 16:1–2, 4–14). Hagar too flees to it only when Sarah's oppression becomes intolerable. To the people of Israel who enter it, the desert is foreign territory. Moses is forced to prevail upon his Midianite brother-in-law Hobab to accompany Israel as a guide. Hobab the Midianite, not Moses the Israelite, knows the desert and its camping places and can keep Israel from losing its way and perishing in the wilderness (Num 10:29–32).

The desert is portrayed by J as a place in which human life is constantly threatened. J's narratives about the desert repeatedly call attention to the precarious plight of Israel there. Israel in the desert is normally in peril, either because of the scarcity of water, as at Marah (Exod 15:22–23, 25a), or because of the scarcity of food (Num 11:4–6). Indeed, the desert is compared constantly and unfavorably, in Israel's complaints, to cultivable land and its agricultural produce, either in the Nile Valley that Israel has left (Num 11:5, 18) or in the Canaanite hills to which it is headed (Num 16:12–14).[17] In the final analysis, J connects the desert with death. Israel is afraid it will die in the desert, a fear that is realized when God punishes the faithless generation for refusing to enter Canaan by death in the wilderness (Num 14:22–23, 16:13).

This is a most telling aspect of J's desert narratives. Life in the desert is above all a sign of divine punishment. Had Israel been obedient and entered the Canaanite hill country willingly, their time in the desert would have been a brief journey, not a lengthy banishment. Just as for Cain, whose punishment meant exile from arable land—a punishment, in his words, too great for a human to bear—so Israel is punished by banishment to the desert until the faithless generation is dead. Once they recognize the punishment that faces them, they change their minds—anything to escape the desert. But it is too late (Num 14:20–25, 39–45).

None of these aspects of J's desert narratives reflects the point of view of a society familiar with the desert and accustomed to living in it. Israel's stay in the desert does not follow the patterns of a nomadic culture adapted to desert life. Nor does Israel's behavior give evidence of a people whose attitudes and values are shaped by the contours of the wilderness environment. The picture is just the opposite: J's narratives depict the desert as an alien and frightful place. Throughout, these stories reflect details and attitudes deriving from the sedentary agricultural society that typified biblical Israel and of which the Yahwist was a member.

The episode in the Yahwist's southern narratives that may appear to run against the grain of this generally negative orientation to the desert is the story of the revelation of God at Mt. Sinai. In the final form of the Pentateuch, which reflects Priestly interests and aims, the encounter between God and Israel at Mt. Sinai is the definitive divine-human encounter. It defines the relationship between God and Israel for all time and establishes the character of Israel as a religious community. Even though the Yahwist's traditions about this desert mountain are much briefer, they include an account of a vivid theophany (Exod 19:2b, 9–13a, 14–16a, 18, 20–25), a code of ritual law (Exod 34:17–26), and a covenant ceremony (Exod 34:1–16, 27–28).

Yet the Yahwist's account of the revelation of God at Mt. Sinai does not depict Israel's deity, who becomes manifest here, as a desert deity, nor does it depict Israel as a desert people who inhabit the environs of this desert sanctuary. J's description of the mountain and of Israel's experiences there are shaped by the same highland agricultural perspective present in the rest of the epic. The imagery for Yahweh's theophany (Exod 19:9, 16a, 18) is drawn from the phenomenon of the thunderstorm typical in the mountains on the eastern rim of the Mediterranean Sea. And the legal code that God delivers to the people at this theophany prescribes a liturgical calendar appropriate for a sedentary agricultural society rather than for nomadic pastoralists (Exod 34: 17–26). Thus, the Yahwist's account of Mt. Sinai in no way mitigates the fearfulness of the desert environment in the southern narratives, nor does it connect Israel's religious ritual with the desert experience. Robert Cohn has suggested that Israel's experience in the wilderness and at Sinai be understood in terms of "liminality," a state at once negative and positive, dangerous and creative; above all, a state of transition between a separation from and a reincorporation into secure space and time.[18] More will be said below about the evidence for the biblical hill country as the environment from which the Yahwist's account of the Sinai theophany and its ritual legislation originate.

Egypt

In the biblical story of the exodus, the land of Egypt is synonymous with oppression and death. According to the narratives at the beginning of the Book of Exodus, Israel's ancestors are forced into slavery and their children killed by the Egyptians among whom the family of Jacob had settled. In the Yahwist's traditions of these events, the tensions and conflict between Egypt and Israel are prominently featured. Yet the negative view of Egyptian political and social policies in the Yahwist's exodus narrative should not be taken as completely representative of the Yahwist's attitude toward the land of Egypt and the Israelite sojourn there. J presents the land of Egypt in a number of favorable ways. By comparison to J's negative attitude toward the desert, J's view of the environment of the land of Egypt—that is, of the Nile Valley where its populace and agricultural land are almost entirely located—is noticeably positive.

As a matter of fact, J describes Egypt's environment in terms that rival and surpass those employed for his homeland in the Israelite hill country. In his first reference to Egypt, J compares the Nile Valley to the paradisaical ecology of the Garden of Eden and of the southern Jordan Valley before its desertification following the disaster in the days of Abraham and Lot (Gen 13:10). During the ancestral era, Egypt is a regular refuge when the precarious enterprise of dry farming in the Canaanite mountains fails because of insufficient rainfall and subsequent famine. In each generation, Israel's ancestors—Abraham (Gen 12:10), Isaac (26:2), and Jacob (Gen 43:1–2, 46:28–31)—either move, or consider moving, to Egypt to escape a period of severe drought and crop failure in the Israelite hills. The land of Egypt is thus an environmental haven that is able to preserve the lives of Israel's ancestors even when their own land fails to do so (Gen 43:8, 47:12).[19] In the desert, the imperiled Israelites are, according to J, more interested in returning to Egypt than in pressing on into their ancestral homeland, primarily because of its bounteous agricultural produce (Num 11:4–5, 14:4). The cliché J reserves for praising the unusual agricultural wealth of his homeland—"a land flowing with milk and honey" (Exod 3: 8–17, etc)—is used by these Israelites as a suitable description of Egypt (Num 16:13).

The Yahwist's positive view of the Egyptian environment reflects certain basic realities about the differing environments of Israel and Egypt. As their own records indicate, the ancient Egyptians regarded Canaan as a rich agricultural area, with abundant grain, fruit, and livestock, which they occasionally exploited as a result of military campaigns or political control.[20] Yet Canaanite agriculture, based as it was on dryland farming, was always more vulnerable to the vagaries of ancient Near Eastern rainfall than was Egyptian agriculture. Due to the huge catchment area in eastern and central Africa, the sources of the Nile supplied a flow of water that was generally abundant and reliable. The Egyptian farmer, himself living in an area with little rainfall, could count on the rising of the Nile for sufficient water to irrigate his crops year after year. And the rising water brought with it alluvial deposits that regularly replenished the soil's nutrients.[21] By contrast, the dryland agriculture of the Canaanite hill country was always completely at the mercy of direct rainfall, which is notoriously irregular in its range, timing, and amount. It was not uncommon throughout history, therefore, for the citizens of Palestine to purchase grain from Egypt during times of famine, which could be brought about by the failure of the rains in any one year.[22] Israel's ancestors, as J describes them, are simply a few examples of an ancient phenonemon: environmental refugees, people forced to relocate because of the failure of their native environment to support human life. Such were the facts with which J was familiar and which lay behind his positive view of the ecological character of the land of Egypt.

In the details of J's description of the Egyptian environment, accurate knowledge of Egyptian society and its environmental setting is blended with other features that reflect the Yahwist's own environment, the Israelite hill country. A good example of this is J's most elaborate plague narrative, the account of the destructive hail storm (Exod 9:13–34). A massive thunderstorm such as this is rare in Egypt, as J twice asserts (vv 18, 24). The country of Egypt is nearly rainless and is characterized by an arid or desert climate, except for a semiarid narrow coastal belt along the Mediterranean.[23] The vivid description of the torrential rain, the hail, and the lightning flashing in the clouds and striking the earth (vv 23–25) is based on the characteristics of this phenomenon in the Israelite hill country where it was not an uncommon occurrence.

J's characterization of the vegetation affected by the hail also reflects the epic's source in the grain-based agricultural economy of the Israelite highlands. The Yahwist focuses particularly on grain, *'ēseb haśśādeh* (vv 22, 25), the field crop that is also the center of interest in the creation narrative (Gen 2:5, 3:18–19).[24] In a detailed explanation of the result of the hail storm on Egypt's crops, J identifies the species that were and were not damaged. Flax (*pištâ*; a fiber crop) and barley (*śĕ'ōrâ*), which mature early, were wiped out, while the wheat varieties, durum (*ḥiṭṭâ*) and emmer (*kussemet*), which mature later, were spared (Exod 9:31–32).[25] J's characterization of Egyptian agriculture as grain-based, and his description of the relative maturation of these crops in the climate of the Nile Valley are accurate, yet one detail, the mention of *ḥiṭṭâ*, betrays his Canaanite orientation. Durum (*ḥiṭṭâ*) and emmer (*kussemet*) wheat were cultivated side by side in Canaan from earliest times, while durum was not introduced into Egypt until the time of the Ptolemies, centuries after J.[26] Here, too, in his description of Egypt's grain economy, J describes the Egyptian environment in precisely the terms with which an Israelite farmer would be familiar. J's narrative of the Egyptian sojourn, as the other narratives of his epic, is firmly rooted in the soil of the Israelite highlands.

Ritual and Law

Within the narratives of Israel's stay in Egypt and at Mt. Sinai in the southern desert, the Yahwist has embedded accounts of the divine establishment of certain specific religious rituals. This does not mean for J, as it does for the Priestly Writer, that religious ritual and proper worship were first established at this period. According to J, Yahweh was worshipped by name and sacrifices were made to him by the first family before the flood (Gen 4:3–5, 26). Yet a number of particulars for worship are laid out in these narratives, particularly in a body of legislation represented by J as part of a covenant between God and Israel at Mt. Sinai (Exod 34:1–28). This ritual legislation provides an illuminating text for exploring further the Yahwist's environmental perspective within his southern narratives.

It has long been recognized that the great body of legislation now associated with the promulgation of the law at Mt. Sinai pertains to sedentary life in the Canaanite hill country rather than to the practice of desert nomadism.[27] This is especially apparent in the Yahwist's own legal and ritual traditions preserved in Exodus 34. In the details of these regulations can be seen the same mixed agricultural economy reflected elsewhere in J's southern narratives and indeed in the epic as a whole.

Prominent in J's ritual legislation are the three festivals (*ḥaggîm*) at which all Israelite males were required to be present, to appear before God (Exod 34:23).[28] First mentioned is the *ḥag hammaṣṣôt*, the festival of unleavened bread (v 18). J identifies this festival as a commemoration of the exodus, yet it is apparent that it is also closely associated by J with the harvest of barley, the first harvest in the Israelite hill country. The *ḥag hammaṣṣôt* is celebrated in the month of *'ābîb* (the end of March and beginning of April), which takes its name from the term for the ripening ear of barley (*'ābîb*). Indeed, J links the times of the barley harvest and the exodus explicitly in the narrative of the plague of hail that destroys the mature barley crop immediately before the escape (9:31–32). The festival of unleavened bread as a commemoration of the barley harvest, together with the exodus, is preserved and made explicit in both Deuteronomic (Deut 16:1–10) and Priestly legislation (Lev 23:9–16).[29] The second festival of J's ritual code, *ḥag šābu'ōt*, the festival of weeks, commemorates the wheat harvest (*qĕṣîr ḥiṭṭîm*) a month or two later in May or June (Exod 34:22). At this festival the worshipper presented to God the first sheaves (*bikkûrîm*) from the year's crop of wheat. The third festival, *ḥag hā'āsîp*, the festival of ingathering, is held at the end of the agricultural year (*tĕqûpat haššānâ;* 34:22). It celebrates the gathering of the fruit harvest—grapes and olives in particular—in the fall.

The Yahwist's religious calendar marked out by these three major festal occasions is based entirely on, and gives sacred meaning to, the agricultural year of sedentary farmers in the Israelite highlands. Each of the great harvests, of grain in the spring and fruit in the fall, becomes the occasion of a sacred festival to celebrate the new produce and present its finest specimens to God. Such a ritual calendar sacralizes the major events of the very agricultural year that God stabilized for Noah and his descendents as his first divine act following the flood (Gen 8:22). It reflects the life of the farmer, not of the nomadic pastoralists in the desert.

A fourth festival mentioned in J's legislation, the *ḥag happāsaḥ (34:25)*, the festival of the Passover, has inspired a great amount of discussion and debate about its nature and origin. It does not appear to be associated in this code with the three major festivals, but it is linked in Deuteronomistic and Priestly legislation with the festival of unleavened bread (Deut 16:1–8; Lev 23:4–21).[30] Julius Wellhausen's explanation has shaped the terms of the debate and remains the starting point for most theories. According to Wellhausen, the Passover, which involves the sacrifice of a lamb, originated in a pastoral nomadic society that had nothing to do with agriculture or its harvests. It involved the presentation to the deity of the first offspring of the flocks in the spring. Because he regarded the Israelites as seminomadic pastoralists in origin, Wellhausen considered the Passover the oldest and only authentic Israelite festival. It was then later combined with the agricultural festivals Israel adopted from the Canaanites as Israel settled down, during their "metamorphasis of shepherds into peasants," as he put it.[31] Such a nomadic pastoral background for Passover is still widely assumed in discussions about its origin and its relation to the festival of unleavened bread. This view has been developed in detail by L. Rost, who considers Passover a rite celebrated by seminomadic pastoralists at the time of change of pasture to insure protection for themselves and their flocks.[32]

Behind the whole history of this analysis of Passover and its relation to the other festivals lies the old dichotomy that was assumed to exist between nomadic pastoralists and sedentary farmers, which in its classic form is reflected neither in ancient societies nor in the perspective of the J writer. The setting of Passover is more likely to be discovered within the context of the mixed agricultural economy of biblical Israel depicted in J's epic and in this ritual legislation in particular. In the first place, the Passover's "secondary" status, outside the three great harvest festivals, reflects properly the subsidary role of pastoralism in the agricultural economy of ancient Israel. Second, the association of Passover with the feast of unleavened bread, loosely made by J and described more directly in Deuteronomic and Priestly tradition, is to be explained ultimately by their roughly simultaneous occurrence in the agricultural year of the Israelite highlands.[33] Whether Passover was celebrated at lambing time to present God with the flock's first born, as Wellhausen suggested, or whether it coincided with the movement of flocks from distant marginal winter pasturage to the stubble of harvested fields nearby, as Rost has proposed, it would have been practiced by highland farmers at roughly the time of the barley harvest festival, *ḥag hammaṣṣôt,* the feast of unleavened bread. This rough chronological coincidence of the festivals of Passover and unleavened bread appears to have been formalized in Deuteronomistic and Priestly legislation, which were concerned to a greater extent than J with standardizing and centralizing cultic practice in Israel.[34]

Just as the major festivals of J's religious calendar reflect a mixed agricultural economy, so also do the prescriptions about first fruits. According to J's code, the first of all produce is to be offered to God. This includes the first harvested produce of the arable land, *ʾǎdāmâ* (34:26; cf. v 22), and firstborn male sheep, goats, and cattle. Firstborn male donkeys, considered unclean, as well as firstborn male humans, are to be substituted with lambs (vv 19–20). The offering to God of the produce from both sectors of the mixed agrarian economy, its crops and herds, is the very ritual practiced by the first family, when Cain and Abel brought to God the fruit of the arable land (*pĕrî hāʾǎdāmâ*) and the firstborn of the flock (*bĕkōrôt ṣōʾn;* Gen 4:3–4). These prescriptions reflect once again the practices of an agricultural society, which supplements its cultivation of cereals and fruits with the herding of sheep and goats.

A final detail in this ritual legislation reveals the agricultural orientation of J's traditions in a particularly striking way. It occurs in the sabbath regulation (Exod 34:21), a decree paralleled in the decalogues preserved by the other pentateuchal authors (Exod 20:8–11 and Deut 5:13–15; cf. Exod 23:12). In each case, the author or editor has chosen to explain the observation of the sabbath in terms of a theme unique to his own perspective and theological goals. The Priestly Writer, for example, explains sabbath rest as the imitation of the deity at creation (Exod 8:11, Gen 2:2–3), thus founding cultic observance in the very structure of the cosmos itself.[35] Deuteronomic tradition, by contrast, is particularly concerned with the welfare of the less fortunate in society, admonishing Israelites to allow their slaves to rest on the sabbath, by reminding Israel that they too were once slaves in Egypt (Deut 5:14–15).[36] By contrast, J's concerns about the sabbath are dictated by the rhythm of the agricultural year. "Six days you shall work/cultivate (*ta'ăbōd*),[37] but on the seventh day you shall rest, (even) during plowing and harvest you shall rest" (34:21). J's specific concern about the rite is that it be observed even in the busiest seasons of the agricultural year, seedtime and harvest, when the demands of grain production were particularly work intensive and when the proper timing in seeding or harvesting could spell success or failure. In this brief detail regarding the sabbath, especially when compared to treatments of it in the other pentateuchal sources, the strong influence of J's agricultural milieu on his view of life and religion becomes particularly apparent.

In the Yahwist's legal and ritual traditions, as in his narrative discourse regarding Israel's experiences in Egypt and the desert, the environmental orientation is consistent. Though describing experiences of Israel's ancestors outside the hill country of biblical Israel, these traditions are all told from the perspective of the typical Israelite farmer in those hills, involved in grain-based dryland agriculture, supplemented by the cultivation of fruit crops and by the herding of sheep and goats. Ritual observances are rooted in the various sectors of such a diversified agricultural economy. And both Egypt, a source of grain during famine in Syria-Palestine, and the desert, a domain of aridity and death, are described from the perspective of the biblical heartland and its village farmers. No desert or nomadic ideal can be gleaned from J's southern narratives. On the contrary, these desert stories depict a temporary, precarious sojourn that possess as its goal and as its narrative point of view the hill country of biblical Israel.

Nature and Religion in the Southern Narratives

The opening episode of the southern narratives, the Israelite exodus from Egypt, has been regarded above all as a social and political event, as a paradigm of human freedom for later generations. This perspective has only been strengthened by the recent adaptation of the exodus as a foundational text for liberation theologies. Within such an interpretive context, the historical dimensions of the exodus narrative are naturally highlighted and emphasized. Indeed, the exodus event has been commonly regarded as the very starting point of Israel's historical religious consciousness.

A few influential proponents of such an approach to the exodus narratives may be cited by way of illustration. G. Ernest Wright, one of the pre-eminent spokesmen for the historical character of Israelite religion, argued in the following way.

> The most probable supposition regarding the origin of Israel's preoccupation with history is that it arose in the earliest days of the nation's history as the only possible explanation available to the people of the manner in which God had made himself known to them. . . . At the center of Israelite faith lay the great proclamation that the God of the fathers had heard the cry of the weak, oppressed people in Egypt. . . . The knowledge of God was an inference from what actually had happened in human history. The Israelite eye was thus trained to take human events seriously,

because in them was to be learned more clearly than anywhere else what God willed and what he was about. Consequently, in all that happened subsequently the Israelite simply interpreted the meaning of events by recognizing and acknowledging in them the God who had formed the nation by the remarkable events at the Exodus and in the wilderness.[38]

In a similar vein, Walther Eichrodt makes the claim that

the roots of this peculiar viewpoint, by which Israel clearly is to be differentiated from all other Near Eastern Peoples, doubtless lie in those happenings of the early time, which gave the impulse to the genesis of the Israelite people, in the events of the time of Moses. . . . This first experience of a Divine encounter was decisive for the fundamental conception of the Divine revelation in Israel. Here one learned to understand the being of God from history and to exhibit his works in the forms of history.[39]

Nahum Sarna introduces his study of the book of Exodus from the same perspective. He too regards history as the realm of God's action and the exodus as the point of crystalization for this theological perspective:

History is the arena of divine activity, and the weal and woe of the individual and of the nation is the product of God's providence, conditioned by human response to his demands. It is no wonder that the Exodus is the pivotal event in the Bible, and that the experiences connected with it—the slavery of the Israelites, their liberation from Egypt, the covenant between God and His people at Mt. Sinai, and the journey in the wilderness toward the Promised Land—all constitute the dominant motif of the Scriptures in one form or another.[40]

In a similar fashion, Emil Fackenheim, in his monograph, *God's Presence in History*, identifies the exodus as a "root experience," an historical event so foundational as to shape a new faith, "affecting decisively all future Jewish generations."[41]

Such claims regarding the historical, social, and political features of the exodus story have been adopted as foundational in recent liberation theologies. "The Exodus is the key event that models the faith of Israel," writes J. Severino Croatto. "Unless we begin from this central event, neither Israel's faith nor the formation of its religious traditions and sacred books are understandable."[42] Such paradigmatic history is contrasted by Croatto to the rhythms of the cosmos, deemed static, tyrannical, and bound to the oppressive structure of the status quo. "Mythic persons are not free," asserts Croatto,

they are subject to the cosmos. . . . Israel had the experience of a *personal* God who acts *in history,* who is independent of nature. . . . On the basis of this experience, Israel elaborates the idea of a God different from the world that he creates. . . . Now human beings do not need to associate themselves with the rhythm of the cosmos in order to imbibe the sacred. God, different from the world, manifests himself in the *events* of history. The Exodus event was indicative in this respect [Croatto's emphasis].[43]

Against the backdrop of such a distinctly historical and political approach to the exodus story, the world of nature assumes a secondary place. At best, it represents a rather insignificant background for the human drama of liberation; at worst, it represents a paradigm for the static, tyrannical powers of oppressive governments like the Pharaoh's court. Neither representation of nature, however, takes into account the substantial way in which the Yahwist's agrarian perspective, detailed in the preceding analysis, has shaped the narrative of events and the code of religious law contained in these southern stories. Nor do they reflect the significant influence of traditions about the storm god in the narratives. When the southern narratives are reread in light of these concerns, the role of nature in these stories and the character of divine activity in the world can be more fully appreciated.

God and the World

An appropriate starting point for reexamining the relationship between nature and history in the Yahwist's southern narratives is an observation by Frank Cross that these narratives draw heavily—in their details and overall form— on a conventional ancient Near Eastern literary cycle describing the establishment of the orders of the cosmos.[44] The core of this conventional cycle is the conflict between two deities, a storm deity and a sea deity, in which the defeat of the sea by the storm subdues chaos and establishes the orders of nature that make life possible.

Examples of such a narrative are available from a broad spectrum of ancient Near Eastern literature. The classic example from Mesopotamia is its great creation epic, *Enuma Elish*, in which the divine warrior Marduk, who fights with the weapons of the thunderstorm, subdues Tiamat, "Sea," and out of her body shapes the world and establishes its natural orders.[45] A Canaanite version of this same conflict, the Baal Cycle from the ancient city of Ugarit, describes the conquest of Prince Sea, alias Judge River, by the storm god Baal, thereby establishing his power over chaos and death and guaranteeing bounty and fertility in the world.[46] In Israelite literature, this narrative form is reflected most clearly in a corpus of archaic poems that picture Israel's deity as a storm in conflict with sea (e.g., Exod 15; Pss 18, 68, 77; Hab 3).[47]

Underlying these particular versions of the story are a set of shared features that point to a conventional narrative pattern. This pattern is a drama composed of two, paired movements. In the first movement, the Divine Warrior, accompanied by the manifestations of the thunderstorm, marches into battle and conquers Sea. At the storm god's advance into battle, nature is shaken and thrown into disarray. In the second movement, the victorious divine warrior returns to his holy mountain to be enthroned as sovereign ruler in the universe. At the storm god's return from battle, nature is restored to order and made fertile and productive.[48]

Cross's observation that this conventional cycle has shaped the selection of events and the overall structure of the Yahwist's southern narrative can be substantiated by examining key details of the Yahwist's story. Action in the first movement of the traditional conflict cycle is initiated when a challenge to the divine warrior's authority is delivered to the residence of the god, in Baal's case, to Mt. Zaphon north of Ugarit.[49] In the Yahwist's exodus drama, divine action also begins at God's sacred mountain, where God first appears to the hero Moses (Exod 3:2–4a, 5).[50] In God's speech to Moses at this initial theophany, God describes the challenge to his authority represented by Pharaoh's oppression of God's people, whose cries have reached his ears. And he describes his intention to go into battle to subdue the Egyptians and deliver Israel (3:7–8, 15–22).

The Yahwist's divine warrior, like the traditional hero of the conflict cycle, marches into battle accompanied by the phenomena of the thunderstorm.[51] God's first appearance to Moses is symbolized by a bolt of lightning (*labbat 'ēš*), which does not consume the tree it sets ablaze (3:2).[52] In the plague narratives, which relate God's mighty acts against the Egyptians on behalf of his people, the most elaborate episode describes God's assault on Egypt in a great storm, with thunder and lightning, which strikes the earth with rain and hail, devastating the land (9:13–34). At the climactic battle between God and the Egyptians at the sea, God appears above the Israelites in a pillar of cloud (*'ammûd 'ānān*; 13:21–22), the towering thunderhead typical of the Mediterranean storm front. At night the storm cloud appears as a "pillar of fire" (*'ammûd 'ēš*; v 21), a great column of cloud filled with lightning that illuminates the contours of the cloud and the land beneath.[53] From this storm cloud, and with its winds, God attacks the Egyptians and destroys them in the midst of the sea (14:19, 20, 21b, 24–25, 27b).[54]

The disintegration of the orders of nature, which accompanies the divine warrior's march into battle in the traditional conflict cycle, is dramatically portrayed in the series of natural disasters recounted in the plague narratives (Exod 7–11). Natural patterns are reversed when water turns to blood (7:14–18, 20b–21a, 23–25) and day becomes night (10:21–26). Nature's limits and balances disintegrate, as frog and insect populations rage out of control (7:26–29; 8:3b–11a, 16–28) and epidemics spread unchecked (9:1–7). "The whole land of Egypt," says the Yahwist, "lay devastated" (8:20). In his analysis of the natural and political implications of the plague narratives, Terrence Fretheim has characterized these catastrophes as the complete reversal of the created order.[55]

In contrast to the comparative examples of the conflict cycle, in which the storm god's adversary is a rival deity, Sea, God's adversary in the Yahwist's narrative is a human figure, the Egyptian Pharaoh. Yet by virtue of the fact that the Yahwist's narrative places the climactic conflict between God and Pharaoh at the sea, and in light of the actual description of the sea in the portrayal of that conflict, the sea takes on much of the character and significance it possesses in the traditional conflict cycle. It assumes a kind of symbolic adversarial role. This can be illustrated, in the first place, by the way in which the sea becomes associated with Pharaoh in the climactic conflict with the storm god. At Pharaoh's demise, his armies and the sea coalesce. In pursuit of Israel, Pharaoh enters the dried sea bed, where his chariots sink into the soft sea bottom (14:24–25). When the sea waters return at dawn, the

Egyptian armies perish within them, their corpses littering the seashore (vv 27b, 30). Furthermore, the imagery with which J describes the sea's response to the storm god's attack shares many features with the description of the sea in comparative literature. Like Tiamat, "Sea," who is pierced by Marduk's storm winds—including north, south, east, and west winds—in Enuma Elish, so the sea in J's epic is driven back by God's powerful east wind (14:21b).[56] Like Prince Sea (yamm), who vanishes when Baal consumes him in the Baal Cycle, so the sea (yām) in J's narrative disappears when God dries it up and turns it into dry ground (v 21b).[57] The victory of the divine warrior in J's epic portrays his power and authority over human governments, represented by Pharaoh, and natural orders, represented by the sea, alike.

God's victory at the sea concludes the first movement of the conventional conflict cycle. The second, paired movement begins with the procession of the victorious deity back to the sacred mountain to assume sovereignty over the world by virtue of his conquest over the forces of chaos.[58] In the Yahwist's epic, this movement is initiated when Israel's victorious deity moves before the people in the storm cloud (Exod 13:21–22), leading them from the sea to Mt. Sinai, the sacred mountain where he had first appeared to Moses. At this holy mountain, God's sovereignty over the world is confirmed through a covenant between God and Israel and through the issuance of a code of law by which the worship of God is to be conducted. In this code, absolute allegiance to Israel's God is demanded (Exod 34:11–16). And a liturgical calendar is prescribed that recalls in ritual not only of God's control of the political realm, such as the deliverance from Egypt (Exod 34:18), but also of God's control of the seasonal cycles that produce Israel's harvests (34:18, 22, 26).

The second movement of the conventional conflict cycle concludes with the restoration of nature, when the victorious God reappears as the thunderstorm, brings nature to life, and prepares a banquet from the earth's produce.[59] In the Yahwist's epic, God's return to Mt. Sinai is marked by a spectacular display of storm phenomena: the dark cloud, thunder, and lightning (Exod 19:9, 16a, 18; 34:5).[60] On either side of the narrative of this great theophany, immediately before and after it, occur narratives in which the desert comes to life and Israel feasts on food provided by God. In the story of Marah, God turns bitter (mārā) water into sweet, drinkable water for the Israelites (Exod 15:22–25a).[61] And in the story of Kibroth-hattaavah, God provides bread and meat to satisfy Israel's hunger (Num 11:4–13, 15, 18–23, 31–35).[62] These accounts of God's provision of water and food for his people, even in the lifeless wilderness, draw heavily, as William Propp has shown, on traditional imagery from the second movement of the ancient Near Eastern conflict cycle.[63]

Having illustrated the influence of the ancient Near Eastern conflict cycle over the form and content of J's southern narrative, we are in a position to reconsider the relationship between history and nature in this narrative. The narrative contains an account of a unique history, Israel's experience of deliverance from Egyptian slavery and covenant making at Mt. Sinai. At the same time, the kinds of events narrated and the sequence in which they occur have been substantially affected by a conventional transcultural pattern designed to describe the establishment of universal cosmic orders. An appraisal of the Yahwist's orientation to nature and history rests ultimately on the way in which the interrelationship between these two features of the Yahwist's narrative is perceived.

The relationship has commonly been described in terminology that reflects the traditional dichotomy between nature and history as well as the association of Israelite religion with history and the religions of its neighbors with nature. While scholars have recognized the presence of elements of the old conflict cycle in biblical texts, they have argued that the narrative of cosmic conflict has been "demythologized" or "historicized" at the hands of biblical writers. This viewpoint is stated clearly by Dennis McCarthy. Biblical writers, he argues, appropriated the conflict drama in a manner which

> shows that there was little feeling of a religious reality behind it. Rather it was simply a convenient source of tropes. . . . The evidence is that such "demythologization" was there from the first because Israel was interested in historical, not cosmic origins, and so it could use mythic themes without hazard. . . . So many motifs are crowded together here: mountain god, storm god, warrior god, *Chaoskampf;* but they are all symbolic, impressive figures of speech and thought for picturing the way Yahweh controls events among men. The point is always political or social order.[64]

In such an approach, the cosmic dimensions of the conflict cycle are discounted, and the natural imagery associated with it is seen as merely instrumental to another purpose: the social and political. Thus the plague narratives, while rooted in a natural phenomena characteristic of the conflict cycle, can be interpreted theologically as "instances of God's harnessing the forces of nature for the realization of His own historic purpose."[65] Occasionally the assessment of cosmic elements in biblical narrative is even negative; they are regarded as possessing "an alien spirit," a purpose that runs against the grain of the Bible's historical aims.[66] According to this position, the cosmic dimensions of the conflict cycle appropriated by biblical writers are recognized, but they are rejected as theologically significant for biblical writers themselves.

If the traditional dichotomies between nature and history and the religions of Israel and its neighbors are set aside for a moment, however, the relationship between the conventional conflict cycle and Israel's own history can be seen from the opposite point of view. From this perspective, the ancient Near Eastern cycle of cosmological conflict and ordering is not an empty shell to be discarded, nor an alien conceptual scheme to be superceded, by Israel's new historical consciousness. Rather, as the source of the larger framework within which the exodus and Sinai stories are narrated and of central images of God and the world contained in these stories, the conflict cycle is employed to provide cosmic depth for historical events. Israel's experiences of liberation and covenant are, by virtue of their narration within the structure of the conflict cycle, grounded in the orders of the cosmos.

Human history is thereby viewed as neither distinct from nor superior to natural orders but rooted in them. And the natural world is viewed as neither a mere instrument nor an alien conception for historical narrative but its foundation and ground. In his analysis of Israel's appropriation of the ancient Near Eastern conflict genre in its archaic poetry, Cross has recognized this type of interrelationship between cosmic ("mythic") and historical themes:

> Israel's early religious evolution was neither simple nor linear. It will not do to describe the process as a progressive historicizing of myth. . . . The power of the mythic pattern was enormous. The Song of the Sea [Exodus 15] reveals this power as mythological themes shape its mode of presenting epic memories. It is proper to speak of this counterforce as the tendency to mythologize historical episodes to reveal their transcendent meaning.[67]

Such an interpretation of the biblical appropriation of the conflict cycle and its cosmological purposes has precedent in the uses of this cycle in comparative literature. The conflict cycle's classic exemplar in Mesopotamian literature, Enuma Elish, provides a useful example. This narrative is certainly about cosmic ordering. After conquering Tiamat, "Sea," Marduk constructs the universe from her body. But Marduk's conquest of Sea is not the basis for the establishment of cosmic orders alone. It is also the basis for the establishment of the city of Babylon and its preeminent political position in the world. Following Marduk's construction of the cosmos, the gods build Babylon and within it, Esagila, the great temple to be Marduk's abode. On this throne in this temple in the city of Babylon, Marduk takes his place as his sovereignty in the cosmos is proclaimed by the deities at the conclusion of the epic.[68]

Noting the brevity of the account of creation, when compared to Marduk's battle with and conquest of Tiamat, and the length of the proclamation of Marduk's names as ruling sovereign in Babylon, Alexander Heidel claims that Enuma Elish, as much as a creation story, is a tribute to Marduk's city Babylon. "Next to the purpose of singing the praises of Marduk comes the desire, on the part of the Babylonian priests, who were responsible for the composition of this epic, to sing the praises of Babylon, the city of Marduk, and to strengthen her claim to supremacy over all the cities of the land."[69] Thus cosmic and political orders are conceived as dimensions of a single reality established and sustained by Marduk.

In this vein, Thorkild Jacobsen has argued that Marduk's adversary, Tiamat, "Sea," represents not only a natural or cosmic phenomena but also an historical one, the "Sealand" (*māt tâmti,* "land of *tâmti/'*Sea'") the territory of ancient Sumer near the Persian Gulf in southern Mesopotamia and Babylon's chief antagonist in the first half of the second millennium.[70] The conquest of Tiamat thus signifies Marduk's control over the powers of the cosmos and over the political powers of southern Mesopotamia as well. This blending of the cosmic and historical in the representation of Marduk's adversary provides an instructive parallel for the coalescence of the Egyptian armies and the sea in God's climatic battle in the Yahwist's exodus narratives. In both narratives, natural and political orders alike are placed under the control of the soverign deity.

Within this interrelationship between cosmological and political themes in Enuma Elish, Jacobsen recognizes "a unifying concept of existence" in which divine orders pervade both nature and society. In this single system of order, in which cosmos and history share a common design, the cosmological sovereignty of Marduk provides "cosmic scope" for the historical and political sovereignty of Babylon.[71] In the same fashion, the Yahwist's narration of Israel's particular history within the context of the conventional ancient Near Eastern genre of cosmological conflict and ordering provides cosmic scope to these events. It locates them within the orders of the universe itself, granting them transcendent meaning.[72]

Within such an interpretive approach, the cosmological motifs in the Yahwist's southern narratives are not alien to Israelite thought or merely convenient tropes for Israel's historical narrative. They reflect a conception of the natural world as the foundation of human existence and the ultimate context within which human history must be regarded. They reflect a conception of reality in which the arenas we speak of as nature and history are dimensions of a single ordered realm under the sovereignty of a deity who guarantees life in the world and to his people.

Religious Ritual and Worship

It has been suggested by Jacobsen that the ultimate origin of the ancient storm-sea conflict drama, which influences the shape J's southern narratives, is the hill country along the eastern coast of the Mediterranean Sea.[73] In this environment, during the rainy season, great thunderheads build up over the Mediterranean and come sweeping in over the sea and into the hill country, where life depends on the rains these storm fronts bring. Thus, in the literary shape and primary images of the southern narratives are reflected the cosmological phenomena native to the biblical highlands that provide the perspective for the Yahwist's epic as a whole.

The same can be said of the legal codes preserved in this part of the epic and of the prescriptions for religious ritual and worship they contain. Just as J's view of God's activity in the world is expressed through the form and imagery of a literary cycle indigenous to the Canaanite highlands, so his understanding of the worship of that deity is expressed in a code of rituals arising from that same milieu. As has already been shown in detail above, J's "decalogue" in Exodus 34 contains a set of prescriptions for Israelite worship that reflect the same mixed agrarian economy presumed throughout the epic. It is necessary now to consider, in conclusion, how these rituals represent the relationship between society and nature.

There can be no doubt that the collection of laws in Exodus 34 is regarded in the Yahwist's epic as Israel's supreme religious obligation to Yahweh. The laws are presented as the code of conduct required of Israel by the covenant drawn up between Yahweh and Moses on Mt. Sinai (vv 1–11). Whereas the Elohist's record of the covenant with God at the mountain in Exodus 24:1–15a included the familiar "ten commandments" in Exodus 20:1–17 as the basis

of Israel's obligations, so Exodus 34 reflects the Yahwist's own record of the
Sinai covenant and Israel's obligations therein.[74]

The most distinctive aspect of J's covenant code is the manner in which
it reflects the agricultural economy and calendar of biblical Israel. The primary religious festivals mandated by J's code, at which all adult males were
required to be present, are harvest festivals: the festival of unleavened bread
at the barley harvest (v 18 cf. 9:31), the festival of weeks at the wheat harvest
(v 22), and the festival of ingathering at the fruit harvest (v 22). If the explicit instructions of the festival of weeks is any indication, these festivals
required the presentation to Yahweh of the first produce of each of these major
crops (v 22). In any case, other regulations make it clear that a primary duty
of all is the contribution to Yahweh of the first produce of the entire agricultural economy, from the firstborn of the herds—cattle, sheep, donkeys
(vv 19–20)—to the initial harvest of the arable land (*ădāmā;* v 26). These regulations represent the heart of J's covenant code, which contains in addition
several key prescriptions found also in the Elohist code—the exclusive worship of Yahweh (v 14), the prohibition of images (v 17), and the observation
of the sabbath (v 21; even, according to J, at seasons of peak agricultural
labor!).

The first observation that can be made about J's conception of worship
on the basis of these ritual regulations is that Israel's service to God was rendered through its agricultural economy. Israel's primary religious responsibility was the offering to God of the first returns of its investment in its fields
and herds. Such a pattern of worship does not derive ultimately from the
experience of divine activity in historical or political events, but from a sense
of divine involvement in the orders of nature, in the processes of fertility that
produced crops and offspring in particular. The realm of nature is regarded
by such ritual not as emptied of divinity and thereby "desacralized" but as
the very arena within which human society fulfills its service to God.

To probe more deeply into the purpose of these agricultural rituals, into
the human intentions that lay behind them, is not as simple an investigation
as it might at first seem. While the offering of first fruits is a common practice around the world in various types of societies—food gatherers, pastoralists, agriculturalists—no single interpretation of the ritual has been accepted
by anthropologists and comparativists.[75] Many, however, find in such ritual,
including its biblical version, two interrelated motives: the expression of
gratitude on the one hand and the interest in gaining the favor and aid of the
deity on the other.[76] This twofold intent of the first fruits offering is aptly
captured in the term *minḥā,* employed for it by J in the story of Cain and
Abel (Gen 4:3,4). *minḥā,* as its usage in the Jacob and Esau story clearly shows
(Gen 32:14, 19, 21; 33:10), is "a present made to secure or retain good will."[77]

As the contents of Israel's offering to God—the first fruits of field and
herd—indicate, the gratitude expressed and the aid desired have both to do
with the processes of fertility in ground and womb. The contribution to God
of the first results of such fertility in the field and in the herd signify the
community's thankfulness to the deity. (The possibility that J conceived of

this contribution as actually feeding the deity has already been examined in chapter 2.) By this act, the worshipper also hoped to influence favorably the divine powers responsible for fertility in the future. Such powers are closely associated with God by J throughout the epic. From its opening sentence identifying God as the source of rain to its elaborate theophany of God as the thunderstorm in these southern stories, from its identification of God with arable land in the Cain and Abel story to its accounts of the victorious storm god's making the desert bloom, the Yahwist's epic has associated the divine with the fertility of the land. Repeatedly, the fertility of the womb is also attributed by J to the work of God (e.g., Gen 4:1, 16:2, 20:18, 29:31–35).

The foundation of Israel's cult in the natural cycles of fertility and production is reflected plainly in J's prescriptions about the altar on which these sacrifices are to be made (Exod 20:22–26).[78] In each sanctuary (*māqôm*) in which Yahweh is worshipped, the altar is to be constructed of arable soil, *ădāmâ* (v 24). Alternatively the altar may be constructed of field stones, but stones, if used, must remain in their natural state. The touch of human tools— the contact with technology—was regarded as profaning the cultic structure (v 25). *ădāmâ*, the preferred material for the Israelite altar, is of course the basis of Israel's agricultural economy. It is the land from which the worshippers' offerings have been produced and the land regarding which the offerer desires Yahweh's future aid. It is the land that defines Israelite society. It represents the focal point of J's landscape and signifies the character of human life, composed as it was from arable soil. Israel's central cultic installation, its altar of arable soil, grounds Israelite worship firmly within its agrarian mode of life.

Having surveyed the natural phenomena that shaped the Yahwistic cult, we must also examine the references to history and politics in J's ritual code. While two of the three major harvest festivals, the festival of weeks at the wheat harvest and of ingathering at the fruit harvest, are exclusively agricultural in nature, the third, the festival of unleavened bread at the barley harvest, includes the commemoration of Israel's escape from Egypt (Exod 34:18). Participation in this festival thus reflects human gratitude both for the first grain harvest of the spring and for Israel's deliverance from Egyptian oppression. Yahweh's activity in both natural and historical realms, so ably expressed by J's use of the conflict genre as the basis for the southern narrative, is here acknowledged in a single religious ritual. This blending of the natural and historical is beautifully symbolized in the key element of this festival, the consumption of unleavened bread. The exclusion of leaven, which has its roots in the eating of the first produce in its original state, untouched by leaven, or in the association of leaven with fermentation, deterioration, and death, is also provided with an historical explanation by J: the haste with which Israel left Egypt did not leave time for its use (Exod 12: 33–39).[79]

A second reference to political realities within J's list of ritual regulations calls to mind a theme of J's ancestral narratives in Genesis: the gift of land as the basis for Israelite nationhood.[80] J's code specifically states that careful observation of its regular rituals will ensure possession of the land God ceded to Abraham, secure borders, and a stable national existence (Exod 34:11, 24). But here, too, the natural and historical are blended in the worshipper's propitiation of the deity. By fulfilling the agricultural obligations prescribed by J's covenant code, the offerer hoped to secure God's continued sovereignty over the soil, regarded as both the foundation of Israel's agricultural economy and physical survival and of its national identity and political security.

One final element in J's legislation deserves attention because it has occasionally been employed in the argument for Israel's exclusive historical orientation and desacralization of the world of nature. This is the prohibition of images for the deity (Exod 34:17; cf. 20:23). According to this proposal, argued eloquently by Gerhard von Rad, the veto on images in Israelite worship rose ultimately from Israel's refusal to associate divinity directly with the world. Since God acted in history rather than in nature, no natural object could represent his presence. As von Rad summarizes the argument, "Nature was not a mode of Jahweh's being; he stood over against it as its Creator. This then means that the commandment forbidding images is bound up with the hidden way in which Jahweh's revelation came about in cult and history."[81]

Israel's aniconic tradition, more and more confirmed by archaeological excavation, has been explained with a variety of theories, none of which has gained a consensus among scholars.[82] The close association between this prohibition and the command for the exclusive worship of Yahweh, within the various codes in which it appears (Exod 34:11–17, 20:3–5; cf. Deut 5:7–10), suggests that the prohibition of images may have most to do with preserving the worship of Yahweh alone and the discouragement of syncretism, to which the use of images may have made worship susceptible (Exod 34: 13–14). Whatever the case, J's thoroughgoing identification of Yahweh with natural phenomena does not justify von Rad's claim that "nature was not a mode of Jahweh's being." For J nature and history alike represent modes of divine being, and Israel's aniconic tradition in no way contradicts this fact.

Throughout Israel's worship, as J conceived it to be, the world of nature plays a foundational role. It is within this realm that Israel serves its God. From this realm are taken its offerings to God and within this realm it desires God's goodwill and blessings. Related integrally to the recognition and celebration of God's presence in this realm is the recognition of God's presence and activity in the historical and political arena as well. When both realms are present in the ritual of worship they are so completely intertwined in the central religious symbols, whether they be land or unleavened bread, that they cannot be separated according to the modern dichotomy signified by the terms *nature* and *history*. For J, Israel's religious ritual reflected a single world revelatory at once of Yahweh's presence within it and sovereignty over it.

5

The Bible and Nature
Ancient Israelite Views and Modern Environmental Theologies

The detailed survey of the Yahwist's landscape in chapters 2, 3, and 4 provides us with a new set of measurements—of J's physical terrain and intellectual perspective—with which to reassess the larger issue that prompted this survey. This is the common belief, widespread in traditional biblical scholarship and recent environmental writing alike, that nature poses a problem for biblical thought. It is a belief, in its scholarly version at least, based solidly on two interrelated concepts: the idea that biblical religion is an historical religion for which the world of nature is of only peripheral interest, and the idea that this viewpoint derived largely from Israel's desert origins.

This traditional and familiar representation of nature in the Bible has been illustrated and analyzed at length in chapter 1, where its theoretical basis in nineteenth-century anthropology and theology has already been documented and critiqued. Throughout the subsequent interpretation of the three major movements of the Yahwist's epic, the text of J has been analyzed in light of the two key themes—the desert and history—that have shaped traditional scholarship. And these key concepts have proven unworkable, as characterizations of the environment of the Yahwist's epic and of the representation of nature and culture expressed within it. In order to bring the results of this reinterpretation of the Yahwist's epic into sharper focus, the Yahwist's perspective on nature and on the human position within it will be summarized below under three headings. Under the first, "Agriculture as Culture: The Human as a Farmer," the issue of the Yahwist's formative environment will be reconsidered. Under the second and third headings, "Creation as Redemption: The Human as a Citizen of the Earth," and "Nature as Measure: The Human as a Servant," the Yahwist's conception of the relationship between nature and society will be reviewed. In each of these cases, the Yahwist's perspective will be explored for its major implications, both for a reconceptualization of the religion of ancient Israel and for a more genuine and authentic treatment of biblical traditions within current discussion of environmental values.

Agriculture as Culture: The Human as a Farmer

A brief review of the concrete details of the Yahwist's landscape, as these have come into focus in the preceding chapters, shows that J's native environment is the agrarian terrain of the biblical hill country, rising from the Mediterranean Sea on the west and the deep Jordan rift on the east. These agricultural highlands provide the scene in which J's epic of Israel's ancestors is, for the most part, set and the point of view from which their story is, in its entirety, told.

At the center of this landscape lies arable soil, the substance out of which all life—plant, animal, human—is created and to which it owes its survival. The Yahwist traces Israel's ancestors, and the human race as a whole, to "the farmer," *hā'ādām*, who was made from arable soil, *'ādāmâ*, and assigned by God to be its cultivator. His descendants—the epic's central characters: Cain, Noah, Abraham, Isaac, Jacob—are all landholders and farmers, at home in the agricultural highlands of biblical Israel. It is these arable highlands that figure most prominently in J's well-known theology of blessing and curse. They bear the curse in the prediluvian age and become the primary element of blessing in the postdiluvian era. In them are grounded the sacred shrines, established by Israel's ancestors at the location of theophanies of Yahweh, that mark the center of the Yahwist's world.

Israel's ancestors are also shepherds, raising sheep and goats on grazing lands contiguous with the richer arable soils in the biblical hill country. Such pastoralism, as it is described by J, is combined with cultivation by single ancestral families to produce the mixed agrarian economy that has typified the Mediterranean highlands since the domestication of plants and animals. From the first family, in which Cain tills the soil—as did his father—and in which his younger brother Abel tends the family's flocks, J's ancestral families are largely sedentary, multipurpose households, seeking to ensure their subsistence by the self-sufficiency such an integrated economy provides. Their animal husbandry includes those species—sheep and goats, cattle, donkeys, and camels—typical of rural Iron Age settlements in the biblical period; and the family's flocks are cared for, as is customary in such agricultural communities, by children and servants.

The desert, in which Israel's origins have more commonly been located, is a real landscape close at hand, with which the Yahwist and his ancestral characters must constantly deal, especially in the final movement of the epic. Yet it remains spatially and intellectually at the periphery of the Yahwist's world. The desert is regarded throughout the epic as a foreign and perilous place, not the indigenous and formative environment of Israel's ancestors. The prospect of life in it is as horrific to the Israelites at the end of the epic as it was to their ancestor Cain at the beginning. When they experience the Sinai theophany in this liminal place, it does not ground them in the desert nor does it reflect a desert religion. At Sinai, Israel's ancestors, as the Yahwist describes them, are encountered by a storm god who binds them by covenant to a ritual life centered on the major harvests produced by the arable soil of the biblical hill country.

The specialized, nomadic pastoralism, associated with the desert and commonly believed to characterize Israel's own beginnings, is not the economic style of life to which the Yahwist traces Israel's origins. While not unknown to J, specialized pastoralism is ascribed in the epic to secondary ancestral lineages (e.g., Jabal, Ishmael) and to Israel's own ancestors only when they are forced to adopt it outside the biblical hill country (e.g., in Syria and Egypt) when they must take up temporary residence as clients, *gērîm*, in foreign countries where they do not own property and cannot farm. Throughout the sweep of J's ancestral narrative, there is no dichotomy between herding and farming, nor is there any evidence for the evolution of J's forbearers from one to the other.

Thus, the Yahwist's epic furnishes no evidence for the traditional view, built heavily on nineteenth-century anthropological theory, that Israel originated in the desert and in the culture of nomadic pastoralism associated with it. Such a view of Israel's origins is rendered suspect, as has already been pointed out in chapter 1, by the problems inherent in the early anthropological models on which it was based. It is also contradicted by the details of J's own landscape. This is especially significant in light of the fact that J's epic has been regarded as Israel's oldest, most extensive account of its origins.

To be in a position to correctly evaluate the biblical view of nature and its place in biblical religion, the reader of the Bible must be resituated geographically, from the ancient Near East's deserts to its arable highlands. It is within this agrarian environment that biblical values toward the natural world arose and were shaped. Precisely, biblical values reflect the realities and demands of an agricultural society, in which grain-based dryland farming was supplemented with fruit and vegetable production and with animal husbandry, the raising of sheep and goats in particular. It is this concrete environment and the experience of the small farmers who inhabited it—not the desert and nomadic pastoralists—that must provide the frame of reference for describing the role of nature in ancient Israelite religion, and for reconsidering the significance of biblical values for contemporary readers, as well.

The most far-reaching consequence of such a reorientation is the undoing of the environmental argument for the uniquely historical shape of biblical religion. The claim that Israelite religion valued history while it devalued nature can no longer be derived from a formative desert experience. It cannot be argued, for example, that Israel lost its bond with the phenomenal world, as the Frankforts put it, because of its beginnings in the stark solitude of the desert. Nor can the claim be made that its deity was a god of people and not of places, related as he was in Israel's infancy to its nomadic ancestors rather than to the natural terrain they traversed.[1] The traditional claim for Israel's historical religion is thus stripped of its major, classic support: Israel's desert origins. And the question then logically follows as to what extent the historical characterization of Israelite religion can be sustained without its traditional ecological foundation. Without it, the imposing reconstruction of the historical character of Israelite religion and law assembled by Alt, for example, would have to be completely dismantled.[2]

When one situates oneself within the environmental location of the Yahwist and views the world from the point of view of an ancient Mediterranean agricultural society, one can see how deeply Israelite religion is bound up with the dynamics of such a natural and social setting. As has been shown in the preceding chapters, the worship of Yahweh in J's epic is closely associated with the places and processes crucial to Israel's agricultural existence. The cult centers established by Israel's ancestors, commemorating in each case divine appearances in which land is bequeathed to them, are located at the center of Israel's agrarian landscape. The liturgical year, mandated in the covenant decalogue promulgated at Mt. Sinai, is based on the three primary harvests of the Mediterranean highlands: barley and wheat in the spring and fruit in the fall. The principal cultic ritual consists in the presentation to the deity of the prime produce of the two sectors of Israel's mixed agricultural economy: the first fruits of the ground and the firstborn of the flocks and herds. Israelite worship as reflected in J's epic—in its location, in its seasonal observance, and in the content of its ritual—has to do with the process of fertility upon which an agrarian society such as Israel's was wholly dependent for its survival.

Such a ritual and theological system is not one that sets God and people apart from natural processes but formalizes through cultic acts their interdependence. These rituals recognize the integral link between divine activity and the soil's fertility. They express thanksgiving to God as the source of nature's bounty. They also enact and sacralize the connection between people and soil. Made by God from arable soil and commissioned by God to farm it, the worshipper offers the soil's produce as service to God, as an act, one might almost say, of self-definition. The point of orientation behind all of this ritual, and the understanding of the human and the divine that they entail, is the recognition of the dependence of human survival on productive soil.

Israelite religion has frequently been distinguished from its neighbors, the Canaanites in particular, in its not being an agrarian religion bound up with the cycles of nature or concerned with the processes of fertility as was Canaanite religion. In fact, the tension between Canaan and Israel in the Bible is often represented as a conflict between two religious worldviews, one based in the natural processes crucial to agricultural existence, the other based in human history. "Settling down in Canaan involved all sorts of social and religious problems," observes Helmer Ringgren in his study of Israelite religion. "The Canaanites were settled farmers; their religion was a fertility cult appropriate to the needs of an agricultural civilization. The immigrating Israelites, in contrast, were probably nomads or semi-nomads, their civilization was primarily pastoral, and their religion was in no position to satisfy the demands made by agriculture."[3] Such a perspective is attributed by Peter Ellis to the Yahwist's epic itself. "While it is true that an anti-Canaanite polemic runs through the saga," he writes, "it is equally true that the Yahwist's specific polemic is religious not national. His animus is against the fertility cult of the Canaanites not against the Canaanites as a people."[4] In studies of the Yahwist, as in analyses of Israelite religion more broadly, the tension with Canaan has been associated with the Bible's problem with nature, with its attempt to exclude nature from the realm of religious reality and ritual.

There is no doubt that the Yahwist draws a sharp distinction between Israelites and Canaanites throughout the epic. In the very first narrative of the postflood age, Canaan is cursed by Noah for his father's indiscretion, and he is placed under the rule of his brothers. Alone among all of the indigenous peoples of Syria-Palestine who figure prominently in J's epic—the Israelites, Ammonites, Moabites, Edomites, and Arameans—the Canaanites are traced through the line of the delinquent Ham rather than through the line of Shem from whom Israel and its neighbors descend. Later, Abraham and his descendants are granted the land of the Canaanites, and Israel is forbidden to intermarry with the Canaanites or to participate in their worship.

This clear boundary between Israel and Canaan, however, is never formulated by J in terms of different orientations toward nature in their respective religions, or in terms of contrasting environments or economies in which these religions were shaped. Rather, Canaan's distinct lineage and subservience are part of the epic's elaborate political agenda, developed in genealogies and genealogical narratives, by which Israel's relationships with its neighbors are mapped out and authorized. J's stories seek to legitimate ethnic distinctions, claims to lands, boundaries between territories, and balances of power between neighboring peoples. Such boundary marking in the Yahwist's epic reflects no criticism of sedentary agricultural society or of religious rituals associated with agrarian life, and it should not be employed to characterize early Israelite religion as hostile toward such a point of view.

In the preceding analysis of the Yahwist's landscape, two ancient Near Eastern environments have been of primary interest: the desert, because it has so often been identified in traditional scholarship as the formative setting of Israelite thought, and the agricultural highlands of biblical Israel, which have been shown in this study to comprise the Yahwist's actual landscape. Before concluding this case for the agricultural orientation of the Yahwist's epic and of the religion of Israel it reflects, a third environment must be briefly considered: the urban landscape. This is necessary in the case of the Yahwist because of the common hypothesis that J's actual social location was not in the rural countryside but in Jerusalem's royal establishment. J has been variously identified as an architect of the Solomonic enlightenment, a propagandist for the Davidic monarchy, and a member of Israel's urban, intellectual elite, all characterizations that would link J and his ideology with royal, urban society rather than with rural agriculture.[5]

There can be little doubt that the Yahwist's epic assumed its final form in the age of the Davidic monarchy and that it represents, in certain of its features, the ideology of the royal family and of a united Israel. Such a scenario, as many have argued, is the only way to account for the preeminence of David's tribal ancestor Judah in the epic and to explain the inclusion in the single family of Jacob (Israel) of the ancestors of the twelve tribes united in the Davidic Kingdom. A monarchic location accounts as well for the elaborate political mapping of the balances of power between the Iron Age Kingdom of Israel and its neighbors—the Ammonites, Moabites, Edomites, Arameans, and Philistines, in particular—which are worked out and authorized in the genealogies and narratives of Genesis.

Yet the ideological claims of the Davidic monarchy are presented by the Yahwist not in urban or royal categories, but in terms of the characters and narratives typical of Israel's highland agricultural society. King David and the ideology of covenant associated with him, for example, are prefigured in the hill country agriculturalist, Abraham.[6] The archetypal ancestral figures, for the Yahwist, are not kings but successful, astute farmers, heads of families— perhaps even of clans or tribes—in whom rested power and prestige in Israel's traditional agrarian culture. The distinctiveness of the agrarian orientation in this representation of the ancestral hero as a farmer is highlighted and brought into sharper focus when Israel's epic literature is compared with those of the neighboring cultures of Mesopotamia and Greece. In these neighboring epics, the values of entrenched urban monarchies are reflected in the characterization of ancestral heroes as kings, for instance, the kings of the Sumerian King List and Gilgamesh in Mesopotamia, and Agamemnon and Odysseus in Greece.[7]

Cities—in particular, Shechem, Bethel, Hebron, and Beersheba—represent a substantive feature of the Yahwist's landscape. Yet their significance to J lies primarily in their religious precincts, precincts encompassing the altars established by Israel's agricultural ancestors. These shrines, each linked to a natural phenomenon—the oak tree, the mountain top, the water source— that mediated the ancestral theophany, represent the sacred centers of the Yahwist's agrarian landscape. They are the sites at which the great harvest festivals mandated in the Yahwist's liturgical calendar were celebrated. As such, these towns are represented by J as extensions of the agricultural economy of the Israelite hill country rather than as centers of a distinct culture based on production or trade.

Such a characterization of the Yahwist's epic fits comfortably with the traditional conception that J's epic traditions were not created de novo by a monarchic scribe but originated in the tribal era of premonarchic Israel.[8] When genealogical and narrative elements sympathetic to the Davidic monarchy entered these traditions as they assumed their final form in the Yahwist's rendition, these new elements were presented in terms of older, sacred tradition. In sum, the Yahwist's landscape and point of orientation to the world is the agrarian countryside and culture in which biblical Israel originated and that provided the basis for its economy into the monarchic age itself.

With these historical conclusions in hand, it is possible to return to the larger issue of the role of the Bible in the formation of values in Western culture and to make some suggestions about a more genuine and substantive understanding of the relationship between biblical and contemporary perspectives on nature. An awareness of the rootedness of biblical values in the Yahwist's ancient agrarian landscape has implications both for assessing the claims that have been made about the Bible in recent ecological literature, and for reaching an informed judgment on the possible value of biblical modes of thought for current theological and ethical reflection on the proper human role in the natural world.

The first fact, surely, that strikes the modern reader about the Yahwist's landscape is its remoteness from modern experience. The Yahwist's landscape and orientation toward it predate the major social and economic revolutions that have repositioned the human in the world and have substantially redefined humanity's understanding of its relationship to the environment in the modern era. J's characters and contemporaries were predominantly rural, largely untouched—in spite of their small hill country towns—by the urban revolution, which has in the United States, for example, pushed 97 percent of the population into cities, leaving only a minuscule 3 percent of the population on the farm. Furthermore, J's economy was agricultural, entirely unaffected by the industrial and technological revolutions that determine the shape of modern economies and that have industrialized modern agriculture itself, introducing machines, fossil fuels, chemical pesticides, herbicides, and fertilizers, and placing the control of production and marketing into the hands of large agribusiness corporations. The operative, archetypal image of the human in terms of which modern society defines itself and its goals is certainly not the Yahwist's primitive subsistence farmer. It has been replaced by the image of the urban entrepreneur.

Even in the Yahwist's own day, when the ancient Near East was dominated by the empires and economies of the great urban, river valley civilizations of Egypt and Mesopotamia, J's landscape was a remote, small, and marginal one. Each aspect of J's economy—the specific kinds and combinations of plants under cultivation, the precise types and numbers of livestock raised, and the balance of these pursuits—was a refined adaptation of traditional Mediterranean farming practices to the particular facts of climate, rainfall, soil, and topography, and of the native flora and fauna of the narrow spine of hills between the Mediterranean Sea and Jordan River. And the key features of the Yahwist's perspective on nature—the position of arable soil at its center and the desert at its periphery, the attention to domestic plants and animals and the fear of the arid wilderness—reflect the struggle for survival in this particular, small place. Israel's liturgical year is grounded in the harvests of these hills. The Yahwist's account of the creation of the world itself is constructed not out of the cosmologies of the great societies that preceded and surrounded it—nor, of course, according to modern scientific theories of the origins of the universe—but out of the concrete details of this little hill country and its small farmers.

It would be difficult to describe, within the historical era, two landscapes further removed from one another than the Yahwist's and the modern reader's. They are so distinctive and the position of the human in them so different that a measure of restraint and caution is required in any attempt to describe their relationship. This is necessary for friends and foes of the Bible alike. Great caution must be exercised whether one wishes to blame the Bible as the source of modern views of humanity and its place in the environment or to promote the Bible as a sort of guidebook for the environmental ethics of modern societies. As a prerequisite for any disqualification of biblical values or appropriation of them, they must be granted an historical authenticity in their own right. They must be recognized as a genuine response to a specific and ancient Mediterranean agrarian setting. Such a radical contextualization of biblical values reflects not only a proper historical sense, but also a sound ecological principle. Proper environmental values and behaviors are always local, not general. They are precise adaptations and responses to precise places. Each society must develop an appropriate response to its particular landscape.

The Yahwist's image of the human as a farmer has in fact hardly been present at all in recent discussions of the Bible and environmental values. These discussions have been entirely taken up with another biblical model, the Priestly Writer's conception of the human as made in God's image and as commissioned to have dominion over the animals and to subdue the earth. This is understandable. Such an image of authority and control is certainly compatible with the modern experience of human power to manage and manipulate nature with its new technological and industrial tools. Contemporary debate has centered not on the general appropriateness of this image of the human being, but on the extent to which it unleashes or restrains human power, or fosters responsible or irresponsible thinking. It is not surprising that in the modern era of the urban entrepreneur, J's image of the human as a small farmer would have little immediate appeal. And, given the vast differences between the Yahwist's ancient rural landscape and the contemporary urban environment just described, one might wish simply to leave it at that, to set J's agricultural view of culture aside as of merely historical interest or at most of only marginal value to modern society.

There are, however, cogent ecological reasons for rescuing the image of the small farmer from relative oblivion, and not only for rescuing it, but for reincorporating it into the self-concept of modern culture. This is the import, at least, of a group of ecologists who would put agricultural concerns at the very core of the environmental agenda. Among these are Wendell Berry and Wes Jackson on the American scene, and Vandana Shiva, Miguel Altieri, and Dean Freudenberger on the international scene.[9] On the basis of the work of individuals such as these, World Bank economist Herman Daly and theologian John Cobb, in their economic blueprint for a sustainable future entitled *For the Common Good: Redirecting the Economy Toward Community, the Environment, and a Sustainable Future,* have arrived at the following conclusion: "If economics is reconceived in the service of community, it will begin with a concern for agriculture and specifically for the production of food."[10]

Such a conclusion rests on two premises: first, that agriculture is the major mode in which humans interact with the environment and the ultimate basis of human survival, and second, that modern industrial agriculture is not working—it is unacceptably destructive to the environment and it is unsustainable. The first of these premises is, of course, a kind of truism: people must eat to live, and farmers provide the food. "No matter how urban our life," writes Wendell Berry, with language drawn partly from the Yahwist himself, "our bodies live by farming; we come from the earth and return to it, and so we live in agriculture as we live in the flesh."[11] But because the actual practice of agriculture is such a distant practical reality for 97 percent of Americans, the truth and significance of this first premise is seldom given serious attention. Thus arises one of the dangerous ironies of modern culture. That upon which its survival is most dependent is that to which least attention is given. "We now have more people using the land (that is, living from it) and fewer people thinking about it than ever before," observes Berry. "We are eating thoughtlessly, as no other entire society ever has been able to do."[12] Timothy Weiskel's reminder is particularly apt: "We live in a highly industrialized, urban culture, but it is important to remember that there is no such thing as a 'post-agricultural' society."[13]

The second reason for reconsidering agriculture, the failure of modern industrial farming, is not a truism—far from it, given the financial and political power of the large agribusiness corporations that support the current system. But a growing body of criticism has demonstrated that current agricultural practices—dependence on oil, a nonrenewable resource, to drive machines and to process and distribute products; the use of chemical pesticides, herbicides, and fertilizers that contaminate water supplies; and the cultivation of massive monocultures, making crops more vulnerable to pests and diseases, while depleting and accelerating the erosion of agriculture's and culture's final resource, topsoil—cannot be sustained. To survive, according to these critics, modern society will have to change its basic approach to the production of food. This is not the place to detail the compelling indictment of industrialized agriculture, nor to outline the new policies that will be demanded. Suffice it to say that such changes will mean the reversal of current trends—the United States "should give up most of the policies that have operated in recent decades," say Daly and Cobb—and require the recovery of an older, traditional way of farming.[14] This "new" sustainable agriculture will have to be small-scale, local, organic, and more dependent on human and animal labor and solar energy than on machines and fossil fuels—in other words, more like agriculture used to be. Such proposals are based not on a romantic view of primitive or rural life but on a sober, scientific assessment of the damages of industrialized farming and the demands and limits of the agrarian landscape.[15]

The inevitable rehabilitation of a more traditional kind of agriculture will demand all of the scientific knowledge that modern society can muster to develop biological alternatives to the toxic chemicals now in use, to develop high-yield perennial polycultures in order to replace the till agriculture that destroys topsoil, and to harness solar energy more effectively. But such a change will also require a new cultural vision, a vision of human life as dependent on small-scale agriculture, a vision, in a real sense, of the human as a small farmer. To this end Wendell Berry has argued that society take as its model for the human nurturer of the environment, in contrast to its exploiter, "the old-fashioned idea or ideal of the farmer."[16]

In such a situation, the Yahwist's conception of the human being as a small farmer takes on a new value. It cannot be regarded as a quaint or marginal perspective, but it must be accepted as a perspective with which modern society must reacquaint itself if it is to restore and revitalize the agricultural base upon which its survival depends. J's agricultural economy is not a program, per se, though it shares many principles with "new" sustainable models of agriculture. It does, however, provide an image of human identity, an image that is sacred and honored by many and that springs from the roots of the Western religious tradition, that can be a resource for reimagining the proper role of the human in the world.

Creation as Redemption: The Human as a Citizen of the Earth

As we have seen, the Yahwist's perspective on nature does not originate in a desert environment but in the agrarian countryside at the heartland of biblical Israel. Consequently, it is within the context of an ancient agricultural society that the larger theological and philosophical issues of nature and history and of their relationship to one another in the Yahwist's epic and in biblical thought must be reconsidered.

The implications of this are substantial, since the treatment of biblical religion in the history of scholarship, as was pointed out in chapter 1, has been so strongly influenced by assumptions about Israel's desert origins. In fact, the common characterization of Israelite religion as an historical religion, in which the natural world was rendered peripheral and reduced ultimately to a theological problem, has been derived largely from certain notions about the character of desert life. According to this line of thought, the worship of a deity associated primarily with human experience rather than with natural phenomena was the natural outgrowth of desert nomadism, in which neither families nor their patron deity could develop a close and lasting attachment to specific sites or phenomena within the physical environment. Common characterizations of Israelite religion that draw a sharp dichotomy between human history and natural phenomena, to the extent that they are based on presuppositions of Israel's desert origins, have to be consciously relinquished in order to recover the Yahwist's point of view on nature and on history.

The clear-cut distinction between history and nature in these traditional reconstructions of early Israelite religion is not in accord with the manner in which J portrays the relationship between ancestral society and its agrarian environment nor with J's characterization of divine activity within this setting. There is certainly no sense of the detachment of society from its environment in J. The picture is very much the opposite. The vital relationship between Israel's ancestors and the arable soil that lies at the center of the Yahwist's landscape is established in a variety of ways throughout the epic. The first human is, of course, fashioned from this topsoil and charged with its cultivation. Thus the agricultural economy of biblical Israel was at creation built into the orders of nature.

In the narrative of ancestral society that unfolds in the first, primeval age, the relationship between these early farmers and their land—in particular, the link between human morality and the soil's fertility—is every bit as important as the relationship between these farmers and their deity. Of course, these relationships are inseparably bound up with one another; one can hardly be characterized as the backdrop for the other. Furthermore, the great etiological narratives of the postflood era, which explain and authorize the realities (or alleged realities) of the Yahwist's age, are designed not just to validate political orders and events, but also to establish bonds between people and their environs. In Israel's case, the connection between its ancestors and the arable highlands of biblical Israel is continually reiterated by these narratives. In fact, this land assumes a central role in the Yahwist's theology of promise and blessing that dominates the postflood age. Outside of this setting, the survival of Israel's ancestors is always in jeopardy, a fact illustrated most vividly in the southern narratives of exile in Egypt and the desert that conclude the epic. From the offerings presented to God by Cain and Abel in the epic's first generation to the great liturgical prescriptions promulgated to the epic's last generation, the agricultural economy of those highlands provides the basis of Israelite worship, its cycles marking out the liturgical year and its produce comprising the ritual service rendered to God.

The traditional, well-defined partition between history and nature is as problematic for describing J's ancestral deity as it is for describing J's ancestral culture. J's God is not a figure whose character and activity can be satisfactorily described within the flow of human history alone, solely in the terms, that is, of the clans of families, social institutions, and political events of the ancestral narratives. The Yahwist's deity is not altogether transcendent of nature but is intimately associated with the epic's landscape and his presence is mediated through the natural phenomena that are particularly characteristic of it.

The connection between God and geographical space in J's epic is illustrated best perhaps by the theophanies at Shechem, Bethel, Hebron, and Beersheba during which the ancestral blessings are bestowed. These divine appearances, in which the relationship between Israel's ancestors and Israel's arable highlands is reiterated, establish the sacral character of the land, of the people's attachment to it, and of these sites of revelation in particular. J's description of these sites—their theophanies, their natural images of the center (e.g., the oak tree, the mountain top), and their ancient, ancestral altars—suggests that J understood them, in the terminology of Eliade, as cosmic centers.[17] They become axes around which the geographical and social space of J's epic is ordered and organized, to which the lives and journeys of Israel's ancestors are anchored, and through which the divine presence is specially mediated. Thus particular spaces, the arable highlands in general and these sacred precincts in particular, assume a unique relationship to the deity and thereby a special sacral character. They become concrete media of revelation.

Characteristically, natural and cultural metaphors blend together in J's representation of God. The God of J is a very personal, anthropomorphic figure, a manner of representing the divine that has become accepted as quintessential of the Yahwist's style and point of view. Sometimes J's God appears, for all intents and purposes, as a man, as he does to Abraham at the oaks and to Jacob at the river. But J's deity appears as well through a remarkable array of natural forms: the tree, the mountain summit, and above all, the thunderstorm, that without which Israel's dryland farming could not exist. Very often, these modes of manifestation are intermingled in a particular theophany, so that it is precarious to associate the revelation narrowly with the historical process or with natural phenomena. God speaks, for example, in the thunder of the storm, or from the oak at Shechem. The lightning bolts are the weapons of the divine warrior in Egypt. God walks in the wind of the Garden. The soil bears and mediates the divine curse uttered to the first man.

Neither J, nor Israel, nor its ancient Near Eastern neighbors considered the divine identical with its modes of manifestation, whether human or nonhuman. God remained in the end distinct from, transcendent, if you will, of all the forms, human and nonhuman alike, by which the divine was known. Yet when J wished to emphasize this essential distinctiveness of the divine, God in God's peculiar Godness—the character of the *mysterium tremendum,* to use Rudolf Otto's phrase—J relied heavily on the language of nature. This is especially true in the Yahwist's two covenant narratives (Gen 15, Exod 19), the accounts of the establishment of a special relationship between the human and the divine. In both, the distance between the human and the divine is carefully preserved: Abraham experiences deep terror, and falls into unconsciousness, the very unconsciousness of 'ādām at creation (cf. Gen 2:21, 15:12). The Israelites are banned from Mt. Sinai because nearing the deity would mean certain death (Exod 19:20–25). In both cases, the power and mystery of God are stressed by the use of awesome natural phenomena: fire and smoke while Abraham slept, and the frightening storm at the summit of Mt. Sinai. In antiquity, the forces of nature, which lay outside of human control but on which human survival absolutely depended, provided the most vivid images of the "other," of the mystery at the heart of the universe.

This brief summary of the results of the foregoing study of the Yahwist's epic reviews just some of the evidence for the need to move beyond the older reconstructions of Israelite religion based on a clear-cut conceptual dichotomy between history and nature. This dichotomy, although linked to Israel's desert origins, derives ultimately from the old idealistic dualism of spirit (human) and matter (nonhuman) in Western culture that, in its Hegelian form, had such a significant influence on early critical biblical scholarship. While old in the West, such dualistic thought was foreign to the Yahwist as it was to the other authors of the Hebrew Bible, and it must be consciously avoided to grasp the complexities of biblical thought. The same must be said for the clichés about Israelite religion—claims that it "historicizes," "demytholo-gizes," "desacralizes"—that have spun off of such idealistic interpretations.

One final example might be retrieved from this study of it in order to illustrate the problems with such dualistic terminology. It is still common to make the claim that Israel "historicized" an older kind of Canaanite worship, taking over what were once nature festivals and adapting them to celebrate historical events. Here is how John Bright, for example, has described early Israelite worship in his history of Israel: "Early Israel's cult, however, did not center in a sacrificial system, but in certain great annual feasts. . . . All these feasts were far older than Israel and, save for Passover, of agricultural origin. Israel . . . gave them a new rationale by imparting to them a historical con-tent. They ceased to be mere nature festivals and became occasions upon which the mighty acts of Yahweh toward Israel were celebrated."[18]

In fact, the liturgical calendar preserved by J (Exod 34) is an agricul-tural calendar. Its three great festivals celebrate Israel's three important har-vests—barley, wheat, and fruit—and its structure is thereby established by the seasonal cycle of Israel's agricultural economy. And this is so not only for J but also in the liturgical calendars preserved by the Deuteronomist (Deuteronomy 16) and Priestly Writer (Leviticus 23) as well. In two respects "historical" concerns are present in J's annual liturgy. The first festival com-memorates both the barley harvest and the departure from Egypt, which occurred exactly when the barley ripened (Exod 9:31, 34:18). And the regu-lar commemoration of these festivals was believed to insure not only agri-cultural bounty but political security as well (Exod 34:24). But there is sim-ply no evidence that such elements were "added" to rituals or traditions without them. They occur here in the earliest levels of Israelite liturgical practice. The "historicization" of this agricultural calendar does not occur until postbiblical Judaism when its feasts all become connected with events in Israelite history.[19] In its biblical form, Israel's liturgical calendar celebrates both of what scholars have referred to as the cyclical time of nature and the linear time of history.

Within such a nonidealistic worldview, the separation of history from nature or redemption from creation cannot be very useful or meaningful. For the Yahwist, the idea of redemption is very much grounded in the world of creation, specifically in the agricultural landscape to which humans were intrinsically related at the beginning of the world. Redemption, well-being, or salvation was conceived of entirely within the concrete agricultural envi-rons in which J, his ancestors, and his contemporaries lived out their lives on this earth. Redemption depended on this fertile and secure land. It con-sisted of a lasting and stable relationship with this land and the bountiful harvests it produced. The attempt to separate out historical experience from natural phenomena within such an understanding of redemption, or the attempt to elevate one over the other, introduces a perspective foreign to J's thought.

The religion of the Yahwist's epic was thus a religion of the earth, more precisely a religion of the agrarian highlands of biblical Israel. The world was regarded as a single metaphysical unity, the only realm within which a meaningful human existence was possible. By consequence, the earth, which defined the character and contours of human life, assumed ultimate value in Yahwistic thought. No philosophical or theological dualism is present by which the world can be conceived in terms of two distinct ontological orders—human and world, history and nature, spirit and body, mind and matter—which may then be weighed against one another to determine their relative value.

Almost in their entirety, the Hebrew Scriptures share the Yahwist's unitary metaphysic. Only with the rise of apocalyptic thought, late in Israelite history, is this unified conception of reality and its absolute valuation of earthly existence modified. The apocalyptic worldview, whose clearest expression in the Hebrew Scriptures is the book of Daniel, despaired of life in this world and conceived of human salvation only through a complete transformation of the world's orders and/or as a new existence in another, supernatural sphere of reality.[20] Apocalyptic thought included, for the first time in biblical history, a clear statement of the notion of life after death. While Jewish apocalypticism takes up and adapts the physical imagery of the earthly worldview out of which it sprang, it nevertheless proposed the possibility of human redemption apart from the world as it is. The earth was no longer the true human home. Ultimate salvation for the faithful was to be found in another world on another metaphysical plane.

Early Christian thought was deeply affected by this apocalyptic consciousness, and the doctrine of two worlds became foundational in the Christian West. Combined in various ways, first with Neoplatonic thought that separated soul from body and later with other forms of idealism, Christianity developed at its heart a profound metaphysical dualism. Here, too, the spiritual world assumed primary importance and the natural world took on secondary or temporary significance. In its more extreme forms, Christian dualism even perceived the material world as alien to authentic human experience and therefore dispensable, if not downright evil.

It is this later dualistic legacy, with its roots in apocalyptic thought and in Greek Idealist philosophy, about which historians and theologians interested in Western environmental values have been primarily concerned. One of the first major criticisms of the ecological values of the Western religious tradition stemming from Judaism and Christianity was Lynn White's charge that this tradition possessed a dangerous "dualism of man and nature." Wendell Berry makes the same point with characteristic literary power. "This separation of the soul from the body and from the world is no disease of the fringe, no aberration," he writes, "but a fracture that runs through the men-

tality of institutional religion like a geological fault. And this rift in the mentality of religion continues to characterize the modern mind, no matter how
secular and worldly it becomes."

Not long after Lynn White's critique appeared, Gordon Kaufman took
up the issue of the dualistic character of theological discourse in an essay
entitled, "A Problem for Theology: The Concept of Nature." Again, the concept of nature as a "problem" is prominent. "The conceptions of God and
man, as they have developed in Western religious traditions," wrote Kaufman,
"work hand in hand toward the distinguishing of man from (the rest of)
nature. Nature is not conceived primarily as man's proper home and the very
source and sustenance of his being, but rather as the context of and material
for teleological activity by the (nonnatural) wills working upon and in it."
Pointing out the philosophical and scientific untenability, by modern stan-
dards, of such classic dualistic philosophy, Kaufman urged "a theological
reconstruction going down to the deepest roots of the Western religious sen-
sibility and vocabulary," a reconstruction that would make it possible to gain
a more unified view "inclusive of what we now call nature and what we now
call history."[21]

In search of patterns of thought more in tune with the ecological realities of human life, its interconnections with and dependence on the entire
ecosystem of which it is a part, theologians are exploring new modes of discourse that emphasize divine and human integration with earthly reality.
Gordon Kaufman, for example, has recently described the nature of human
life as "biohistorical," a term by which he wishes to integrate within a unified view of the human, the recognition "of our interconnectedness and interdependence with all other forms of life (on the one hand), and of our cultural creativity in history, producing a thoroughly cultural form of existence
(on the other)."[22]

Many other attempts to develop new conceptual models for overcoming
this entrenched Western dualism have been proposed. Father Thomas Berry,
a Passionist priest at the forefront of the environmental movement, has called
for a new creation story that would capture "the integrity and harmony of the
total cosmic order." He urges a more integral vision of the world in which we
would recognize that "we bear the universe in our beings as the universe bears
us in its being," a vision he regards as a "new paradigm of what it means to be
human. . . . Until the human is understood as a dimension of the earth," writes
Berry, "we have no secure basis for understanding any aspect of the human.
We can understand the human only through the earth."[23] Sallie McFague has
employed the metaphor of the world as God's body in order to try to overcome the ontological dualism between the divine and the world in Western
thought.[24] The World Council of Churches, in order to underline the need
for more holistic thinking in the church's vision, has chosen as the title for its
environmental program, "The Integrity of Creation."[25]

The Yahwist's perspective is important in the context of this contemporary struggle with the dualistic orientation of Western theology because it
reminds us that this dualism has not been the sole model for understanding

the place of the human in the world. At its origin in biblical thought, Western religion viewed humanity as part of a single realm of reality in which the earth was considered the proper human home. Salvation was conceived as a stable, healthy relationship with the earthly environment, not as the transcendence of it. In this respect, Lynn White's early claim that Western dualism has its origins in the biblical creation stories is misdirected. Even the Priestly Writer, who had a rather more exalted view of the human as created in God's image, did not see this as an ontological statement but as a functional one, a point of view to which we will return in a moment.

This unitary mode of thought within the biblical point of view has been noted by John Cobb. In a recent essay he withdraws his earlier criticism of the Bible, based on the argument of Lynn White, in his early environmental book, *Is It Too Late?* He now regards the "premodern" thought of the Bible in "much richer continuity" with the "postmodern" thought he believes is demanded to overcome the anthropocentrism, individualism, and dualism of modernity. This is how Cobb describes his more recent position: "It was modern biblical scholarship that had imposed on the Scriptures the dualism of nature and history, derived not from them but from modern philosophy and theology. Such dualism was as alien to ancient Israel as it should become to us . . . I have gradually learned that an honest return to the Bible can be a positive resource rather than an obstacle to the kind of thinking and acting now required."[26]

John Cobb does not advocate an attempt to return to premodern thought, and rightly so. It is impossible and, in certain respects, quite undesirable. But it is important within the contemporary search for less dualistic modes of thought to become reacquainted with those viewpoints at the origin of the Western intellectual tradition that stress integration over separation. These viewpoints, such as the Yahwist's, may serve to anchor and to empower modern modes of thought and speech. They may also serve to remind us about basic truths of existence that modern philosophy and technology have effectively hidden from us. This is, of course, the enduring value of the past as a mirror in which to see ourselves more fully.

Nature as Measure: The Human as a Servant

Within the Yahwist's agricultural landscape, the human being assumes a position in relation to the natural world quite different from the one depicted in traditional biblical scholarship. The original Israelite is not the desert nomad whose social structures and religious experience are detached from the (hostile) environment and conceived in terms of historical categories of thought. Rather, the original Israelite, as was the first human being, is the small farmer whose society and its well-being, and whose religious life itself, are solidly rooted in the arable land of the biblical hill country and in the rhythms of the agricultural economy that it sustained.

The Yahwist's view of the human position in the world contrasts not only with the view in these traditional reconstructions of Israelite origins, but also with the views of other biblical authors. Among these is the most famous of all biblical images of the human, the view of humanity as created in God's image and given dominion over the world, found in the Priestly account of creation in Genesis 1. Of all biblical texts, none has been discussed more in recent ecological literature than Genesis 1:26–28, in which this view of the human is portrayed. Such widespread attention to a single image stems from and contributes to the belief that this is *the* biblical view. And thus almost all intellectual energy has been poured into the debate about whether this par-ticular picture will work or not, whether it is an image of unbounded power that must be abandoned or an image of responsible stewardship that must be recovered.

The discussion of the biblical view of the human position within the natural world would be broadened and enhanced if other views were enter-tained and examined with greater interest. Of these, the Yahwist's is one of the most important. J understands the human place within nature quite dif-ferently from the Priestly Writer, a point that has been astutely recognized and explored in some interesting directions by a nonbiblical scholar, J. Baird Callicott.[27] He attributes his insight, actually, to remarks once made by John Muir about the Yahwist's account of creation in Genesis 2. The insights of Muir and Callicott may be developed by drawing together here some of the key details of the Yahwist's perspective.

The character and distinctiveness of the Yahwist's view of the human place within the natural world can be seen most clearly by contrasting it point by point with the more familiar Priestly perspective. For P, the quintessen-tial fact about human nature is that it bears the image of God (Gen 1:26–27). In all likelihood, given the lack of the dualism between spirit and matter, soul and body, in Israelite thought, this image did not attribute to humans a spe-cial ontological status in creation, but rather assigned to humanity a special function, that of God's representative or steward over the created order. But it does draw the human into a unique association with the divine and in this regard it distinguishes the human clearly from all other forms of life. This special status in relation to God is echoed in Psalm 8, a hymn with parallels to Genesis 1, in which humans are placed between God and other life, "a little less than God (or divine beings)," but with "everything under their feet" (vv 6–7; Eng vv 5–6).

By contrast, the quintessential fact about human nature for J is that it derives from the arable soil (2:7). Humans are made from this soil, they return to it at death, and they cultivate it during their lives. In their basic nature, therefore, humans are associated with the earth rather than with the deity, with creation rather than with the creator. And in this regard humans share the lot of all of life, since this life too—animals and plants alike—is fashioned by God out of arable soil. The breath blown into the first human by God gives humanity no special divine essence, since this is the breath by which all animals live (2:7; cf. 6:3, 7:22).

These differing conceptions of human nature, as can already be seen, are associated with different conceptions of the relationship between human and animal life. P's view is conspicuously hierarchical. At creation humans are commanded by God to rule (*rādā*), to exercise dominion over other animate life (1:28). Whether one wishes to construe such rule as benevolent or harsh— and both are possible within the limits of the term in biblical usage—there can be no doubt that *rādā* represents control and power, since it is used customarily of kings and always of those with authority over others.[28] By contrast, J conceives of this relationship in more communal terms. As animals and humans alike are made from the earth's topsoil, they possess no distinct ontological status, both being referred to simply as living beings (*nepeš ḥayyâ;* 2:7,19). Humans and animals share speech and knowledge, as the wise snake reveals (3:1–2). Above all, animals are regarded as helpers (2:18), companions in the art of agriculture. This is the reason for which they were created in the Yahwist's account. The act of naming them (2:19), as was argued in chapter 2, is not employed in this account as a demonstration of power or control but of identification and relationship. Only the long shadow cast by the Priestly account, not the character of the Eden narrative itself, can account for the traditional attribution of power to this act.

The relationship between humans and the earth in the Priestly and Yahwistic perspectives differs in striking respects as well. To the Priestly Writer agricultural production is viewed as subduing (*kābaš*) the earth (1:28). The verb *kābaš* is a powerful word, employed in the Bible to describe the forceful subjection of another, the coercion into bondage and service. It is used to describe defeating an adversary in war, making slaves, and raping women.[29] The land for P is, to all intents, an adversary to be pressed into service. By contrast, agriculture is viewed by the Yahwist as serving (*'ābad*) the land (2:5,15; 3:23; 4:2). J's term for cultivation is the common Hebrew word for service rendered to a superior, that is, to a human master or to God. For J, therefore, the land is a sovereign to be served. Two opposite views of the relationship between humanity and the earth are present here: for P the human is the land's master, coercing it into service, while for J the human is the land's servant, performing the duties demanded by its powers and processes.

The issue of human reproduction and the population of earth by the human species is also viewed from different perspectives by Priestly and Yahwistic authors. For P, human reproduction is viewed as a human obligation upon which no limits are placed. Reproduction is the first command delivered to the human couple at creation, and it is delivered in unrestricted terms: "Be fruitful, become numerous, and fill the earth" (1:28). Following the flood, this is the first command, according to P, that is delivered by God to Noah and his family (9:1). For J, human reproduction is viewed as a more complex and paradoxical phenomenon. On the one hand, descendants are promised to Abraham in unimaginable numbers—like the dust of the earth or the stars of the sky (13:16, 15:5). On the other hand, human reproduction is placed under severe restraints at creation. Conception and childbirth alike are prescribed as precarious and difficult, as the experiences of the matriarchs in J's narratives frequently attest.

These contrasting views of the position of humanity in the created order, one of power and control, the other of humility and limit, are symbolized by the altars that stand at the centers of Priestly and Yahwistic worship. The Priestly altar, constructed according to detailed instructions delivered by God to Moses at Mt. Sinai, is an elaborate artistic achievement (Exod 27:1–8, 38:1–7). It is a large square installation, ten feet on a side, constructed of acacia wood and overlaid with bronze. It is accompanied by an array of vessels and instruments, themselves forged from bronze, to be used by the Priests when offerings are burnt upon the altar. Offerings are thus presented to the deity by the Priests on an altar reflecting the most refined achievements of human technology in wood and metal work, in the shaping of natural materials to human use.

By contrast, the Yahwistic altar is to be built of earth alone, in particular of the fertile topsoil (*'ădāmâ*) on which Israel's agricultural economy was based (Exod 20:24). Field stones are also allowed, but should they be used they are not to be dressed by the tools of the stonecutter. Any presence of human artifice, the stroke of a metal tool on the stone, is considered a profanation of the altar. It must remain in its pristine, natural form unshaped by human technology (20:25). The altar thus symbolizes the material of nature on which people are dependent rather than the achievements of people to shape those materials to their ends. Wes Jackson, who has adopted the Yahwist's altar as a symbol of human modesty in the modern age, has a fine sense of its archaic function. "This scripture must mean," he writes, "that we are to be more mindful of the creation, more mindful of the original materials of the universe than of the artist. The altar was to stand as a reminder that we could not improve on the timeless purpose of the original material . . . that the scientist and the artist must remain subordinate to the larger Creation."[30]

Two distinct postures within creation are assumed by the human being in Priestly and Yahwistic perspectives. The Priestly human occupies a superior position within the created order. Created in God's image, humans are distinguished from the rest of creation and granted unique authority over it. They are to exercise this authority by populating the earth, ruling its animals, and subduing its land. As was argued in chapter 2, this archetypal human is in fact a priestly figure. The human of Genesis 1 shares many of the characteristics of the priestly role itself. This was the role of a distinct, elite party in Israelite society, closely allied to royalty, that regarded itself as the mediator of divine rule to Israel and to creation itself. The ornate altar on which its worship was conducted represented the greatest refinements of human power and technological achievement.

By contrast, the human being in the Yahwist's epic occupies a subordinate role within the created order. Created out of the arable soil, the Yahwist's human is united with the rest of creation and placed in a subservient relationship to it. This subservience is expressed in the image of the soil as the beginning and the end of human life and in the depiction of the cultivation of the soil as "serving" rather than "subduing." In this agricultural task, the animals—made of the same soil—are helpers and companions. As has been argued throughout this study, this human is above all a typical Israelite farmer, the role of the majority in Israelite society and the role attributed to its ancestors in the Yahwist's epic. The altar on which their worship is conducted is composed of the soil itself, deliberately untouched by human artifice. Basic to this image of the human is the ancient farmer's sense of dependence upon the soil, of the necessity of meeting its demands and cooperating with its processes, and of the ultimate lack of control over nature's own orders and powers.

The title given by modern interpreters to the role played in nature by the Priestly human is the "steward," an individual granted authority by a superior to manage and supervise the estate placed under his control. To identify the contrasting role played in nature by the Yahwist's human, I have chosen the title of "servant," taking this designation from the Yahwist's own vocabulary in which the cultivation of the soil—that central act that defines for J the relationship between people and the earth—is described by the verb "to serve," *'ābad*. In such a role, human responsibility is viewed not as the administration and control of nature but as the respect for nature's orders and compliance with its rules.

The recovery of the Yahwist's modest view of the human place within the world from the very long shadow cast by the Priestly viewpoint in the history of scholarship and in modern environmental theology broadens our understanding of ancient Israelite thought. It provides an additional example, from Israel's earliest reflections on its position in the world, of the modest view of human life more commonly associated with the Book of Job. A major point of God's great speeches from the whirlwind to Job, speeches full of the wild powers of nature, is to convince Job of his miniscule position in the larger scheme of things.[31] These two works point to a tradition in Israelite thought in which humanity is viewed as much smaller in creation than portrayed in the well-known Priestly image of Genesis 1.

In several respects, the Yahwist's position can provide added perspective to current discussions about the resourcefulness of Western religious traditions for a contemporary theology of nature. To begin with, the contrast between the Priestly and Yahwistic views of the human role in creation illustrates the age and magnitude of a debate that continues to shape the contemporary discussion of environmental values. Many illustrations of these two views of the human—the steward and the servant of creation—could be taken from current writing on environmental issues. I have selected only two by way of example, and these two because they represent to some extent the same social locations, in modern form, reflected in the ancient Priestly and Yahwistic perspectives.

One of these is the Passionist priest, Thomas Berry, a prominent religious leader in the environmental movement for many years. Thomas Berry has argued that the West's traditional stories of creation be replaced with a new creation story, a story expansive enough to incorporate the most recent scientific knowledge about the spatial and chronological scope of the evolution of the universe and about the emergence of humanity as the culmination within that process. While Thomas Berry urges us, on the basis of this

new story, "to see the human itself as an integral member of the earth community, not as some lordly being free to plunder the earth for human util-
ity," his primary image of the human is a lofty one. Influenced deeply by the
philosopher Teilhard de Chardin, he regards the human as the climax of
evolutionary activity, "that being in whom the universe in its evolutionary
dimension became conscious of itself." Such a view represents for Thomas
Berry a new paradigm of the entire earth–human order—"a shift in earth–
human relations, for we now in large measure determine the earth process
that once determined us." Humans possess a special power and with it a
special responsibility: "While this capacity for self-formation is a high privi-
lege, it is also a significant responsibility, since the powers we possess also
give us extensive control over a wide range of earthly affairs." The modern
tragedy, for Thomas Berry—that is, the failure of the human race—has been
"to become not the crowning glory of the earth, but the instrument of its
degradation."[32] While Thomas Berry's story of creation and paradigm of the
human is certainly new as he claims it to be, it nevertheless reflects, in modern philosophical terminology, the ancient Priestly sense of the preeminence
of humanity in the scheme of creation.

To illustrate the opposite viewpoint, the Yahwist's conception of the
human occupying a subordinate position in creation, I have chosen Wendell
Berry, a writer and farmer from Henry County, Kentucky. "Good farmers,"
writes Berry, "have always . . . been careful students" of their environs, of
natural vegetation, soil depth and structure, slope, and drainage. They have
recognized with special clarity that in any biological system the first principle is restraint and that to survive humans must live within the precise limits
nature has established. "We can make ourselves whole," in Wendell Berry's
opinion, "only by accepting our partiality, by living within our limits, by being
human. . . . The message seems essentially that of the voice out of the whirlwind in the Book of Job," he goes on to observe. "The Creation is bounteous
and mysterious, and humanity is only part of it—not its equal, much less its
master. . . . The Creation provides a place for humans, but it is greater than
humanity and within it even great men are small. Such humility is the consequence of an accurate insight, ecological in its bearing, not a pious defer-
ence to 'spiritual' value." The current crisis, according to Wendell Berry, stems
in part from modern society's forgetfulness of this fact and its refusal to recognize human limits. To respond adequately to the contemporary crisis,
Wendell Berry asserts, "we must address ourselves seriously, and not a little
fearfully, to the problem of human scale."[33]

In a new industrial and technological age and in a contemporary philosophical milieu, the contrasting views of the human position in creation held
by the ancient Priestly and Yahwistic writers continue to be discussed and
debated, critiqued and defended, reimagined and reused. Yet it is also the
case that, of these two, the Priestly point of view has attracted the most attention, the most rigorous analysis, and the most spirited defense and ani-
mated criticism. This is certainly understandable. As the Bible's initial statement—majestically and memorably phrased—on the place of humanity in

the world, the Priestly point of view has historically been accepted as the normative biblical viewpoint.

Furthermore, the Priestly view of the human as possessing the status and authority to rule and administer the world of creation appears to have gained striking new support as a result of the power modern science and technology have given humans to manipulate and change the natural environment. Indeed, it is now no secret that humans are altering the environment—eliminating diseases, rainforests, topsoil, and species; reconfiguring genes, rivers, deserts, and the atmosphere—with a speed almost unimaginable within natural evolutionary processes. During the last century, humans have acquired unparalleled power to intervene in natural processes and adapt them to human use.

In such a climate, the Priestly image of superiority and control naturally acquires a new legitimacy simply as a description of the contemporary human place in the world. It resonates with modern experience. The Priestly view has also come to be regarded by many, who endorse the idea of human preeminence, as a positive and constructive model for the responsible use of power.[34] It has been properly pointed out by those who advocate the Priestly image of stewardship that the exercise of human authority in Genesis 1 is restricted by the divine creator who installed the human race and expects it to mediate God's own creative will and design within the world.[35] In the preindustrial agrarian world of the Priestly Writer, of course, humans had precious little power or control over their environs. These limits necessarily make of the Priestly Writer's claim a very modest proposal in practice.

At the same time, an old and significant tradition in the environmental movement has argued that the image of human control, reflected already in the Priestly perspective, is an inaccurate description of the actual position of the human being in the natural world and that it is an improper model for human behavior. Those who have taken this position believe that a suitable environmental ethic must be based on a much more modest conception of the human position in nature, a conception that resembles in many respects the Yahwist's view of the human in a subordinate role, subservient to nature's orders and requirements. This viewpoint can be seen, for example, in the thought of the early environmentalist Aldo Leopold, whose new land ethic envisioned the human not in a "conqueror role" within the biological community, but as a "plain member and citizen" of it.[36] It is Leopold's model of "citizenship" that J. Baird Callicott, in fact, believes best captures the Yahwist's conception of the human posture in creation.[37]

In order to illustrate the manner in which this alternative view of the human posture in creation has influenced recent practitioners of a new environmental ethic, I have selected representatives from two sectors of the American economy, agriculture and business. The first is Wes Jackson, whose Land Institute in Salina, Kansas, is attempting to create a new sustainable agriculture based on information "learned from natural ecosystems and subsistence human societies." A central component in the work of the Land Institute is the recovery and development of native, perennial grains that, in a diverse polyculture, would not require annual cultivation, which destroys topsoil, nor the heavy application of chemical fertilizers, herbicides, and pesticides. When Wes Jackson discusses the philosophy that undergirds his work, he contrasts it with the managerial approach of modern industrial agriculture, and he calls for a perspective in which humans take nature as the standard to which humans must subordinate themselves and their behavior. "What links our activities together," he maintains,

> is the idea of using *nature as our measure or guide* in the search for sustainability. The prairie ecosystem is what nature produced in the Great Plains of the United States, and it is a near perfect example of sustainability . . . through our perennial polyculture work we try to imitate the vegetative structure of the prairie. . . . Ecosystem principles represent the 'nature's wisdom' end of the spectrum of knowledge, and that's what we are thinking about and researching here at The Land. It is this end which has to dominate the 'human cleverness' end of the spectrum. None of us wants human cleverness to disappear. We just want to move it once and for all into a subordinate role.[38]

A second representative of this alternative perspective on the human location in nature is Paul Hawken, past chief executive officer of Smith and Hawken. In a recent book on *The Ecology of Commerce,* Hawken outlines the steps he believes business and industry will have to take to create a sustainable economy. In the course of laying out the specific political and fiscal policies he believes are necessary for sustainability, Hawken returns repeatedly to the concept of nature as the measure by which the human economy must be ruled and regulated if it is to be healthy and restorative. Business must be reconceptualized, according to Hawken, not as the managerial enterprise it became with the industrial revolution, but as a "commercial culture that is so intelligently designed and constructed that it mimics nature at every step. . . . The restorative economy," argues Hawken, "unites ecology and commerce into one sustainable act of production and distribution that mimics and enhances natural processes. It proposes a newborn literacy of enterprise that acknowledges that we are all here together, at once, at the service of and at the mercy of nature, each other, and our daily acts."[39] Such literacy is, as Hawken rightly observes "newborn." It is not new in itself, but rather an old perspective on the human position in the world that should be born again in an ecological age.

The paradoxical position of the human race today, with its new technological power and its old place as a single species in an immense and complex ecosystem that it does not entirely understand and cannot control, means that these two competing views of the human as steward and as servant will undoubtedly be debated for some time to come. The power of the image of the human as servant, already present in the Bible's oldest account of creation, is the insight that, however clever and powerful humanity may become, it cannot survive if it does not subordinate itself to nature's own principles and processes. Humanity cannot survive, that is, if it does not recover in some fashion an old sense of humility, as old as the beginnings of the Western religious tradition itself.

Appendix

Table A.1 Sources of the Pentateuch

This table provides a basic guide to the sources of the Pentateuch, so that readers can identify those sections of the larger narrative that make up the Yahwist's work and provide the basis for the analysis in this book. The Yahwist's work is found in the J column, the Elohist's in the E column, and the Priestly Writer's in the P column. In the majority of cases, the division of sources outlined here reflects the general consensus of source critics that has developed over the last one hundred years. In its details, however, this source outline reflects the author's own judgments.

GENESIS	J	E	P
Creation			1:1–2:4a
	2.4b–3:24		
Cain and Abel	4:1–16		
Cain's Genealogy	4:17–26		
Adam's Genealogy			5:1–28
	5:29		
			5:30–32
Heroes	6:1–4		
Flood	6:5–8		
			6:9–22
	7:1–5		
			7:6
	7:7–8		
			7:9
	7:10		
			7:11
	7:12		
			7:13–16a
	7:16b–17		
			7:18–21
	7:22–23		
			7:24
			8:1–2a
	8:2b–3a		
			8:3b–5
	8:6		
			8:7
	8:8–12		
			8:13a
	8:13b		
			8:14–19
	8:20–22		

(continued)

Table A.1 (continued)

GENESIS	J	E	P
Covenant with Noah			9:1–17
Curse on Canaan	9:18–27		
			9:28–29
Genealogy of Noah and Sons			10:1–7
	10:8–19		
			10:20
	10:21		
			10:22–23
	10:24–30		
			10:31–32
Tower of Babel	11:1–9		
Genealogy of Shem			11:10–27
Abraham and Nahor	11:28–30		
			11:31–32
Abraham's Migrations	12:1–4a		
			12:4b–5
	12:6–9		
Abraham in Egypt (wife/sister)	12:10–20		
Abraham and Lot	13:1–5		
			13:6
	13:7–11a		
			13:11b–12a
	13:12b–18		
[Special Source: Abraham and the Kings]	[14:1–24]		
Covenant with Abraham	15:1–21	(15:13–16?)	
Hagar and Ishmael	16:1–2		
			16:3
	16:4–14		
			16:15–16
Covenant with Abraham			17:1–27
Three Visitors	18:1–33		
Sodom and Gomorrah	19:1–28		
			19:29
Lot, Moab, and Ammon	19:30–38		
Abraham in Gerar (wife/sister)		20:1–17	
	20:18		
Isaac's Birth	21:1–2a		
			21:2b–6
	21:7		
Hagar and Ishmael		21:8–21	
Abraham, Abimelech, & the Beersheba Wells		21:22–31	
	21:32–34		
Binding of Isaac		22:1–14a	
	22:14b–19		

Table A.1 (*continued*)

GENESIS	J	E	P
Nabor's Genealogy	22:20–24		
Machpelah Cave			23:1–20
Rebekah	24:1–67		
Keturah's Children	25:1–6		
Abraham's Death; Ishmael's Descendants			25:7–20
Jacob and Esau	25:21–34		
Isaac in Gerar (wife/sister) & Beersheba Wells	26:1–33		
Esau's Wives			26:34–35
Blessing of Jacob & Esau	27:1–45		
Jacob sent to Syria			27:46
			28:1–9
Jacob at Bethel	28:10		
		28:11–12	
	28:13–16		
		28:17–18	
	28:19		
		28:20–21a	
	28:21b		
		28:22	
Jacob, Leah, and Rachel	29:1–30		
Jacob's Children	29:31–35		
		30:1–24a	
	30:24b		
Jacob's Flocks	30:25–43		
	31:1		
		31:2	
	31:3		
		31:4–16	
Jacob's Return			31:17–18
		31:19–42	
Treaty with Laban		31:43–48	
	31:49		
		31:50–54	
		32:1–3	
Reunion with Esau	32:4–22		
Wrestling with God	32:23–33		
Reunion with Esau	33:1–17		
Shechem	33:18a		
			33:18b
		33:19–20	
Dinah	34:1–31		
Jacob in Bethel		35:1–8	
			35:9–13
		35:14	
			35:15
		35:16–20	

(*continued*)

Table A.1 (continued)

GENESIS	J	E	P
Reuben and Bilhah	35:21–22a		
Jacob's Sons & Isaac's Death			35:22b–29
Esau's Children			36:1–30
	36:31–43		
Joseph Sold			37:1–2
	37:3–4		
		37:5–13	
	37:14ab		
		37:14c–17	
	37:18		
		37:19–22	
	37:23		
		37:24	
	37:25–27		
		37:28a	
	37:28b		
		37:29–30	
	37:31–35		
		37:36	
Judah & Tamar	38:1–30		
Potiphar's Wife	39:1–23		
Butler's and Baker's Dreams		40:1–23	
Pharaoh's Dreams, Joseph's Elevation		41:1–57	
Joseph and Brothers		42:1–3	
	42:4–5		
		42:6–25	
	42:26–28		
		42:29–37	
	42:38		
	43:1–34		
	44:1–34		
	45:1–2		
		45:3	
	45:4–5a		
		45:5b–15	
Jacob Moves to Egypt	45:16–28		
Jacob's Vision at Beersheba		46:1–4	
	46:5		
Ancestors in Egypt			46:6–27
Meeting Pharaoh: Shepherds	46:28–34		
	47:1–6		
			47:7–11
Joseph Centralizes Control in Egypt	47:12–26		
			47:27–28
	47:29–31		

Table A.1 (*continued*)

GENESIS	J	E	P
Blessings on Ephraim & Manasseh		48:1–2	
			48:3–7
		48:8–22	
[Old Poetry: Blessings on All Sons]	[49:1–28]		
Jacob's Death			49:29–33
Jacob's Burial	50:1–11		
			50:12–13
	50:14		
Reconciliation; Joseph's Death		50:15–26	
EXODUS			
Family of Jacob			1:1–7
Oppression	1:8–12		
			1:13–14
		1:15–21	
Moses' Birth and Flight	1:22		
	2:1–23a		
			2:23b–25
Revelation at the Mountain		3:1	
	3:2–4a		
		3:4b	
	3:5		
		3:6	
	3:7–8		
		3:9–15	
	3:16–22		
Moses' Protest	4:1–31		
Pharaoh's Harsher Policies	5:1–23		
	6:1		
Revelation of Name			6:2–13
Israel's Clans			6:14–25
Moses & Aaron before Pharaoh			6:26–30
			7:1–13
The Plagues			
Blood	7:14–18		
			7:19–20a
	7:20b–21a		
			7:21b–22
	7:23–25		
Frogs	7:26–29		
			8:1–3a
	8:3b–11a		
			8:11b
Flies			8:12–15
Swarms	8:16–28		

(*continued*)

Table A.1 (continued)

EXODUS	J	E	P
Pestilence	9:1–7		
Boils			9:8–12
Hail	9:13–34		
			9:35
Locusts	10:1–19		
			10:20
Darkness	10:21–26		
			10:27
	10:28–29		
Death of Firstborn			
Announced	11:1–9		
			11:10
Passover			12:1–20
	12:21–27	(12:24–27?)	
			12:28
Death of Firstborn	12:29–39		
			12:40–51
Unleavened Bread and			
Consecration of Firstborn			13:1–2
	13:3–16	(13:3–16?)	
Flight		13:17–19	
Cloud	13:20–22		
Sea			14:1–4
	14:5–7		
			14:8–12
	14:13–14		
			14:15–18
	14:19–20		
			14:21a
	14:21b		
			14:21c–23
	14:24–25		
			14:26–27a
	14:27b		
			14:27c–29
	14:30–31		
[Special Source: Old Poem]	[15:1–18]		
			15:19
		15:20–21	
Water: Marah	15:22–25a		
		15:25b–26	
Elim			15:27
Wilderness of Sin			16:1–3
		16:4–5	
Quail and Manna			16:6–36
Rephedim			17:1
Water: Massah and Meribah	17:2–7	(17:2–7?)	

(*continued*)

Table A.1 (*continued*)

EXODUS	J	E	P
Fight with Amelek		17:8–14	
	17:15–16		
Jethro and Appointment of			
Judges		18:1a	
	18:1b		
		18:2–7	
	18:8–11		
		18:12–27	
Mt. Sinai: Theophany			19:1–2a
	19:2b		
		19:3–8	
	19:9–13a		
		19:13b	
	19:14–16a		
		19:16b–17	
	19:18		
		19:19	
	19:20–25		
Ten Commandments		20:1–17	(20:1–17[ed.])
Theophany		20:18–21	
Altar	20:22–26		
[Special Source: Covenant			
Code]	[21:1–23:19]		
Canaanites	23:20–33	(23:20–33?)	
Covenant at Sinai		24:1–15a	
			24:15b–18a
		24:18b	
Tabernacle, Sabbath, Tablets			25:1–31:18
Golden Calf		32:1–14	
			32:15–16
		32:17–35	
Departure Announced	33:1–3a		
Tent of Meeting		33:3b–11	
Theophany to Moses	33:12–23		
Theophany & Ten			
Commandments	34:1–28		
Moses' Face			34:29–35
Construction of Tabernacle			35:1–40:38
LEVITICUS			
Legal Material			1:1–27:34
NUMBERS			
Census & laws			1:1–10:28
Departure with the Ark	10:29–36		
Fire of God		11:1–3	
Quail	11:4–13		
Elders/Prophets		11:14	

(*continued*)

Table A.1 (*continued*)

NUMBERS	J	E	P
Quail	11:15		
Elders/Prophets		11:16–17	
Quail	11:18–23		
Elders/Prophets		11:24–30	
Quail	11:31–35		
Miriam, Moses, and Aaron		12:1–16	
Scouting out Canaan:			
First Attack			13:1–16
	13:17–20		
			13:21
	13:22–24		
			13:25–26
	13:27–31		
			13:32
	13:33		
People Refuse to Attack			14:1a
	14:1b		
			14:2–3
	14:4		
			14:5–10
	14:11–25		
			14:26–38
	14:39–45		
Laws about Sacrifice			15:1–41
Rebellion (P: Korah;			16:1a
J: Dathan & Abiram)	16:1b–2a		
			16:2b–11
	16:12–15		
			16:16–24
	16:25		
			16:26–27a
	16:27b–32a		
			16:32b
	16:33–34		
			16:35
Aaronids & Levites			17:1–18:32
Red Heifer			19:1–22
Water: Meribah			20:1–13
Approach to Canaan:			
Skirting Edom	20:14–21		
Aaron's Death at Mt. Hor			20:22–29
Defeat of Canaanites at Arad	21:1–3		
Serpents		21:4–9	
Itinerary to Pisgah			21:10–20
Defeat of Sihon/Amorites			
and Og/Bashan	21:21–35		
Balaam (parts: E and Old			
Poems)	22:1–24:25	(parts)	

(*continued*)

Table A.1 (continued)

GENESIS	J	E	P
Baal Peor	25:1–5		
Midianites			25:6–18
Census			26:1–65
Daughters of Zelophehad			27:1–11
Joshua Appointed			27:12–23
Laws About Worship			28:1–29:39
Women's Vows			30:1–17
Midianites			31:1–54
Tribal Allotments			32:1–42
Stations			33:1–49
Tribal Allotments			33:50–36:13
DEUTERONOMY = D			1:1–34:12

Table A.2 Sections with Hebrew/English Verse Number Differences

In a few places, the numbering system of chapters and verses in the Hebrew text and in modern English translations differs. This is not true for the new English translation put out by the Jewish Publication Society or for the Jerusalem Bible, where chapter and verse numbers correspond to those in the Hebrew text. But for many other modern English translations—the Revised Standard Version, the New Revised Standard Version, the New English Bible among them—there are occasional discrepancies between the numbering systems in the Hebrew and English texts. The following instances are the places where the English numbering of some translations differs from the Hebrew:

GENESIS	J	E	P
[end of] Treaty with Laban		31:50–55	
		32:1–2	
Reunion with Esau	32:3–21		
Wrestling with God	32:22–32		
EXODUS			
Frogs	8:1–4		
			8:5–7a
	8:7b–15a		
			8:15b
Flies			8:16–19
Swarms	8:20–32		
NUMBERS			
Aaronids and Levites			16:36–18:32
Laws about Worship			28:1–29:40
Women's Vows			30:1–16

Notes

Chapter 1

1. Gerhard von Rad, "The Theological Problem of the Doctrine of Creation," trans. E. W. Trueman Dicken, in *The Problem of the Hexateuch and Other Essays* (London: SCM, 1966) 131–43.

2. Ibid., 138–39.

3. Ibid., 135.

4. Ibid., 138.

5. G. Ernest Wright, *God Who Acts: Biblical Theology as Recital* (London: SCM, 1952) 43.

6. Ibid., 38.

7. Ibid., 38, 43.

8. Ibid., 19.

9. Ibid., 19–21.

10. Ibid., 15–20.

11. H. and H. A. Frankfort et al., *Before Philosophy: The Intellectual Adventure of Ancient Man* (New York: Penguin, 1949) 237–62.

12. Ibid., 11–36, 237–62. Much of what Yehezkel Kaufmann had to say about the distinctive character of Israelite religion and its rejection of mythic thought reflects categories and argumentation much like those in the Frankforts' analysis. See Kaufmann's *The Religion of Israel*, trans. and abr. Moshe Greenberg (New York: Schocken, 1972) 7–121.

13. H. W. Robinson, *Inspiration and Revelation in the Old Testament* (Oxford: Clarendon, 1946) 2. Compare Luis I. J. Stadelmann's comment about Israel in *The Hebrew Conception of the World* (Rome: Pontifical Biblical Institute, 1970): "Their contemplation of the world, then, begins with the experience of the facts of salvation history" (p. 4).

14. Sigmund Mowinckel, *The Psalms in Israel's Worship*, vol. 1, trans. D. R. Ap-Thomas (Nashville: Abingdon, 1967) 139.

15. U. Cassuto, *A Commentary on the Book of Genesis*, vol. 1, trans. Israel Abrahams (Jerusalem: Magnes, 1961) 8.

16. Nahum M. Sarna, *Genesis*, The JPS Torah Commentary (Philadelphia: Jewish Publication Society, 1989) xiv.

17. James Barr, "Revelation Through History in the Old Testament and in Modern Theology," *Interpretation* 17 (1963) 193–94.

18. Mircea Eliade, *The Myth of the Eternal Return or, Cosmos and History* (Princeton: Princeton University, 1954), esp. 102–12, 147–62.

19. Hans J. Klimkeit, "Spacial Orientation in Mythical Thinking as Exemplified in Ancient Egypt: Considerations Toward a Geography of Religions," *History of Religions* 14 (1975) 267, 269.

20. Robert L. Cohn, *The Shape of Sacred Space: Four Biblical Studies* (Chico, CA: Scholars, 1981) 1.

21. Albrecht Alt, "The Settlement of the Israelites in Palestine," trans. R. A. Wilson, in *Essays on Old Testament History and Religion* (Garden City, NJ: Archer Books, 1968) 173–221. Originally published as *Die Landnahme der Israeliten in Palästina; Territorialgeschichtliche Studien* (Leipzig: Werkgemeinschaft, 1925); reprinted in *Kleine Schriften zur Geschichte des Volkes Israel* (Munich: C. H. Beck).

22. Albrecht Alt, "The God of the Fathers," trans. R. A. Wilson, in *Essays on Old Testament History and Religion* (Garden City, NJ: Archer Books, 1968) 1–100. Originally published as *Der Gott der Väter; ein Beitrag zur Vorgeschichte der israelitischen Religion*, Beiträge zur Wissenschaft vom Alten und Neuen Testament, III, 12 (Stuttgart: W. Kohlhammer, 1929); reprinted in *Kleine Schriften zur Geschichte des Volkes Israel* (Munich: C. H. Beck, 1953) I. 1–78.

23. Albrecht Alt, "The Origins of Israelite Law," trans. R. A. Wilson, in *Essays on Old Testament History and Religion* (Garden City, NJ: Archer Books, 1968) 101–71. Originally published as *Die Ursprünge des israelitischen Rechts*, Berichte über die Verhandlungen der Sächsischen Academie der Wissenschaften zu Leipzig. Philologische-historische Klasse, 86, 1 (Leipzig: S. Hirzel, 1934); reprinted in *Kleine Schriften zur Geschichte des Volkes Israel* (Munich: C. H. Beck).

24. Alt, "God of the Fathers," 54–55.

25. Ibid., 78–79.

26. H. and H. A. Frankfort, *Before Philosophy*, 246, 247.

27. John Van Seters discusses the scholarly tradition of nomadic origins in *Abraham in History and Tradition* (New Haven: Yale University, 1975) 9–10, and offers a critique of it (13–38). Israel Finkelstein surveys the heirs of Alt's settlement theory in *The Archaeology of the Israelite Settlement* (Jerusalem: Israel Exploration Society, 1988) 302–6, and presents his own adaptation of it (336–56). In his recent study of nature in the Bible, *World and Environment* (Nashville: Abingdon, 1980), O. H. Steck still relies heavily on Alt's reconstruction of early Israelite environment and religion (63–64, 115–27).

28. Roland de Vaux, *Ancient Israel: Its Life and Institutions*, trans. John McHugh (New York: McGraw-Hill, 1961).

29. Ibid., 3–4.

30. See also, by way of illustration, K. Budde, "The Nomadic Ideal in the Old Testament," *New World* 4 (1895) 726–45; John W. Flight, "The Nomadic Idea and Ideal in the Old Testament," *JBL* 42 (1923) 158–226; Samuel Nyström, *Beduinentum und Jahwismus: eine soziologisch-religionsgeschichtliche Untersuchung zum Alten Tes-*

tament (Lund: C. W. K. Gleerup, 1946); and Morris S. Seale, *The Desert Bible: Nomadic Tribal Culture and Old Testament Interpretation* (London: Weidenfeld and Nicolson, 1974).

31. Wright, *God Who Acts* 19–29.

32. J. Severino Croatto, *Exodus: A Hermeneutics of Freedom* (Maryknoll, NY: Orbis, 1981) 13, 34–35. A similar view is expressed by Dorothee Soelle in *To Work and To Love: A Theology of Creation* (Philadelphia: Fortress, 1984); see esp. chapter 2, 7–21.

33. Harvey Cox, *The Secular City*, rev. ed. (Toronto: MacMillan, 1966) 19–21. Cf. James Barr's description of this viewpoint and his critique of it in "Man and Nature: The Ecological Controversy and the Old Testament," in *Ecology and Religion in History*, ed. David and Eileen Spring (New York: Harper & Row, 1974) 49–59. Barr's essay was originally published in the *Bulletin of the John Ryland's Library* 55 (1972) 9–32.

34. Lynn White, Jr., "The Historical Roots of Our Ecologic Crisis," *Science* 155 (10 March 1967) 1203–7; reprinted in *Ecology and Religion in History*, ed. David and Eileen Spring (New York: Harper & Row, 1974) 15–31.

35. Ibid., 1205.

36. Thomas Berry, "Economics: Its Effects on the Life Systems in the World," in *Thomas Berry and the New Cosmology*, ed. Anne Lonergan and Caroline Richards (Mystic, CT: Twenty-Third Publications, 1987) 5–26, esp. 15, 17; previously published in *Cross Currents* 35 (Winter 1985–86) as "Wonderworld as Wasteworld;" and *The Dream of the Earth* (San Francisco: Sierra Club Books, 1988) 123–37.

37. George Hendry, *Theology of Nature* (Philadelphia: Westminster, 1980) 18–19.

38. Paul Santmire, *The Travail of Nature: The Ambiguous Ecological Promise of Christian Theology* (Philadelphia: Fortress, 1985) 1–3.

39. Kenneth Woodward, *Newsweek* (June 5, 1989) 70–72.

40. G. W. F. Hegel, *Lectures on the Philosophy of Religion*, 3 vols., trans. E. B. Speirs and J. Burdon Sanderson (London: Routledge and Kegan Paul, 1962).

41. Ibid., 2.128, 189.

42. Ibid., 2.199.

43. Julius Wellhausen, *Prolegomena to the History of Ancient Israel*, trans. Black and Menzies (New York: Meridian Books, 1957) 102–4, 437–38; for a recent brief discussion of Hegel's influence on Wellhausen, see Joseph Blenkinsopp's comments in *The Pentateuch* (New York: Doubleday, 1992) 8–11; and for an attempt to distance Wellhausen from Hegel, see Lothar Perlitt's *Vatke und Wellhausen* (Berlin: Alfred Topelmann, 1965).

44. Wright, *God Who Acts*, 42.

45. Eliade, *Myth of the Eternal Return*, 148.

46. Gerhard von Rad, "Some Aspects of the Old Testament World-View," trans. E. W. Trueman Dicken, in *The Problem of the Hexateuch and Other Essays* (London: SCM, 1966) 144; originally published as "Aspekte alttestamentlichen Weltverständnisses" *Evangelische Theologie* 24 (1964) 57–73.

47. Ibid., 154–55.

48. Ibid., 154

49. Bertil Albrektson, *History and the Gods: An Essay on the Idea of Historical Events as Divine Manifestations in the Ancient Near East and in Israel* (Lund: C. W. K. Gleerup, 1967).

50. Barr, "Revelation Through History," 193-205.

51. Rolf Knierim, "Cosmos and History in Israel's Theology," *Horizons in Biblical Theology* 3 (1981) 59–123; H. H. Schmid, "Creation, Righteousness, and Salvation: 'Creation Theology' as the Broad Horizon of Biblical Theology," trans. and abr. Bernhard W. Anderson and Dan G. Johnson, in *Creation in the Old Testament* (Philadelphia: Fortress, 1984) 102–17; see also H. H. Schmid's collection of essays, *Altorientalische Welt in der alttestamentlichen Theologie* (Zürich: Theologischer Verlag, 1974), where this essay in its German original appears (9–30) together with others related to this issue.

52. A. M. Khazanov, *Nomads and the Outside World*, trans. Julia Crookenden (Cambridge: Cambridge University, 1983) 1–14, 85–118; "Introduction," in *Pastoralism in the Levant: Archaeological Materials in Anthropological Perspective*, ed. Ofer Bar-Yosef and Anatoly Khazanov (Madison, WI: Prehistory, 1992) 1–6.

53. Clarence J. Glacken, *Traces on the Rhodian Shore: Nature and Culture in Western Thought from Ancient Times to the End of the Eighteenth Century* (Berkeley: University of California, 1967) 6.

54. Among the most exhaustive recent treatments of pastoral nomadism are A. M. Kazanov's broadly synthetic *Nomads and the Outside World* and the collection of essays from archaeologists and anthropologists assembled by Ofer Bar-Yosef and Anatoly Khazanov in *Pastoralism in the Levant*.

55. Bar-Yosef and Khazanov, *Pastoralism*, 5–6.

56. Richard Meadow, "Inconclusive Remarks on Pastoralism, Nomadism, and Other Animal Related Matters," in *Pastoralism in the Levant: Archaeological Materials in Anthropological Perspective*, ed. Ofer Bar-Yosef and Anatoly Khazanov (Madison, WI: Prehistory, 1992) 267.

57. Emmanuel Marx, "Are There Pastoral Nomads in the Middle East?" in *Pastoralism in the Levant: Archaeological Materials in Anthropological Perspective*, ed. Ofer Bar-Yosef and Anatoly Khazanov (Madison, WI: Prehistory, 1992) 257.

58. Bar-Yosef and Khazanov, *Pastoralism*, 1–6; Khazanov, *Nomads*, 17–25; see also Emmanuel Marx's studies of pastoralism: "Pastoral Nomads," 255–60 and "The Tribe as a Unit of Subsistence," *American Anthropologist* 79 (1977) 343–63.

59. Bar-Yosef and Khazanov, *Pastoralism*, 1–6; Fredrik Barth, "A General Perspective on Nomad-Sedentary Relations in the Middle East," in *The Desert and the Sown: Nomads in the Wider Society*, ed. Cynthia Nelson, Institute of International Studies Research Series, No. 21 (Berkeley: University of California, 1973) 11–21.

60. Bar Yosef and Khazanov, *Pastoralism*, 3–4.

61. See, for example, the study by Oystein LaBianca on the historical fluctuations between intensive agriculture and intensive herding in the vicinity of the Transjordanian site of Hesbon, *Sedentarization and Nomadization: Food system cycles at Hesbon and vicinity in Transjordan* (Berrien Springs, MI: Institute of Archaeology and Andrews University, 1990).

62. George E. Mendenhall, "The Hebrew Conquest of Palestine," *BA* 25 (1962) 66–87; *The Tenth Generation* (Baltimore: Johns Hopkins Univ., 1973), esp. chapters 1, 5, and 7. Norman K. Gottwald, *The Tribes of Yahweh: A Sociology of the Religion of Liberated Israel, 1250–1050 B.C.E.* (Maryknoll, NY: Orbis, 1979) 435–63; "Domain Assumption and Societal Models in the Study of Pre-Monarchic Israel," *VT Supp* 28 (1975) 89–100.

63. Mendenhall, "Conquest," 66–71.

64. Gottwald, *Tribes*, 436.

65. A critique of Israel's nomadic origins has also been undertaken by John Van Seters as part of another agenda, the argument for a late, exilic dating of the patriar-

chal traditions in the old epic sources, the Yahwist and Elohist, in *Abraham in History and Tradition*, 13–38.

66. Among the ablest early respondents to the criticisms of Lynn White was Bernhard W. Anderson, who has addressed ecological issues in biblical literature in a series of essays, including "Human Dominion Over Nature," in *Biblical Studies in Contemporary Thought*, ed. Miriam Ward (Burlington, VT: The Institute; Somerville, MA: distributed by Greeno, Hadden, 1975) 27–45; "Creation and Ecology," *American Journal of Theology and Philosophy* 1 (1983) 14–30, reprinted in *Creation in the Old Testament*, ed. Bernhard W. Anderson (Philadelphia: Fortress, 1984) 152–71; and "'Subdue the Earth,' What Does It Mean?" *Bible Review* (October 1992) 4,10; Many of his essays on these issues have now been collected in *From Creation to New Creation* (Minneapolis: Augsburg Fortress, 1994). See also note 51 above.

67. In addition to Julius Wellhausen's *Prolegomena*, see his *Die Composition des Hexateuchs und der historischen Bücher des alten Testaments* (Berlin: Walter de Gruyter, 1963). The most thorough presentation of the documentary hypothesis is still that of J. Estlin Carpenter and George Harford-Battersby, *The Hexateuch*, 2 vols. (London: Longmans, Green, 1902). Two recent introductions to the documentary hypothesis are Richard Friedman's *Who Wrote the Bible?* (New York: Summit Books, 1987) and Anthony F. Campbell and Mark A. O'Brien's *Sources of the Pentateuch* (Minneapolis: Augsburg Fortress, 1993), which reflects broadly the perspective of Martin Noth's classic, *A History of Pentateuchal Traditions*, trans. B. W. Anderson (Englewood Cliffs, NJ: Prentice-Hall, 1972; reprint, Chico, CA: Scholars, 1981; German Original, 1948).

68. Peter Ellis, *The Yahwist: The Bible's First Theologian* (Collegeville, MN: The Liturgical Press, 1968).

69. Robert Coote and David Ord, *The Bible's First History* (Philadelphia: Fortress, 1989); John Van Seters, *Prologue to History: The Yahwist as Historian in Genesis* (Louisville, KY: Westminster/John Knox, 1992) and *The Life of Moses: The Yahwist as Historian in Exodus-Numbers* (Louisville, KY: Westminster/John Knox, 1994); Harold Bloom, *The Book of J* (New York: Grove Weidenfeld, 1990).

70. E.g. Kåre Berge, *Die Zeit des Jahwisten* (Berlin: Walter de Gruyter, 1990); H. H. Schmid, *Der sogenannte Jahwist: Beobachtungen und Fragen zur Pentateuchforschung* (Zürich: Theologischer Verlag, 1976), a study which actually calls the traditional view of J into question; Christoph Levin, *Der Jahwist* (Göttingen: Vandenhoeck & Ruprecht, 1993).

71. The new literary critics, such as Robert Alter, have criticized the "excavative" approach of traditional scholarship and have advocated a more unitary reading. See Alter's *The Art of Biblical Narrative* (Basic Books, 1981); cf. Meir Sternberg, *The Poetics of Biblical Narrative* (Bloomington, IN: Indiana University, 1985). Those who have proposed new explanations for a composite Pentateuch include R. N. Whybray, *The Making of the Pentateuch: A Methodological Study* (Sheffield: JSOT, 1987); Rolf Rendtorff, *The Problem of the Process of Transmission in the Pentateuch*, trans. John J. Scullion (Sheffield: JSOT, 1990); and Joseph Blenkinsopp, *The Pentateuch*. There have, of course, been critics of the documentary hypothesis from the beginning, a prominent representative of whom is Umberto Cassuto, *The Documentary Hypothesis and the Composition of the Pentateuch*, trans. Israel Abrahams (Jerusalem: Magnes, 1961).

72. While scholars of late have usually placed J in the early monarchy, John Van Seters has argued for an exilic date (*Prologue to History*; *The Life of Moses*). For a defense of a date in the early monarchy, see Coote and Ord, *The Bible's First History*, 5–7.

73. Bloom, *Book of J*, 9.

74. Ellis, *Yahwist*, 21.

75. Otto Eissfeldt, *The Old Testament: An Introduction*, trans. P. R. Ackroyd (New York: Harper & Row, 1965) 195. This view of nomadic and agricultural sources behind J goes back to Rudolf Smend's *Die Erzählung des Hexateuch auf ihre Quellen untersucht* (Berlin: G. Reimer, 1912).

76. Georg Fohrer, *Introduction to the Old Testament*, trans. David Green (Nashville: Abingdon, 1968) 165.

77. Claus Westermann, *Genesis 1–11*, trans. John H. Scullion (Minneapolis: Augsburg, 1984) 187, 206, 267. For a similar approach to the Cain and Abel story, see J. Maxwell Miller, "The Descendants of Cain: Notes on Genesis 4," *ZAW* 86 (1974) 164–74.

78. Ellis, *Yahwist*, 127; cf. pp. 28–32, 61–65, 88–100, 140–41, 163–72.

79. This characterization comes out most clearly in Wellhausen's analysis of the development of Israel's religious festivals (*Prolegomena*, 83–120). It is in some tension with Wellhausen's analysis of J's narrative elsewhere, when he tends to emphasize its interest in human affairs in contrast to the world of nature (303–15). Wellhausen's view of the development of Israelite religion is indebted to Hegel, as has been noted, as well as to his predecessor Wilhelm Vatke (*Die biblische Theologie wissenschaftlich dargestellt* [Berlin: G. Bethge, 1835]), as he openly acknowledges (13).

Chapter 2

1. Paul Ricoeur, "Myth: Myth and History," *ER* 10.273. Compare the comments on the Yahwist by Odil Hannes Steck, *World and Environment* (Nashville: Abingdon, 1980) 65–66, 143–146.

2. Some major alternative treatments of creation in the Bible are Psalms 8, 19, 74, 89, 95, 104, 148; Isaiah 40, 51; Job 38–40; Proverbs 8.

3. Translations of the Bible are the author's unless otherwise indicated.

4. Harold Bloom has recently called attention to and inveighed against the "strong misreadings of J" to which the work of later editors has led; see *The Book of J* (New York: Grove Weidenfeld, 1990) 9–23. Joseph Blenkinsopp's recent argument that the Yahwistic elements in the primeval narrative are later supplementary additions to a primary Priestly account—*The Pentateuch* (New York: Doubleday, 1992) 54–97—is to my mind less persuasive than the older and more widely held view that J predates P.

5. The argument for interpreting *'ādām*, the first human, as male is developed later in this chapter in the discussion of "Agriculture in the Garden." The Yahwist actually employs *'ādām* as a common noun, not as a name, throughout the Eden narrative and at the beginning of the Cain and Abel story, using it regularly with the definite article, *hā'ādām*, "the man." (One should, I believe, repoint the vowels in 2:20, 3:17, and 3:21, and add the definite article in 4:25.) I have tried to reflect this accurately in the interpretation of the Garden of Eden narrative, but I have departed from this careful practice later in the chapter where, for ease of discussion, I employ Adam as a proper name (as the Priestly Writer seems to do in 5:1–5).

6. Not "to the east of the Garden of Eden" as most translators. The term *miqqedem* means "to the east," that is, east of the couple's new home (cf. Gen 13:11; also 2:8, 11:2). The phrase *lĕgan-'ēden* means "at the garden," reading the preposition *lĕ* as expressing locality (BDB, 511). J uses the expression *qidmat-'ēden* for "east of Eden" (Gen 4:16).

7. Julius Wellhausen thought the Yahwist must have said more about nothingness, but that it was edited out by the Priestly reviser: "[It was all a dry waste] when Jehovah formed the earth . . ." *Prolegomena to the History of Ancient Israel* (New York: Meridian Books, 1958) 299. John Skinner refers to the Yahwist's "conception of the primal condition of the world as an arid, waterless waste," *Genesis*, 2 ed., ICC (Edinburgh: T. & T. Clark, 1980) 51. Gerhard von Rad believed J to be describing the primordial state as a desert: "Whereas in ch. 1 creation moves from the chaos to the cosmos of the entire world, our account of creation sketches the original state as a desert in contrast to the sown," *Genesis* (Philadelphia: Westminster, 1972) 76. Theodor H. Gaster sees J's opening clauses as a retrojection into cosmogony of the climatic conditions that obtain in the autumn at the beginning of the agricultural year, with the earth dry, no rain, and only the springs for water, "Cosmogony," *IDB*, 1.704-5; "Earth," *IDB*, 2.3.

8. The idea of a more detailed creation account preceding the Yahwist's opening sentence was present during the formation of the classical outlines of the documentary hypothesis at the beginning of this century. See J. Estlin Carpenter and George Harford-Battersby, eds., *The Hexateuch* (London: Longmans, Green and Co., 1902) 1.97. This approach has become popular again in some recent treatments of the Yahwist, for example, David Damrosch, *The Narrative Covenant* (Ithaca, NY: Cornell University, 1987) 121; Bloom, *Book of J*, 28–31.

9. Translated by E. A. Speiser in *ANET*, 60–61. For another example of this convention, see the preface to an incantation recited for the purification of Ezida, the temple of Nabû at Borsippa in Alexander Heidel, *The Babylonian Genesis* (Chicago: University of Chicago, 1951) 61–63.

10. See Claus Westermann's useful discussion of this literary convention in *Genesis 1–11: A Commentary* (Minneapolis: Augsburg, 1984) 43–47. The motif of conflict between storm god and sea is appropriated by the Yahwist not at the beginning of the epic but in its final section describing the Exodus and Sinai experiences, as will be discussed in detail in chapter 4.

11. The use of *'ădāmâ* as a special designation for arable land is unique to the Yahwist. The Elohist uses it only twice, as a designation for the earth (Exod 32:12; Num 12:3), and the Priestly Writer only six times, four of them in the cliché "that which creeps on the ground," *remeś hā'ădāmâ* (Gen 1:25, 6:20, 7:8; Lev 20:25), and twice for a territory (Lev 20:24; Num 32:11). In only a few cases, out of its forty-two uses—when the Yahwist employs it for the holy ground at the southern mountain (Exod 3:5) and the ground that swallows Dathan and Abiram with their families (Num 16:30–31), for the land flooded (Gen 6:7), and for the land of Israel (Gen 28:15) or the land of others (Gen 12:3)—could *'ădāmâ* be translated more broadly, but given its normal technical meaning, it probably maintains that sense in these cases, too.

Both Luis J. J. Stadelmann in *The Hebrew Conception of the World* (Rome: Pontifical Biblical Institute, 1970) 128–129, and Frank Crüsemann in "Die Eigenständigkeit der Urgeschichte," in *Die Botschaft und die Boten*, ed. J. Jeremias and L. Perlitt (Neukirchen-Vluyn: Neukirchener Verlag, 1981) 11–29, esp. 17ff., have noted the specific use by the Yahwist of *'ădāmâ* for arable land, but neither has suggested the consistent and thorough employment of *'ădāmâ* in this way throughout the epic.

12. Of its 195 occurrences in the Yahwist's epic, only 7 connect *'ereṣ* specifically with agricultural production, where the Yahwist might be expected to use *'ădāmâ* (Gen 8:22; 26:12; 27:28, 39; 43:11; Exod 10:12; Num 13:20). Even in these

cases, however, the more general sense communicated by 'ereṣ may have been preferred by the Yahwist over the narrower 'ădāmâ.

13. Examples include Eve (Gen 3:20), Cain (Gen 4:1), Noah (Gen 5:29), Jacob
(Gen 32:29), Jacob's sons (Gen 29:31–35), and Moses (Exod 2:10). These are "folk
etymologies," that is, J sees a connection between the name and the Hebrew root
used to explain it not necessarily because the name can be linguistically derived from
the root, but simply because the name sounds like the root.

14. Westermann's observation is pertinent: "The wordplay . . . 'dm-'dmh points
to the basic relationship between the soil and the person which in reality characterizes agricultural life. . . . Soil and people are associated with each other in agricultural life in such a way that each is determined by the other" (Genesis 1–11, 199).
The Hebrew root 'dm can mean "red," and this sense may not be unrelated to the
terms 'ădām and 'ădāmâ in the Yahwist's mind. For the Yahwist, 'ădāmâ must refer
primarily to terra rosa, the commonest and most fertile soil in the hills that made up
the heartland of biblical Israel. Derived from the limestone underlying these hills,
terra rosa is a vivid reddish-brown color, not dissimilar from the deep-reddish brown
Mediterranean complexion of the inhabitants of this part of the world for millennia.
This similarity in complexion between soil and skin may have provided the link
between 'ădāmâ and 'ădām with an added nuance for the Yahwist. While the Yahwist
does not make the connection in this case, he does play on this sense of 'dm in the
story of Esau/Edom (Gen 25:30).

15. Translated, with restorations, by Thorkild Jacobsen in "The Eridu Genesis,"
JBL 100 (1981) 516–17, n. 7.

16. Yehuda Karmon, Israel: A Regional Geography (London: John Wiley & Sons,
1971) 27. The reference to the spring ('ēd) in v 6 anticipates the garden ecology and
is really part of that story rather than one in the series of details describing the author's
own world. The spring will be discussed further below in relation to the garden
ecology.

17. The meaning of 'ēśeb as "grain" may in fact also be indicated by the Priestly
Writer's use of it. P describes it as producing seed, as grain does in the head, in contrast to fruit, which contains its seed within it (Gen 1:11, 12). For P it is also the
primary food of human beings (Gen 1:29,30; 9:3), as bread in fact was in ancient
Israel's grain-based agricultural economy.

U. Cassuto, largely on the basis of the parallelism in Genesis 3:18–19 between
'ēśeb and bread (leḥem), reaches the same conclusion that 'ēśeb must refer to the
grains, wheat and barley; see his A Commentary on the Book of Genesis I (Jerusalem:
Magnes, 1978) 102. 'ēśeb is also understood in this way by E. A. Speiser in Genesis,
AB (Garden City, NY: Doubleday, 1964) 14; and Robert B. Coote and David Robert
Ord in The Bible's First History (Philadelphia: Fortress, 1989) 42, 52. The translation "grasses" comes close to this sense (JPSV, NAB), but the misunderstanding that
this is wild vegetation still persists (NEB, JB).

18. On agriculture in Iron Age Israel, see Lawrence E. Stager, "The Archaeology of the Family in Ancient Israel," BASOR 260 (1985) 1–35; Oded Borowski, Agriculture in Iron Age Israel (Winona Lake, IN: Eisenbrauns, 1987); and David C.
Hopkins, The Highlands of Canaan: Agricultural Life in the Early Iron Age (Sheffield:
JSOT/ Almond, 1985). In biblical references to the produce of the Israelite hill country, the grains, wheat and barley, are regularly mentioned first (e.g., Deut 8:7–9).

19. Michael Zohary, Plants of the Bible (Cambridge: Cambridge University 1982) 72.

20. On the relationship between cultivation and herding in the ancient Israelite agricultural economy, see for example, Hopkins, Canaan, 245–50. While the

understanding of *śîaḥ* as the wild vegetation of arid regions, as biblical usage implies, is not uncommon (Skinner, *Genesis,* 54, Westermann, *Genesis 1–11,* 199; *JB*), the connection with pasturage has not been suggested. Coote's and Ord's "fruit bearing tree" is puzzling (*First History,* 42, 52).

The term *śādeh,* "field," in both expressions— *'ēśeb haśśādeh,* "grain of the field," and *śîaḥ haśśādeh,* "shrub of the field"—refers to the open areas outside the village (cf. 4:8). Compare the clear distinction made between the inhabited village and the surrounding countryside in Susan Freeman's study of the agricultural village of Valdemora, *Neighbors: The Social Construct in a Castilian Hamlet* (Chicago: University of Chicago, 1970) 182.

21. On the form and function of the typical Israelite farmhouse, see Stager, "Archaeology," 11–24. For the key features of Israelite agriculture, see also Borowski and Hopkins. Westermann sees much the same picture in Genesis 2:5: "These few sentences . . . give us an outline of the world in which the narrative was conceived. It is a world where people cultivate the soil surrounded by steppe and desert, where life depends on the rain that gives growth to the shrubs of the steppe and to the seed of the cultivated land. It is a world which corresponds to that of the Palestinian farmer" (*Genesis 1–11,* 199–200). O. H. Steck also believes J represents the world in his primeval narrative from the point of view of the "small farmer" or "Palestinian peasant," but he combines this observation with an argument for J's universal perspective that goes considerably beyond the position taken here (*World,* 64–80). The attempt to differentiate agricultural from nomadic elements within the Eden narrative disregards both the literary integrity of the text and the character of biblical agriculture. See Westermann, *Genesis 1–11,* 264–65, for a review of the debate.

22. Meron Benvenisti, *The West Bank and Gaza Atlas* (Jerusalem: West Bank Data Base Project; Boulder: Westview Press, 1988) 25.

23. A widely held modern view, this interpretation was put into its classic form by J. Wellhausen in *Die Composition des Hexateuchs und der historischen Bücher des alten Testaments* (1885; reprint, Berlin: Walter de Gruyter, 1963), 8–9; and Bernard Stade, "Beiträge zur Pentateuchkritik. 1) Das Kainszeichen," *ZAW* 14 (1894) 250–318. This view has been adopted in BDB (884) and by many commentators in the twentieth century to explain at least one level in the history of the story. See, for example, Baruch Halpern, "Kenites," *ABD* 4. 17–22. As Halpern notes (18–19), the Kenites are described as a community in the wilderness south and southeast of Judah in such biblical references as Numbers 24:21, 22, and 1 Samuel 15:6, with a possible branch in the north (Judg 4:11,17; 5:24).

24. Peter Ellis, *The Yahwist: The Bible's First Theologian* (Collegeville, MN: The Liturgical Press, 1968) 167, 199.

25. Westermann, *Genesis 1–11,* 292–96, 317–18; von Rad, *Genesis,* 104, 108–9; Cassuto, *Commentary,* 203; E. A. Speiser, *Genesis,* AB (Garden City, NY: Doubleday, 1964) 31; Nahum M. Sarna, *Genesis,* JPS Torah Commentary (Philadelphia: Jewish Publication Society, 1989) 32.

26. See the critique of older views of the dichotomy between sedentary agriculture and nomadic pastoralism in chapter 1.

27. Laws of primogeniture in Israel guaranteed the major part of the family estate to the firstborn son (e.g., Gen 27; Deut 21:15–17). The younger son customarily had to watch the family's flock (e.g., 1 Sam 16:11). In modern anthropological studies of the culture of Mediterranean villages with mixed subsistence economies, cultivation is always more highly regarded than herding, a task consigned to children and the elderly, or to specialists. See Abdulla M. Lutfiyya, *Baytin: A Jordanian*

Village (The Hague: Mouton, 1966), 28, 30; Freeman, *Neighbors*, 175–87 (cf. Job 30:1). This understanding of the work of Cain and Abel is taken by Coote and Ord (*First History*, 68) and to some extent by Sarna (*Genesis*, 32). Coote and Ord, however, add to their interpretation a new version of the old dichotomy: Cain is the archetype of Egyptian sedentary farmers; Abel is the archetype of the Bedouin identity that the Yahwist, according to them, imputes to Israel.

28. This is the kind of folk etymology typical of the Yahwist (see n. 13); it is based on the similarity of sounds between *qayin* (Cain) and *qānâ* ("create") rather than on an actual linguistic relationship between the terms. Cain and "create" stem from different roots, Cain from *qyn*, "create" from *qnh*. On the basis of the Hebrew term *qayin* meaning "spear" in 2 Samuel 21:16 and of cognate evidence connecting the root *qyn* with metal work, commentators have generally linked the name Cain with "smith" or "metalworker" (e.g., BDB, 883–84; Westermann, *Genesis*, 289), but this is not the way in which J understands the meaning of Cain's name. Abel's name, *hebel*, "vapor, breath, unsubstantialness," may point to his insignificance in the story.

29. The parallels between the stories of Adam in Genesis 2:4b–3:24 and of Cain in Genesis 4:1–16 are so numerous and striking that these two accounts appear to be composed as a kind of diptych, two pictures meant to be viewed side by side. Some of the major similarities are surveyed by Westermann (*Genesis 1–11*, 285–86).

30. Exile is a common penalty for an infraction against the norms of behavior expected in a kinship society. See Lutfiyya, *Baytin*, 92–100.

31. For example, Hermann Gunkel, *Genesis* (Göttingen: Vandenhoeck & Ruprecht, 1910) 43, *The Folktale in the Old Testament* (1911; Sheffield: Almond, 1987) 150–51; and J. Maxwell Miller, "The Descendants of Cain: Notes on Genesis 4" *ZAW* 86 (1974) 169–70.

32. See n. 23. J. Maxwell Miller sees two narratives behind the Cain and Abel story, a proshepherd-antifarmer tale (vv 1–8) and an etymology for the Kenites (vv 9–16; 169–70).

33. The relationship between the Yahwistic and Priestly genealogies has been much discussed. See Westermann, *Genesis 1–11*, for a review of the debate (345–62).

34. See for example, Gunkel, *Genesis*, 51; *Folktale*, 151–52; von Rad, *Genesis*, 110–11; and Westermann, *Genesis 1–11*, 324, 330–37. A series of scholars since Rudolf Smend published *Die Erzählung des Hexateuch auf ihre Quellen untersucht* (Berlin: G. Reimer, 1912), 20–22, has attributed Cain's genealogy, in whole or in part, to a separate Pentateuchal source more ancient than J with a pronounced nomadic character, among them Otto Eissfeldt, *The Old Testament: An Introduction* (New York: Harper & Row, 1965) 194–99; and Georg Fohrer, *Introduction to the Old Testament* (Nashville: Abingdon, 1968) 111–12, 159–65, who has identified it as the Nomadic Source Stratum (N).

35. Because the antecedent of the verbs in v 17b is unclear, scholars have disagreed about the actual city builder: was it Cain or his son Enoch? For a summary of the arguments, see Westermann, *Genesis 1–11*, 326–27, who opts in the end for Enoch. Since the Yahwist gives so little attention to the city, the issue of the actual builder does not appear to be crucial to him. Such suggestions regarding the city's name as those made by Westermann (Enoch, from *ḥnk*, "dedicate"; 327) and William W. Hallo (*'īrād*, Enoch's son [v. 18], from Mesopotamian Eridu) in "Antidiluvian Cities," *JCS* 23 (1970) 64, while of legitimate scholarly interest, do not appear to be part of J's concern. When he wished to, as he frequently did, he provided explanations for names.

36. G. Wallis, "Die Stadt in den Überlieferungen der Genesis," *ZAW* 78 (1966)

133–35; Coote and Ord, *First History*, 66–73; and Frank. S. Frick, *The City in Ancient Israel* (Missoula, MT: Scholars, 1977) 205–6.

37. Westermann, *Genesis 1–11*, 327–28; Sarna, *Genesis*, 36; Hallo, "Cities," 64.

38. G. Wallis considers the book of Genesis to be always negative about city culture, which was founded by the first murderer Cain, since early Israel was, in his view, a nomadic, pastoral society ("Die Stadt," 133–48). Cf. Coote and Ord, *First History*, 74–81; Harold Bloom, *Book of J*, 188; and Frick, *The City*, 205–7.

39. Hallo, "Cities," 57–68.

40. Jacobsen, "Eridu Genesis," 519, 526; Hallo, "Cities," 58–60.

41. Jacobsen, "Eridu Genesis," 518. The half-bushel baskets reflect the function of these cities as distribution points for the agricultural produce from the surrounding territory (519).

42. Genesis 5:29 is universally recognized as a Yahwistic text that has been incorporated by the Priestly Writer into his genealogy in Genesis 5.

43. The cryptic phrases describing the occupations of Lamech's sons in vv 20, 21, and 22 have occasioned some consternation and occasional emendation from commentators. While the designations of the occupations are in general clear, the grammar in which they are formulated is difficult at points. Here the terms *ʾōhel ûmiqneh* are probably to be understood as genitives of nearer definition (GKC, 116h, 358).

44. On the modern Bedouin, see Emmanuel Marx, "The Tribe as a Unit of Subsistence: Nomadic Pastoralism in the Middle East," *American Anthropologist* 79 (1977) 343–63. On pastoral nomadism in antiquity, see Lawrence E. Stager, "Archaeology, Ecology, and Social History: Background Themes to the Song of Deborah," *VTSup* 40 (1988) 227–28; and Norman K. Gottwald, *The Tribes of Yahweh* (Maryknoll, NY: Orbis, 1979) 435–63.

45. Cf. NRSV, *NEB*. Most commentators describe the occupation of Tubal-Cain as metalworking in general. See, for example, Sarna, *Genesis*, 38; Westermann, *Genesis 1–11*, 332–333.

46. *lōṭēš* is one who sharpens or hammers metal (e.g., in 1 Sam 13:20 a plowshare, in Ps 7:13 a sword), hence, a "blacksmith." *ḥōrēš* is one who plows (Isa 28:24, Amos 9:13), from a root that the Yahwist also uses for the plowing season, *ḥārîš* (Exod 34:21). For the instrumental use of *nĕḥōšet ûbarzel*, "with bronze and iron (implements)," see GKC, 144m, 461.

47. On the structure and function of the Iron Age plow, see Borowski, *Agriculture*, 48–51; Stager, "Family," 10–11. On metalworking as a specialized occupation in the agricultural villages of early Israel, see Joseph A. Calloway, "A Visit with Ahilud," *BAR* 9, no. 5 (1983) 42–53.

48. The presentation by epic bards of their own occupation in their epic narratives is a common feature of this art form. See, for example, Homer's interest in the blind bard in Book 8 of the Iliad. The Homeric epic was performed to the accompaniment of a stringed instrument held by the singer, as are contemporary Eastern European epic songs; see Albert B. Lord, *The Singer of Tales* (New York: Atheneum, 1976) 13–29. The use of the *kinnôr*, "lyre," for accompanying narrative song in ancient Israel is mentioned in Exodus 15:1 and Judges 5:1, 3; cf. 2 Samuel 6:5, 1 Kings 10:12. The translation of the other instrument attributed to Jubal, the *ʿûgāb*, is uncertain. While some (BDB) have suggested "pipe," following the rendering in the Targum and Vulgate, the parallel use of *ʿûgāb* with *kinnôr* in other biblical texts (Job 21:12, 30:31; cf. Ps 150:4) as here may just as well point to a stringed instrument similar to the *kinnôr*, as the Septuagint and Syriac versions understood it.

49. Cf. Zohary, *Plants*, 26.

50. Franz Delitzsch, *A New Commentary on Genesis*, trans. Sophia Taylor (1888; reprint, Minneapolis: Klock & Klock, 1978) 292–93; Skinner, *Genesis*, 183; Ellis, *Yahwist*, 140–41, 168, 199.

51. This distinction is common: *NEB*: Genesis 9:20, "became drunk;" 48:34, "grow merry;" *JB*: Genesis 9:20, "be drunk;" 43:34, "be happy;" *JPSV*: Genesis 9:20, "become drunk;" 43:34, "drink one's fill."

52. Many commentators subscribe to one version or another of this notion of development in the Yahwist's characterization of early civilization and its agricultural practices. See for example, Westermann, *Genesis 1–11*, 487; von Rad, *Genesis*, 136.

53. A translation Cassuto attributes to Nahmanides (*Commentary*, 159). Cf., for example, Speiser, *Genesis*, 60–61; Coote and Ord, *First History*, 83; NRSV; NEB; JPSV.

54. For the Yahwist's customary expression of "the first to . . ." with the Hiphil of ḥll and a second verb in the infinitive form preceded by the preposition lĕ, see Genesis 4:26, 6:1, 10:8, 11:6; Numbers 25:1. In only one other biblical text is ḥll (Hiphil) linked by the *waw* consecutive to another verb (Ezra 3:8). There too the second verb should not be rendered with the infinitive sense.

55. Thorkild Jacobsen, *The Sumerian King List* (Chicago: University of Chicago, 1939) 55–68, 71–77; ANET, 265.

56. Benvenisti, *West Bank Atlas*, 66–67; Alison Powell, *Food Resources and Food Systems in Two West Bank Villages* (Jerusalem: Arab Thought Forum, 1987) 69; Lawrence E. Stager, "The First Fruits of Civilization," in *Palestine in the Bronze and Iron Ages*, ed. Jonathan N. Tubb (London: Institute of Archaeology, 1985) 176.

57. Cf. Cassuto, *Commentary*, 2.160.

58. The Epic of Gilgamesh, XI. 1–25, translated by E. A. Speiser in *ANET*, 93. The flood story is in fact a global motif, representing in its different versions the various environments of its narrators. See Alan Dundes, ed., *The Flood Myth* (Berkeley: University of California, 1988).

59. A rare word in biblical Hebrew, occurring only here and in Job 36:27, 'ēd is probably related to Akkadian id (Sumerian id), the subterranean fresh water stream; see W. F. Albright, "The Babylonian Matter in the Predeuteronomic Primeval History (JE) in Gen 1–11," *JBL* 58 (1939) 102–3; and P. Kyle McCarter, "The River Ordeal in Israelite Literature," *HTR* 66 (1973) 403–12. The translation "spring," (already adopted by the translators of the Septuagint, Vulgate, and Peshiṭta) is warranted by this comparative evidence and by the description in Genesis itself of the waters rising ('ālā) from the earth (2:6). For a discussion of the issues and alternatives, see Howard N. Wallace, *The Eden Narrative* (Atlanta: Scholars, 1985), 73–74.

60. Cf. Deuteronomy 11:10; Isaiah 27:3; Ezekiel 17:7, 32:6; Joel 4:18; Psalm 104:13; Ecclesiastes 2:6.

61. Skinner, *Genesis*, 62. Many concur with his conclusion "that the resources of philology and scientific geography are well-nigh exhausted . . . and that further advance towards a solution of the problem of Paradise will be along the line of comparative mythology" (65). Cf. Westermann, *Genesis 1–11*, 210–11; Cassuto, *Commentary*, 118; Wallace, *Eden*, 88.

62. For the comparative evidence for the Garden of Eden, with its extraordinary trees and subterranean water source, as a divine dwelling, see Wallace, *Eden*, 70–88. On the residence of the Canaanite God 'El at a water source, see further Frank Moore Cross, *Canaanite Myth and Hebrew Epic* (Cambridge: Harvard University, 1973) 36–39. For comparative Mesopotamian (and Egyptian) data regarding water sources and divinity, see W. F. Albright, "The Mouth of the Rivers," *AJSL* 35(1919) 161–95. The connection of trees and water sources with divinity is broader than

ancient Near Eastern mythology; see Mircea Eliade, *Patterns in Comparative Religion* (New York: New American Library, 1958) 188–215, 265–330, 367–87.

63. W.F. Albright, "The Location of the Garden of Eden," *AJSL* 39 (1922–1923) 17.

64. Useful descriptions and evaluations of the Babylonian theory are provided by Albright ("Eden," 15–18) and Skinner (*Genesis*, 62–66). It has been defended by such scholars as Wellhausen (*Prolegomena*, 308), Gunkel (*Genesis*, 38–39), Stadelmann (*Hebrew Conception*, 11), as well as Speiser in "The Rivers of Paradise," in *Oriental and Biblical Studies*, ed. J. J. Finkelstein and M. Greenberg (Philadelphia: University of Pennsylvania, 1967) 23–34, and *Genesis*, 20; and Richard J. Clifford, *The Cosmic Mountain in the Old Testament* (Cambridge: Harvard University, 1972) 98–103.

65. Albright, "Eden", 18. Anatolia has in fact been adopted by some as an alternative to Mesopotamia for this reason; see Skinner's survey of the Anatolian option on pp. 63–65.

66. Albright, "Eden", 18–24; Cassuto, *Commentary*, I:115–120.

67. Because of Eden's association here with Gîḥôn, Jerusalem's spring, and elsewhere with Mount Zion (e.g., Ezek 28:11–19), Jon Levenson has argued that some in Israel identified the Garden of Eden with Zion and the temple mount; see *Theology of the Program of Restoration of Ezekiel 40–48* (Missoula, Mont.: Scholars, 1976) 25–36, and *Sinai and Zion: An Entry into the Jewish Bible* (San Francisco: Harper & Row, 1985) 127–37.

68. While this verse fits well within the Yahwist's narrative, explaining Lot's choice by referring to preceding and succeeding episodes, it has been dismissed by some as overloaded and full of secondary glosses; see Skinner, *Genesis*, 253; and Claus Westermann, *Genesis 12–36* (Minneapolis, MN: Augsburg, 1985) 177–78.

69. Evidence from studies of plant and pollen remains suggests that the climate and ecological character of the ancient Near East throughout the post-Pleistocene Epoch, that is, the last twelve thousand years, have closely resembled present conditions (Hopkins, *Canaan*, 99–108). Thus the Yahwist's tradition of a radical ecological change occurring in historical times does not conform to the actual ecological history of the Jordan Valley and Dead Sea. In much earlier periods, during the Pleistocene Epoch (the age of the glaciers), the ecology of the ancient Near East varied considerably, alternating between moist rainy periods and dry periods, likely to be correlated with glacial and interglacial periods; see Yohanan Aharoni, *The Archaeology of the Land of Israel* (Philadelphia: Westminster, 1982) 9–11.

70. For a brief description of the ecology of the Nile Valley, see Bruce B. Williams, "Nile (Geography)," *ABD* 4.1112–1116. Cf. Deuteronomy 11:10, which refers to Egypt as an irrigated (*šqh*) garden (*gan*).

71. *gōprît* refers to asphalt found in its natural state. It is highly combustible, as its use for "kindling" in Isaiah 30:33 and its common association with fire (Ezek 38:22; Ps 11:16; Deut 29:22) as here in Genesis 19:24 indicate. In Isaiah 34:9 *gōprît* is paired with *zepet*, an asphalt-based substance used for waterproofing (Exod 2:3). For the presence of natural asphalt deposits near the Dead Sea, see Ephraim Orni and Elisha Efrat, *Geography of Israel*, 4th rev. ed. (Jerusalem: Israel Universities, 1980) 477, 479, 485.

Herein lies further evidence for the common attribution of Genesis 14 to a source outside the major documents of the Tetrateuch, J, E, and P. Chapter 14 at least does not fit properly into the Yahwist's narrative, since the asphalt pits that originate only with the firestorm in Genesis 19 according to the Yahwist, are already present in chapter 14's account of the war in the valley (14:10).

72. Zoar is probably to be identified with modern Sâfî, a large oasis with ample water near the southeast end of the Dead Sea. See Michael C. Astour, "Zoar," *ABD* 6.1107; and Avraham Negev, ed. *The Archaeological Encyclopedia of the Holy Land*, rev. ed. (Nashville: Thomas Nelson, 1986) 412. For a map of the oases of the southern Jordan Valley, see Zohary, *Plants*, 27. Martin Noth recognized these oases as remnants of the "paradisical" ecology that covered the valley floor before the catastrophe: *A History of Pentateuchal Traditions* (Chico, CA: Scholars, 1981) 112.

73. The only suggestion of a possible connection between Eden and the Jordan Valley of which I am aware was made by Jon Levenson in *Ezekiel 40–48*, 32: "the stream of Ezek 47:1–12, which sweetens the Dead Sea, is probably related to another Garden-paradise tradition in Israel, which located the "Garden of YHWH" in the vicinity of Sodom and Gomorrah and believed it was diminished or obliterated in the destruction of those cities (Gen 13:10)."

74. Hopkins, *Canaan*, 213–35.

75. The garden's name, *'ēden*, likely reflects this description of it as a place of abundance and fertility. While *'ēden* has been related to Akkadian *edinu* (Sumerian *eden*), "steppe, plain," it is more likely derived from the West Semitic root *'dn* "luxury, delight"; see A. R. Millard, "The Etymology of Eden," *VT* 34 (1984) 103–6; Howard Wallace, "Eden, Garden of," *ABD* 2.281–82, and *The Eden Narrative*, 84. The name may even carry more specifically the sense of fertility. This appears to be the primary nuance in the Yahwist's use of *'dn* elsewhere to describe Sarah's pregnancy (Gen 18:12). To be compared to this usage are Isaiah 47:8 and possibly the use of *'dn* in an Old Aramaic text from Tell Fekheriyeh in Syria; see A. R. Millard and P. Bordreuil, "A Statue from Syria with Assyrian and Aramaic Inscriptions," *BA* 45 (1982) 135–41. The root *'dn* is also employed in women's names where it appears to mean "fertility"; see Frank Cross's discussion of *'Abi'eden* in "A Report on the Samaria Papyri," *VT Sup* 40 (1986) 23.

76. Stager, "Family," 3–11; Aharoni, *Archaelogy*, 158–59; Israel Finkelstein, *The Archaeology of the Israelite Settlement* (Jerusalem: Israel Exploration Society, 1988). The hill country has been inhabited from earliest times but not as extensively settled as during the early Iron Age.

77. Aharoni, *Archaeology*, 23.

78. The population explosion in the hill country during the early Iron Age results in part in the influx of settlers (Stager, "Family," 3). The source of these settlers is debated: were they pastoralists settling down or urbanites moving to the frontier, or some combination? For a recent survey of varying views, see Finkelstein's, *Archaeology*, 293–314.

79. *miqqedem* means "to the east, eastward," not "from the east," as its usage by the Yahwist in Genesis 13:11 clearly illustrates. The root *qdm* may be used with a chronological sense to refer to the distant past (e.g., Mic 5:1; Isa 45:21), an attractive possibility for a narrative about primeval time; see Wallace, *ABD*, 2.283; Westermann, *Genesis 1–11*, 210–11. Yet when used by the Yahwist in self-evident contexts, its spatial, geographical sense is obvious (Gen 2:14; 13:11). This spatial usage is likely the meaning intended by the term throughout the primeval narratives. Cf. n. 6.

80. Walther Eichrodt has recognized in Ezekiel's vision the idea of the transformation of the world in the age of salvation as a return to the garden of paradise; see *Ezekiel* (Philadelphia: Westminster, 1970) 585. When Ezekiel's vision is taken up by the author of the book of Revelation, the vision of Eden becomes even more strongly Jerusalem centered: the stream and the garden are shifted to the streets of Jerusalem itself (22:1-2).

81. Levenson, *Sinai and Zion*, 116. Many have suggested that Genesis 2:10–14 is a later addition to the Eden narrative. See Westermann, *Genesis 1–11*, 216–19.

82. W. F. Albright, "The Mouth of the Rivers;" Stadelmann, *Hebrew Conception*, 9–10; Exodus 20:4; Deuteronomy 5:8.

83. See n. 67; for *nāhār* as a subterranean flow, see Job 28:11.

84. W. F. Albright, "The Mouth of the Rivers," esp. 172–73. This understanding of *rā'šîm* as the heads or sources of rivers is preferable to the common translation of the term in Genesis 2:10 as "branches" (Cassuto, *Commentary*, I.115; Westermann, *Genesis 1–11*, 216; NRSV, JPSV, *NEB*).

85. Westermann, *Genesis 1–11*, 217: "Neither description [*pîšôn, gîhôn*] is particularly suited to great rivers, but rather to springs like the spring of Gihon in Jerusalem." Cf. Cassuto, *Commentary*, 1.166; Levenson, *Sinai and Zion*, 129, 130. Wallace hints at the foregoing explanation of Eden's waters ("Eden, Garden of," 283).

86. Phyllis Trible, *God and the Rhetoric of Sexuality* (Philadelphia: Fortress, 1978) 72–143; Carol Meyers, *Discovering Eve: Ancient Israelite Women in Context* (New York: Oxford University, 1988) 72–94.

87. Powell, *Food Resources*, 16–17, 40–42, 64–75; Lutfiyya, *Baytin*, 20–35, 145–51; Freeman, *Neighbors*, 175–200.

88. Gunkel, *Genesis*, 11; Westermann, *Genesis 1–11*, 225–29; Skinner: "The naïveté of the conception is extraordinary" (*Genesis*, 67).

89. For the Yahwist's use of "flesh" (*bāśār*) to refer to a kinship relation, see Genesis 29:14, 37:27.

90. The name *hawwâ* derives from the root *hwh*, one of whose meanings was likely "to live" (=*hyh*). For the Phoenician use of *hwh*, "live," see KAI 10.1 and 89:1. The Yahwist, of course, is basing the etymology of *hawwâ* in Genesis 3:20 on the similarity of sound with *hāy*, "the living," not on its linguistic history.

91. Carol Meyers has argued that the prescription for the female role outside Eden focuses on increased work as well as childbearing (*Discovering Eve*, 95–121).

92. I. Engnell, "'Knowledge' and 'Life' in the Creation Story," *VTSup* 3 (1955) 103–19, esp. 110–14, 117–18; Walter Brueggemann, "From Dust to Kingship," *ZAW* 84 (1972) 1–18; Manfred Hutter, "Adam als Gärtner und König (Gen 2, 8. 15)," *Biblische Zeitschrift* 30 (1986) 258–62; Coote and Ord, *First History*, 42–64; Borowski, *Agriculture*, 101, 136. The fact that the figure in Ezekiel 28:12–19, another portrait of Eden, is a king has strongly affected the reading of the Yahwist. For an argument that J's human is not a royal figure, see John Van Seters, "The Creation of Man and the Creation of the King," *ZAW* 101 (1989) 335–341.

93. See the contrast between Yahwistic and Priestly portraits of the human below in the second part of this chapter under the topic "Nature."

94. Cf. Deuteronomy 20:16, Joshua 11:14, 1 Kings 15:29, and the discussion of *nešāmâ* by H. Lamberty-Zielinsi in *TDAT* 5.669–74.

95. The anachronistic and incorrect translation of *nepeš* with "soul" has unfortunately been preserved generally in the New Revised Standard Version, though not in this particular text.

96. See Hermann Gunkel's, *The Folktale in the Old Testament*, 51–54 for other examples of this phenomenon in biblical literature. Howard Eilberg-Schwartz has explored the close relationship between human and animal in Israelite thought by examining the variety of ways in which Israelite society understood itself in terms of the animal world; see "Israel in the Mirror of Nature: Animal Metaphors in the Ritual and Narratives of Ancient Israel," *Journal of Ritual Studies* 2/1 (1988) 1–30.

97. The universe as possessing two realms, the world of the gods and the world

of human beings, is a common formulation for describing ancient cosmologies, discussed recently in relation to the biblical view of nature by Rolf Knierim in "Cosmos and History," *Horizons in Biblical Theology* 3 (1981) 74–80. See Frank Cross's discussion of this conception of the world in Greek and Hebrew epic in "The Epic Traditions of Early Israel: Epic Narrative and the Reconstruction of Early Israelite Institutions," in *The Poet and the Historian: Essays in Literary and Historical Biblical Criticism*, ed. Richard Elliott Friedman (Chico, CA: Scholars, 1983) 13–19.

98. Particularly useful in describing the cosmology of P's creation account, this model is employed for the study of traditional societies by among others Mircea Eliade in *Images and Symbols: Studies in Religious Symbolism* (New York: Sheed and Ward, 1969) 27–56, and for the study of biblical cosmology by Luis I. J. Stadelmann in *The Hebrew Conception of the World*.

99. The conception that immortality could be gained by humans through the consumption of a concrete substance is widespread in the ancient Near East. The plant Gilgamesh failed to gain possession of (XI.263–91; *ANET*, 96) and the bread and water of life offered to Adapa (I. 60–70; *ANET*, 102) are examples. See H. and H. A. Frankfort's comments in *Before Philosophy* (New York: Penguin, 1949) 23. For the conception of immortality in this text, see James Barr, *The Garden of Eden and the Hope of Immortality* (London: SCM, 1992) 1–20.

100. This is illustrated in J by the fact that God can name humans (Gen 32:28–29 [Eng. vv 27–28]) but that humans can also name God (Gen 16:13). On the topic of naming in this text see George W. Ramsey, "Is Name-Giving an Act of Domination in Genesis 2:23 and Elsewhere?" *CBQ* 50 (1988) 24–35.

101. J's phrase "one flesh" (*bāśār 'eḥād*, 2:24) probably refers both to sexual union and to a kinship alliance since J uses the term *bāśār* elsewhere for relations between kin (Gen 29:14; 37:27).

102. Mary Douglas, *Purity and Danger* (London: Routledge and Kegan Paul, 1966) 41–57; Howard Eilberg-Schwartz, "Creation and Classification in Judaism: From Priestly to Rabbinic Conceptions," *History of Religions* 26(1986/87) 357–81; Robert B. Coote and David Robert Ord, *In the Beginning* (Minneapolis: Augsburg Fortress, 1991) 57–66.

103. See Westermann's survey of the proponents of this interpretation of humans bearing the image of God in *Genesis 1–11*, 151–55, as well as alternatives (147–58); and Phyllis A. Bird, "'Male and Female He Created Them': Gen 1:27b in the Context of the Priestly Account of Creation," *HTR* 74 (1981) 129–59.

104. Gerhard von Rad, *The Problem of the Hexateuch and Other Essays* (London: SCM, 1984) 64.

105. Westermann, *Genesis 1–11*, 47–56, 66–67. Cf. John Van Seters, *Prologue to History: The Yahwist as Historian in Genesis* (Louisville, KY: Westminster/John Knox, 1992) 189–91.

106. Gerhard von Rad regards these pronouncements as "the real goal and climax toward which the narrative is directed in its present form" (*Genesis*, 92). Westermann takes a different position (*Genesis 1–11*, 257).

107. Jacobsen, "Eridu Genesis," 526.

108. William L. Moran, "Atrahasis: The Babylon Story of the Flood," *Biblica* 52 (1971) 51–61. Cf. Anne Kilmer, "The Mesopotamian Concept of Overpopulation and Its Solution as Reflected in the Mythology," *Orientalia* 41 (1972) 160–77; and Tikva Frymer-Kensky, "The Atrahasis Epic and Its Significance for Our Understanding of Genesis 1–9," *BA* 40 (1977) 147–55.

109. Moran, "Atrahasis," 56–59.

110. Bird finds the phrase "male and female he created them" (Gen 1:27b) to be concerned neither with the nature of the image of God nor with the roles of men and women in society, but rather with human reproduction ("Male and Female"). Frymer-Kensky contrasts this Priestly ideology of population in the primeval narrative with the opposite view in Atrahasis ("The Atrahasis Epic").

111. For instance, Westermann, *Genesis 1–11*, 397.

112. The Baal Cycle is translated in *ANET*, 129–42. See also the translation by Michael Coogan in *Stories From Ancient Canaan* (Philadelphia: Westminster, 1978) 86–115 and his discussion of Baal as a storm god on pp. 75–85. On Yahweh and Baal as storm deities, see Frank Cross's essay "Yahweh and Ba'l" in *Canaanite Myth and Hebrew Epic*, 145–94.

113. For summaries of the gift theory of sacrifice see Gary A. Anderson, "Sacrifice and Sacrificial Offerings (OT)" *ABD* 5.871–72; and Joseph Henninger, "Sacrifice," *ER* 12.544–57, esp. 550–51.

114. On the understanding of the *minḥâ* "offering," as a gift, see Anderson, "Sacrifice," 873–75. The Priestly Writer used *minḥâ* with the more specific meaning, "cereal offering."

115. W. G. Lambert and A. R. Millard, *Atra-Ḥasīs: The Babylonian Story of the Flood* (Oxford: Clarendon, 1969) 8–9, 12, 15.

116. Atrahasis, III.v.30–41. Cf. The Epic of Gilgamesh, XI.155–61. Scholars have ordinarily been scandalized by this parallel: see Westermann, *Genesis 1–11*, 454; and Alexander Heidel, *The Gilgamesh Epic and Old Testament Parallels* (Chicago: University of Chicago, 1946) 256.

117. That J conceived of sacrifice as feeding the deity is accepted by Wellhausen (*Prolegomena*, 62). Cf. Anderson, 872–78.

118. A. M. Khazanov, *Nomads and the Outside World* (Cambridge: Cambridge University, 1984) 85–86.

119. Wellhausen, *Prolegomena*, 315.

120. Ibid., 314; Gunkel, *Legends*, 13.

121. George Coats, *Genesis* (Grand Rapids, MI: Eerdmans, 1983) 35. Cf. Yehezkel Kaufmann's assessment of the primeval narrative: "The Hebrews . . . did not extend Israel's past to primordial times. Neither the people, its religion, nor its cities and temples are represented as primeval. The Babylonian antediluvian kings became, in accord with Israelite conceptions, 'patriarchs.' These 'patriarchs,' however, are not the ancestors of Israel, but of mankind." Kaufmann, *The Religion of Israel* (New York: Schocken, 1960) 200–1.

122. See for example, Noth, *Pentateuchal Traditions*, 237; Westermann, *Genesis 1–11*, 4; Walter Brueggemann, "Genesis," in *Books of the Bible*, ed. Bernhard Anderson (New York: Charles Scribner's Sons, 1989) 30. O. H. Steck's treatment of J's primeval world recognizes the particularity of it but still employs heavily the language of universal humanity (*World*, 64–80).

123. See, for example, W. G. Lambert, "The Babylonian Background of Genesis," *JTS* 14 (1965) 287–300; Sigmund Mowinckel, "The Babylonian Matter in the Predeuteronomic Primeval History (JE) in Gen 1–11," *JBL* 58 (1939) 87–91, and William F. Albright's response, 91–103; and Heidel, *Gilgamesh,* 224–69.

124. von Rad, *Hexateuch*, 63–67. Cf. Westermann, *Genesis 1–11*, 2.

125. Gunkel, *Legends*, 14.

126. Wellhausen already saw this distinction (*Prolegomena*, 314). Westermann considers time in the primeval era as distinct from historical time in which events happen only once (*Genesis 1–11*, 4, 9). Cf. Isaac M. Kikawada, "Primeval History,"

ABD 5.462; and Richard M. Maze, "In the Beginning: Myth and History in Genesis and Exodus," *JBL* 109 (1990) 577–98.

127. Gunkel, *Legends*, 13–18. Cf. Brevard S. Childs, *Myth and Reality in the Old Testament* (London: SCM, 1960) 15; and Kees W. Bolle, "Myth: An Overview," *ER* 10. 261.

128. Childs, *Myth and Reality*, 16–29; Robert A. Oden, Jr., "Myth and Mythology," *ABD* 4.948–49; Bolle, "Myth," 261; Paul Ricoeur, "Myth," 273.

129. Eliade, *Myth and Reality* (New York: Harper, 1963) 5–6.

130. Childs, *Myth and Reality*; Ricoeur, "Myth," 281.

131. John Van Seters, *Prologue to History*, 1–44. Having identified J's work as "antiquarian historiography," Van Seters continues to use the terms "myth," "history," "demythologizing," and "historicizing" in a manner that reintroduces the problems he is rightly attempting to clarify. Cf. Meir Sternberg's treatment of biblical narrative as "historiography" in *The Poetics of Biblical Narrative* (Bloomington, IN: Indiana University, 1985) 23–34.

132. Frank M. Cross, "The Epic Traditions of Early Israel," 18.

133. Westermann's treatment of *Genesis 1–11* in a separate volume in his three-volume commentary on Genesis is paradigmatic of biblical scholarship. The two scholars who have gone the furthest toward recognizing the epoch-making status of the flood, but without accepting its definitive position in the end, are Malcolm Clark, "The Flood and the Structure of the Pre-Patriarchal History," *ZAW* 83 (1971) 204–10; and Rolf Rendtorff, "Genesis 8,21 und die Urgeschichte des Jahwisten," *Kerygma und Dogma* 7 (1961) 69–71.

134. On the putative exception to this, the Cain-Kenite hypothesis, see the discussion of the Cain and Abel story at the beginning of this chapter.

135. *ANET*, 265.

136. Moran, "Atrahasis," 56–61.

137. Gunkel (*Legends*, 123–44) and his form-critical heirs have always seen J as a collector rather than an author, bringing together disparate, independent tales in his narrative. Cf. von Rad, *Hexateuch*, 64. Some who have taken a more unified approach to the primeval narrative include David Damrosch, *The Narrative Covenant*, 88–143; Kikawada, "Primeval History," *ABD* 5.461–66; and Tikva Frymer-Kensky, "The Atrahasis Epic and Its Significance for our Understanding of Genesis 1-9," in *The Flood Myth*, ed. Alan Dundes (Berkeley: University of California, 1988) 61–73.

Chapter 3

1. Julius Wellhausen, *Prolegomena to the History of Ancient Israel* (1883; New York: Meridian Books, 1957) 7.

2. Harold Bloom, *The Book of J* (New York: Grove Weidenfeld, 1990) 32.

3. Peter Ellis, *The Yahwist: The Bible's First Theologian* (Collegeville, MN: Liturgical Press, 1968) 33.

4. Gerhard von Rad, *The Problem of the Hexateuch and Other Essays* (1938; London, SCM, 1966) 62.

5. Martin Noth, *A History of Pentateuchal Traditions* (1948; Chico, CA: Scholars, 1981) 46–62; Claus Westermann, *Genesis 1–11: A Commentary* (Minneapolis: Augsburg, 1984) 2; Ellis, *Yahwist*, 181; Robert Coote and David Ord, *The Bible's First History* (Philadelphia: Fortress, 1989) 9–10; John Van Seters, *Prologue to History: The Yahwist as Historian in Genesis* (Louisville, KY: Westminster/John Knox, 1992), 331 (note the title of the book).

6. von Rad, *Hexateuch*, 1–78.

7. Albrecht Alt, "The Settlement of the Israelites in Palestine" (orig. pub. 1925) and "The God of the Fathers" (orig. pub. 1929), trans. R. A. Wilson, in *Essays in Old Testament History and Religion* (Garden City, NY: Doubleday, 1968) 1–100, 173–221.

8. See the discussion of "Reexamining Presuppositions: The Desert versus the Sown" in chapter 1.

9. von Rad, *Hexateuch*, 57; Noth, *Pentateuchal Traditions*, 55; and *The History of Israel* (New York: Harper & Row, 1958) 53–84, 121–27.

10. Wellhausen, *Prolegomena*, 320. Cf. Yehezkel Kaufmann, *The Religion of Israel* (New York: Schocken Books, 1960) 170, 201; Roland de Vaux, *Ancient Israel* (New York: McGraw-Hill, 1961) 1–15.

11. W. F. Albright, "Abram the Hebrew: A New Archaeological Interpretation," *BASOR* 163 (1961) 36–54, and *Yahweh and the Gods of Canaan* (1968; Reprint: Winona Lake, IN: Eisenbrauns) 64–73; C. H. Gordon, "Abraham and the Merchants of Ura," *JNES* 17 (1958) 28–31, and "Abraham of Ur," in *Hebrew and Semitic Studies Presented to Godfrey Rolles Driver*, ed. D. W. Thomas and W. D. McHurdy (Oxford: Oxford University, 1963) 77–84.

12. Coote and Ord, *First History*, esp. pp. 15–41, 100–101, 201–30.

13. M. B. Rowton has explored the topic in more than a dozen articles in various journals. The best basic presentation is in "Enclosed Nomadism," *Journal of the Economic and Social History of the Orient* 17 (1974) 1–30. See also "Dimorphic Structure and Typology," *Oriens Antiquus* 15 (1976) 17–31 (a bibliography of his own work is provided on p. 17, n. 4). J. T. Luke, "Pastoralism and Politics at Mari in the Mari Period," (Ph.D. diss, University of Michigan, 1965). Victor H. Matthews, *Pastoral Nomadism in the Mari Kingdom, ca. 1830-1760 B.C.* (Cambridge, MA: American Schools of Oriental Research, 1978).

14. M. B. Rowton, "Dimorphic Structure and the Parasocial Element," *JNES* 36 (1977) 187–98; V. H. Matthews, "Pastoralists and Patriarchs," *BA* 44 (1981) 215–18; "The Wells of Gerar," *BA* 49 (1986) 118–26; J. T. Luke, "Pastoralism and Politics at Mari."

15. William J. Dever, "The Patriarchal Traditions. Palestine in the Second Millennium B.C.E.: The Archaeological Picture," in *Israelite and Judean History*, ed. John H. Hayes and J. Maxwell Miller (London: SCM, 1977) 70–119, and "Pastoralism and the End of the Urban Early Bronze Age in Palestine," in *Pastoralism in the Levant: Archaeological Materials in Anthropological Perspectives*, ed. Ofer Bar-Yosef and Anatoly Khazanov (Madison, WI: Prehistory, 1992) 83–92; C. Westermann, *Genesis 12–36: A Commentary* (Minneapolis: Augsburg, 1985) 74–79; cf. John Bright, *A History of Israel*, 3rd ed. (Philadelphia: Westminster, 1981) 80–83.

16. Both John Van Seters, *Abraham in History and Tradition* (New Haven: Yale University, 1975) 13–38 and Norman K. Gottwald, *The Tribes of Yahweh: A Sociology of the Religion of Liberated Israel 1250–1050 B.C.E.* (Maryknoll, NY: Orbis, 1979) 435–63, esp. 451–53, have criticized traditional notions of Israel's ancestors as pastoral nomads.

17. For J's use of the theme, see Genesis 12:1, 6–7; 13:14–17; 15:7–21; 24:7; 26:2–5; 28:13–16; 31:3; 32:10; Exodus 3:8, 16–17; 13:4–5, 11; 33:1–3a; Numbers 11:12; 14:23. For the Elohist, divine land grant is not a major concern, being mentioned only twice (Gen 50:24, Exod 32:13), the latter possibly a J interpolation into an E story. The Priestly Writer employs the theme, but with a lower profile and in language characteristic of P: Genesis 17:8; 35:12; 48:4; Exodus 6:4 (cf Lev 25:2, 23–24; Num 31:11). The Deuteronomistic Historian, of course, also gives this theme

prominence, casting it in his own distinctive language and placing it in the speeches of his major characters (e.g., Deut 1:7–8; 6:10–11; 30:20; Josh 1:6).

18. Twice J uses 'ǎdāmâ in the ancestral narratives within the expression mišpĕḥōt hā 'ǎdāmâ, "clans of the arable land," when he is describing the blessings Abraham and his descendants will contribute to those with whom they come into contact (Gen 12:3, 28:14). By this designation J likely has in mind the typical rural neighborhood made up of a village and its agricultural environs, as described by N. K. Gottwald (Tribes of Yahweh, 316) and Lawrence E. Stager, "The Archaeology of the Family in Ancient Israel," BASOR 260 (1985) 22. When speaking of larger national entities in such blessing contexts, J employs the alternative, gôyê hā 'āreṣ, "nations of the land," (Gen 18:18; 22:18; 26:4). Only twice elsewhere does J employ 'ǎdāmâ before the ancestors move to Egypt, once to identify the soil to which Jacob will return from Syria (28:15; possibly because of its mention in the phrase mišpĕḥōt hā 'ǎdāmâ in the previous verse, 28:14), and once to describe the devastation of the arable land in the Jordan Valley in the Sodom and Gomorrah narratives (Gen 19:25); see the discussion of this event in chapter 2.

19. See the analysis of 'ǎdāmâ and 'ereṣ in the discussion of "Adam and Eve" in chapter 2.

20. For analysis of the gēr as resident alien, see Lawrence E. Stager, "Archaeology, Ecology, and Social History: Background Themes to the Song of Deborah," VTSup 40 (1988) 229–32.

21. On the relationship of the designation bêt 'āb, "house of the father/household," to the actual structure of the family compound in the Israelite village, see Stager, "Family," 18–23.

22. Such an idiomatic sense appears to be present in a text like 1 Kings 12:16 where the phrase "To your tents, O Israel" (lĕ 'ōhālêkā yiśrā 'ēl) must be understood as "Back to your homes." The northerners at this audience with Rehoboam in Jerusalem were not nomadic pastoralists.

23. Gottwald, Tribes of Yahweh, 440–41.

24. See, for example, Rowton's "Dimorphic Structure and Typology," and "Dimorphic Structure and the Problem of the 'Apirû- 'Ibrîm," JNES 35 (1976) 13–20.

25. The couplet "the dew of the skies/the plenty of the earth" (ṭal haššāmayim/ šĕmannê hā 'āreṣ) is an archaic formula present also in Ugaritic literature. See Stanley Gevirtz, Patterns in the Early Poetry of Israel (Chicago: University of Chicago, 1963) 35–47.

26. Westermann: "It is a blessing typical of agricultural civilization" (Genesis 12–36, 441). Commentators are generally in agreement that Isaac's subsequent "blessing" on Esau deprives him of these same agricultural bounties (27:39), though the style is awkward. See Westermann, Genesis 12–36, 443; E. A. Speiser, Genesis AB (Garden City, NY: Doubleday, 1964) 210; and Gerhard von Rad, Genesis (Philadelphia: Westminster, 1972) 279. Edomite terrain is certainly less conducive to agriculture than the hill country west of the Jordan.

27. leḥem, common bread, is the usual term used in these contexts, though 'ūgôt, "cakes" (18:6), and maṣṣôt, "unleavened bread" (19:3), are also mentioned.

28. On this crop, see Michael Zohary, Plants of the Bible (Cambridge: Cambridge University, 1982) 82; and Oded Borowski, Agriculture in Iron Age Israel (Winona Lake, IN: Eisenbrauns, 1987) 94–95.

29. Genesis 49:2–27 is clearly an archaic poetic composition that has been incorporated by J. See F. M. Cross and D. N. Freedman, Studies in Ancient Yahwistic Poetry (Missoula, MT: Scholars, 1975) 69–93.

30. Almonds, another hill country tree crop, were also cultivated (or their fruit gathered) by Israel's ancestors (Gen 30:37; 43:11).

31. Salo (Shlomo) Hellwing, and Yitzhak Adjeman, "Animal Bones," in Israel Finkelstein's *'Izbet Ṣarṭah: An Early Iron Age Site Near Rosh Ha'ayin*, (Oxford: B.A.R., 1986) 141–52. This article also includes data from Beer-Sheba, Tell-Masos, Shiloh, Lachish, and Tell Michal (151). Melinda Zeder, "Animal Exploitation at Tell Halif," in *Preliminary Reports of ASOR-Sponsored Excavations, 1983–87*, ed. Walter E. Rast (Baltimore: Johns Hopkins University, 1990) 24–29. Lawrence T. Geraty and Øystein S. LaBianca, "The Local Environment and Human Food-Procuring Strategies in Jordan: The Case of Tell Hesbon and Its Surrounding Region" in *Studies in the History and Archaeology of Jordan II*, ed. Adnan Hadidi (Amman: Department of Antiquities, 1985) 323–30. The same pattern of animal populations can also be observed in the recent mixed agricultural economy of the West Bank: see Israel Finkelstein, *The Archaeology of the Israelite Settlement* (Jerusalem: Israel Exploration Society, 1988) 129–39 for data from the early 1970s. Note that the sedentary Shechemites (Gen 34:28) own the same animals as Israel's ancestors (flocks, herds, donkeys).

32. See also Genesis 13:15; 24:35; 32:6, 18; 33:13; 46:32; 47:1. The only exception is Genesis 32:6.

33. See also Genesis 30:43. Once donkeys (32:6) and once camels (32:18) appear earlier in the list.

34. Geraty and LaBianca, "Food-Procuring Strategies," 325–27; Paula Wapnish and Brian Hesse, "Urbanization and the Organization of Animal Production at Tell Jemmeh in the Middle Bronze Age Levant," *JNES* 47 (1988) 88; Volkmar Fritz, "The Israelite 'Conquest' in Light of Recent Excavations at Khirbet el-Meshâsh," *BASOR* 241 (1981) 70–71; Abdulla M. Lutfiyya, *Baytin: A Jordanian Village* (The Hague: Mouton, 1966) 115, 119. Both Gottwald (*Tribes of Yahweh*, 452) and Van Seters (*Abraham*, 16) have called attention to the ancestors' cattle as an indication of a sedentary existence. Westermann tries to get around this data and preserve his view of the ancestors as seminomadic pastoralists by calling the references to cattle by J "interpolations from a later perspective" and claiming that "the mention of cattle is a rare exception" (*Genesis 12–36*, 76–77); both assertions are undermined by J's frequent and patterned references to cattle.

35. David C. Hopkins, *The Highlands of Canaan: Agricultural Life in the Early Iron Age* (Decatur, GA: Almond, 1985) 245–50.

36. A. M. Khazanov, *Nomads and the Outside World* (Cambridge: Cambridge University, 1984) 16–18; Lutfiyya, *Baytin*, 30, 119–21; Susan Tax Freeman, *Neighbors: The Social Contract in a Castilian Hamlet* (Chicago: University of Chicago, 1970) 175–87. Gottwald notes this implication of the ancestors' specialized herders (445–46; 452–53) as does Van Seters (*Abraham*, 16, 18) who calls attention to parallels with Nabal in 1 Samuel 25.

37. Lutfiyya, *Baytin*, 28–34; Freeman, *Neighbors*, 175–87.

38. Coote and Ord, *First History*, 15–16, 197; Westermann, *Genesis 37–50: A Commentary* (Minneapolis: Augsburg, 1986) 167–70; Matthews, "Pastoralists," 217.

39. Hermann Gunkel, *Genesis* (Göttingen: Vandenhoeck & Ruprecht, 1910) 464, and before him B. D. Eerdmans, *Komposition der Genesis* (Giessen: A. Töpelmann, 1908) 42, both noticed this implication of Joseph's instructions. Cf. John Skinner, *Genesis* (Edinburgh: T & T Clark, 1930) 495–96. It should be noted that cattle, draft animals for sedentary farmers, are among the ancestors' herds (46:32; 47:1).

40. Meron Benvenisti, *West Bank and Gaza Atlas* (Jerusalem: West Bank Data Base Project; Boulder: Westview Press, 1988) 67–68; Stager, "Family," 17.

41. Nabal (1 Samuel 25) provides a good example. A wealthy southern sedentary farmer (v 2) Nabal cultivated grain, vineyards, and figs (v 18), yet his wealth is first illustrated by the size of his herds (v 2).

42. For instance, Westermann, *Genesis 12–36*, 78, 162, 172, 309; von Rad, *Genesis*, 171; de Vaux, *Ancient Israel*, 3–15.

43. Emmanuel Marx, "The Tribe as a Unit of Subsistence: Nomadic Pastoralism in the Middle East," *American Anthropologist* 79 (1977) 343–63.

44. For analysis of the patriarchal narratives as a reflection of tenth-century realities and Israel's self-understanding in this period, see Benjamin Mazar, "The Historical Background of the Book of Genesis," *JNES* 28 (1969) 73–83; and P. Kyle McCarter "The Patriarchal Age: Abraham, Isaac and Jacob," in *Ancient Israel*, ed. Hershel Shanks (Englewood Cliffs, NJ: Prentice-Hall, 1988) 1–29.

45. Wellhausen, *Prolegomena*, p. 334, n.1.

46. The Elohist carries the more detailed account of this border treaty: Genesis 31:43–48, 50–54.

47. Genesis 12:10–20 represents the entire Egypt experience *in nuce*. Abraham moves to Egypt because of a famine in Canaan, becomes wealthy there but runs afoul of the Pharaoh who, after a series of plagues, sends Abraham from Egypt back to the land of Canaan. Baruch Halpern refers to 12:10–20 as "a doublet for the exodus"; see *The Emergence of Israel in Canaan* (Chico, CA: Scholars, 1983) 25.

48. In the Elohist source, the entire Gerar narrative is narrated with Abraham as the hero: Genesis 20:1–17, 21:22–31.

49. Bright, *History*, 87–92.

50. See P. Kyle McCarter's critique in "The Patriarchal Age," 6–11. For a critique of the traditional Amorite hypothesis see also Dever, "Pastoralism," 83–92.

51. McCarter, "Patriarchal Age," 19, 21. Fredrik Barth, ed. *Ethnic Groups and Boundaries* (Boston: Little, Brown, 1969) contains further discussions of this phenomenon.

52. Genesis 9:18–27; 10:15–19, 12:6; 13:7; 15:19–21; 24:3, 35, etc.

53. Gottwald, *Tribes of Yahweh*, 451–53.

54. Westermann, *Genesis 1–11*, 1–2.

55. Speiser, *Genesis*, liii, 87.

56. Walter Brueggemann, *Genesis* (Atlanta: John Knox, 1982) 105.

57. For a brief summary of the *Heilsgeschichte* movement in biblical theology, see Gerhard Hasel, *Old Testament Theology: Basic Issues in the Current Debate* (Grand Rapids, MI: Eerdmans, 1972) 29–47. Cf. Henning Graf Reventlow's remarks in his recent article "Theology (Biblical), History of," *ABD* 6. 497–98.

58. von Rad, *Hexateuch*, 65–67. Cf. John Bright's claim in his *A History of Israel*: "As the Bible presents it, the history of Israel began with the migration of the Hebrew patriarchs from Mesopotamia to their new homeland in Palestine" (23).

59. Perhaps the premier figure in this endeavor was W. F. Albright, who addressed this issue in many of his writings. See, for example, *The Biblical Period from Abraham to Ezra* (1949; New York: Harper & Row, 1963) 1–9, and *Yahweh and the Gods of Canaan*, 53–109. A good survey of the major scholarly positions that have been taken may be found in William Dever's "The Patriarchal Traditions," 70–119. Among those who have reopened the discussion in recent years are T. L. Thompson, *The Historicity of the Patriarchal Narratives* (Berlin: W. de Gruyter, 1974); and John Van Seters, *Abraham in History and Tradition*. P. Kyle McCarter's recent article represents a summary and critique of scholarly effort in this endeavor.

60. See the discussion of "Myth versus History" in chapter 2.

61. Kurt Galling, *Die Erwählungstraditionen Israels* (Giessen: A. Töpelmann, 1928) 56; cf. von Rad, *Genesis*, 166. The history of scholarship on the promises to the patriarchs has been summarized recently by John Van Seters, *Prologue to History*, 215–26. J's treatment of the promise theme has been summarized by Norman Habel, *Literary Criticism of the Old Testament* (Philadelphia: Fortress, 1971) 43–64.

62. J's promise texts include Genesis 9:26–27; 12:1–3, 7; 13:14–17; 15:5, 18–21; 18:17–19; 22:16–18; 26:2–5, 24; 28:13–15.

63. On *gôy* as "nation," see E. A. Speiser, "'People' and 'Nation' of Israel," *JBL* 79 (1960) 157–63.

64. Cf. 1 Kings 5:1. Frank Moore Cross, *Canaanite Myth and Hebrew Epic* (Cambridge: Harvard University, 1973) 262–63.

65. Lutfiyya, *Baytin*, 102.

66. Vv 7 and 14 both refer to the spring at which this divine annunciation took place to provide the tale with a literary *inclusio*. While J had a specific oasis in mind (note: "*the* spring," *hā'ayin*), it is no longer possible on the basis of J's explanations to locate it precisely. David R. Seely, "Shur, Wilderness of," *ABD* 5.1230; Dale W. Manor, "Kadesh-Barnea," *ABD* 4.1–3; Rudolph Cohen, "Did I excavate Kadesh-Barnea?" *BAR* 7.3 (1981) 20–33.

67. On the stereotypes of marginal populations, see Fredrik Barth, *Ethnic Groups and Boundaries* (Boston: Little, Brown, 1969) 30–32. Cf. Freeman, *Neighbors*, 179–80, 201–204. *'al-pĕnê*, "in front of," may mean here "east of," which it usually does (BDB, 818), thus referring to the deserts east of biblical Israel.

68. In the Elohist's version of Ishmael's origins (Gen 21:8–21), a doublet of J's account in Genesis 16, the child Ishmael and his mother are actually expelled to the desert and take up residence there.

69. Hermann Gunkel, *The Legends of Genesis* (New York: Schocken, 1964) 34, and *Genesis*, 214–17.

70. Efraim Orni and Elisha Efrat, *Geography of Israel* (Jerusalem: Israel Universities, 1980) 31; J. R. Bartlett, "Edom," *ABD* 2.287.

71. BDB, 973; Ernst Axel Knauf, "Seir," *ABD* 5.1072–73.

72. Speiser, *Genesis*, 196; cf. Gunkel, *Genesis*, 297–99.

73. Khazanov, *Nomads*, 85–90.

74. Westermann, *Genesis 12–26*, 417, cf. pp. 414–15. See V. Maag, "Jakob-Esau-Edom," *Theologische Zeitschrift* 13 (1957) 418–29. The same dichotomy is presumed by Gunkel (*Genesis*, 297–99), Skinner (*Genesis*, 361), and von Rad (*Genesis*, 265–66) to cite just three examples.

75. Hellwing and Adjeman, "Animal Bones," 141–52; Zeder, *Animal Exploitation*, 24–31.

76. The Hebrew syntax of v 39 is somewhat awkward, but the sense is clear.

77. Reading *kaptōrîm* before *'ăšer* in Genesis 10:14 (cf. Amos 9:7). On the Philistines see Lawrence E. Stager, *Ashkelon Discovered* (Washington, DC: Biblical Archaeology Society, 1991) 2–19, and "Merneptah, Israel, and the Sea Peoples: New Light on an Old Relief," *Eretz-Israel* 18 (1985) 61–62. Compare Trude Dothan, "The Arrival of the Sea Peoples: Cultural Diversity in Early Iron Age Canaan," and Moshe Dothan, "Archaeological Evidence for Movements of the Early 'Sea Peoples' in Canaan," in *Recent Excavations in Israel: Studies in Iron Age Archaeology*, Annual of the American Schools of Oriental Research 49, ed. Seymour Gitin and William J. Dever (Winona Lake, IN: Eisenbrauns, 1989) 1–22, 59–70; and Trude Dothan, *The Philistines and Their Material Culture* (New Haven: Yale University, 1982).

78. Albrecht Alt, "The God of the Fathers." For a brief summary of commen-

tary since Alt on the religion of Israel's ancestors, see Westermann, *Genesis 12–36*, 105–108, 113–21.

79. Alt, "The God of the Fathers," 10–11; *'ēl bêt-'ēl*, Genesis 31:13 (E), 35:7 (E); *'ēl 'ôlām*, Genesis 21:33 (J); *'ēl rŏ'î*, Genesis 16:13 (J).

80. Alt, "The God of the Fathers," 54–55. On the basis of this dichotomy between a sedentary, natural religion and a nomadic, historical one, Alt saw a distinction in J's promise theology between the guarantee of land, a theme of a sedentary, natural religion, and the guarantee of descendants, a theme of a nomadic, historical religion (84). A more nuanced but similar dichotomy is present in Westermann's treatment of promise (Westermann, *Genesis 12–36*, 111–12).

81. Alt, "The God of the Fathers," 79.

82. Noth, *Pentateuchal Traditions*, 55; cf. von Rad, *Hexateuch*, 57; *Genesis*, 21–23.

83. Westermann, *Genesis 12–36*, 105–13, 575–76.

84. See "Reexamining Presuppositions: The Desert versus the Sown," in chapter 1.

85. Cross, *Canaanite Myth and Hebrew Epic*, 3–43; cf. 44–75.

86. The Niphal of *rā'â* employed with reflexive force, an interpretation dictated by the related prepositional phrase *'el-'abrām*, "to Abram," and by the theophanic context.

87. For example, Wellhausen, *Prolegomena*, 325; Gunkel, *Legends*, 27–34; Skinner, *Genesis*, 246–47. Claus Westermann unfortunately rejects this traditional interpretation, arguing that these religious centers do not include a temple, the cultic characteristic of sedentary societies, and must therefore only represent the once holy sites of small wandering groups (110–11, 153–57). The patriarchs are therefore not cult founders in his view. Since the Yahwist source is fundamentally etiological, this nonetiological reading is problematic from the start.

88. For *māqôm* as sanctuary, see BDB, 880; Skinner, *Genesis*, 246.

89. For instance, Wellhausen, *Prolegomena*, p. 31 n. 1; U. Cassuto, *A Commentary on the Book of Genesis, II* (1949. Jerusalem: Magnes Press, 1964) 324; Speiser, *Genesis*, 86; Westermann, *Genesis 12–36*, 154.

90. In the case of Bethel, the sanctuary Abraham establishes does appear to be located on a mountain outside the city to the east (12:8). In the case of Shechem, Hebron, and Beersheba, the holy sites are the cultic centers of the cities themselves.

91. In a few additional cases, the Yahwist does not specify the location of the divine appearance or audition in relation to a natural feature (12:1; 25:21–22; 31:3).

92. For *'ēlôn* as oak (Quercus), not terebinth (Pistacia), see Zohary, *Plants*, 108–11, who differs in this respect from older interpretations (e.g., BDB, 18).

93. While J regards trees as a legitimate medium of divine revelation, other biblical authors such as Hosea (4:13) associate them with apostasy (cf. 1 Kings 17:10). Whether these are criticisms of non-Yahwistic worship at these sites or of the sites themselves is difficult to tell.

94. Zohary, *Plants*, 108, 110.

95. *môrĕh*, as the Hiphil participle of *yārâ*, "teach, instruct," is employed here in customary attributive fashion: "The teaching oak." On the other hand, the possibility that J is actually connecting *môrĕh* with *rā'â*, "see," as Cassuto has suggested (*Commentary*, 327), is very good, since it is usual for J to employ folk etymologies that rely on similar sounds rather than genuine linguistic derivations. J may also connect the name of the oak at Hebron, *mamrē'*, with the verb *rā'â* (and divine revelation), as the occurrence of these terms together in Genesis 18:1 might suggest.

The genuine etymology of *mamrē'* may be impenetrable. For two attempts to unravel its actual derivation, see Yoël L. Arbeitman, "Mamre," *ABD* 4.492–93; and E. Lipiński, "'Anaq-Kiryat 'Arba'-Hébron et ses sanctuaires tribaux," *VT* 24 (1974) 41–55.

96. Zohary, *Plants*, 115. The tamarisk at Beersheba was planted by Abraham (Gen 21:33).

97. On the mountain and its significance in Israel and the ancient Near East, see Richard J. Clifford, *The Cosmic Mountain in Canaan and the Old Testament* (Cambridge: Harvard University, 1972); Shemaryahu Talmon, "*har, gibh'āh*," *TDOT*, III, 427–47; Robert L. Cohn, *The Shape of Sacred Space: Four Biblical Studies* (Chico, CA: Scholars, 1981) 25–41; Jon D. Levenson, *Sinai and Zion: An Entry into the Jewish Bible* (San Francisco: Harper & Row, 1985). Cf. Diana Eck, "Mountains," *ER* 10.130–34.

98. The mountain on which Abraham bound Isaac and encountered God (Gen 22:1–14a), which figures prominently in the Elohist's traditions, is also believed by J to be a site of divine revelation, as his reference to this story indicates (22:14b–19).

99. The Jabbok is the modern Wadi Zerqa (*Nahr ez-Zerqa*), the northern boundary, according to J, of Ammonite territory (Num 21:24). See Randall W. Younker, "Jabbok," *ABD* 3.593–94.

100. See "The Garden of Eden" in chapter 2. Cf. Jean Rudhardt, "Water," *ER* 15.350–58.

101. Mircea Eliade, *Patterns in Comparative Religion* (New York: Meridian Books, 1958) 367–87; *Images and Symbols* (New York: Search Books, 1969) 27–56.

102. The history of scholarship on Genesis 15 is surveyed briefly by Claus Westermann (*Genesis 12–36*, 209–16). For the social and historical understanding of the covenant assumed here, see Frank Cross's discussion in *Canaanite Myth and Hebrew Epic* (272–73, cf. 265–71). To this perspective may be compared the detailed studies of Genesis 15 by R. E. Clements, *Abraham and David: Genesis XV and Its Meaning for Israelite Tradition* (Naperville, IL: Alec R. Allenson, 1967); and Norbert Lohfink, *Die Landverheissung als Eid: Eine Studie zu Gn 15* (Stuttgart: Katholisches Bibelwerk, 1967). The same covenant ceremony and its signficance is mentioned by Jeremiah when he accuses Israel and its leaders of transgressing the divine covenant (Jer 34:17–22, esp. vv 18–19). For a discussion of the extrabiblical parallels, see Speiser, *Genesis*, 112–14.

103. Eliade, *Images and Symbols*, 27–56.

104. On Beersheba as the traditional southern boundary of Israel, cf., for example, Judges 20:1, 1 Samuel 3:20; Amos (5:5; 8:14) mentions it as an important religious site.

105. In the Elohist's version of Jacob's departure and return, the use of Bethel as a portal is worked out in an elaborate scheme of a dream at Bethel (28:11–12, 17–18, 20–21a, 22), a second dream in Syria in which Jacob is instructed to return to Bethel (31:10–13), and Jacob's construction of an altar at Bethel upon his return (35:1–7). Like Abraham in J's epic itinerary, so Jacob in E's epic stops at Shechem first before proceeding on to Bethel when he returns from Syria (Gen 33:19–20, 35:1–7). Michael Fishbane has proposed a slightly different scheme in which Bethel (Gen 28) and the Jabbok (Gen 32) represent the theophanic portals for Jacob's trip providing "a certain spatial frame for the movement of the text as a whole"; see his "Composition and Structure in the Jacob Cycle (Gen. 25:19–35:22)," *JJS* 26 (1975) 15–38, esp. 28–30.

106. This is a central thesis of chapter 2; for arguments against the story of

Cain and Abel as a political etiology explaining the origin of the Kenites, see the discussion of "Cain and Abel."

107. Walter Brueggemann, *The Land* (Philadelphia: Fortress, 1977).

108. Ibid., 3.

109. Ibid., 6.

110. Ibid., 6, 14.

Chapter 4

1. Gerhard von Rad, "The Form-Critical Problem of the Hexateuch," trans. E. W. Trueman Dicken, in *The Problem of the Hexateuch and Other Essays* (London: SCM, 1984) 1–78, esp. 8, 50–52, 60, 78.

2. Martin Noth, *A History of Pentateuchal Traditions*, trans. Bernhard W. Anderson (Chico, CA: Scholars, 1981) 46–50. Noth, who considered the books of Deuteronomy and Joshua to be part of another historical work—the Deuteronomistic History—and not the continuation of Genesis through Numbers, shifted the core of Pentateuchal traditions from the settlement, where von Rad placed it, to the exodus from Egypt.

3. See, for example, Norman K. Gottwald, *The Hebrew Bible: A Socio-Literary Introduction* (Philadelphia: Fortress, 1985) 144–47; and Bernhard W. Anderson, *Understanding the Old Testament*, 4th ed. (Englewood Cliffs, NJ: Prentice-Hall, 1986) 9–14.

4. Claus Westermann, *Genesis 1–11: A Commentary* (1974. Minneapolis: Augsburg, 1984) 2.

5. Robert B. Coote and David Robert Ord, *The Bible's First History* (Philadelphia: Fortress, 1989) 9–10.

6. Peter Ellis, *The Yahwist: The Bible's First Theologian* (Collegeville, MN: Liturgical, 1968) 181.

7. The parallel between these accounts has not gone unrecognized by scholars. See, for example, U. Cassuto, *A Commentary on the Book of Genesis*, part II (1949. Jerusalem: Magnes, 1964) 334–69. See also the discussion of "Sacred Geography" in chapter 3.

8. The traditional identification of Jebel Musa, at whose base St. Catherine's Monastery is located, as Mt. Sinai goes back only to the Byzantine era (324–638 C.E.). Israel's old poetry and epic sources appear to associate the southern mountain with Midianite territory in the Transjordan; see Theodore Hiebert, *God of My Victory* (Atlanta: Scholars, 1986) 83–92.

9. According to the Elohist, the divine name is revealed to Moses at his first theophany at the sacred mountain, Horeb (Exod 3:15). The Priestly Writer records the revelation of the divine name to Moses in the land of Egypt preceding his mission to confront Pharaoh with the divine demands (Exod 6:2–9).

10. K. Budde, "The Nomadic Ideal in the Old Testament," *New World* 4 (1895) 726–45; John W. Flight, "The Nomadic Idea and Ideal in the Old Testament," *JBL* 42 (1923) 158–226; Samuel Nyström, *Beduinentum und Jahwismus: Eine soziologisch-religionsgeschichtliche Untersuchung zum Alten Testament* (Lund: C. W. K. Gleerup, 1946).

11. Paul Humbert, "Osée, le prophète bedouin," *Revue de l'Histoire et Philosophie de la Religion* 1 (1921) 97–118, and "La logique de la perspective nomade chez Osée et l'unité d'Osée 2, 4–22," in *Vom Alten Testament* (Karl Marti Festschrift), ed.

K. Budde (Giessen: A. Töpelmann, 1925) 158–66; E. Sellin, *Das Zwölfprophetenbuch*, vol I., (Leipzig: A. Deichert, 1920) 236.

12. H. and H. A. Frankfort, et al., *Before Philosophy: The Intellectual Adventure of Ancient Man* (New York: Penguin, 1946) 246. Compare Robert Cohn's judgment: "It is not at all improbable that the wilderness was the breeding ground for a new socio-religious movement. . . . In the harsh environment of the wilderness, the air was first cleared and the Israelite revolution began"; *The Shape of Sacred Space: Four Biblical Studies* (Chico, CA: Scholars, 1981) 21–23.

13. George H. Williams, *Wilderness and Paradise in Christian Thought* (New York: Harper, 1962); Herbert N. Schneidau, *Sacred Discontent: The Bible and Western Tradition* (Berkeley: University of California, 1976); Max Oelschlaeger, *The Idea of Wilderness: From Prehistory to the Age of Ecology* (New Haven: Yale University, 1991) 31–67.

14. Shemaryahu Talmon, "The 'Desert Motif' in the Bible and in Qumran Literature," in *Biblical Motifs: Origins and Transformations*, ed. A. Altmann (Cambridge: Harvard University, 1966) 31–63. Cf. M. Weber, *Ancient Judaism* (Glencoe: The Free Press, 1952) 13; E. Voegelin, *Order and History, I. Israel and Revelation* (Baton Rouge: Louisiana State University, 1956) 208–19; and H. P. Smith, *Religion of Israel* (New York: Scribner, 1914) 12.

15. Writes Talmon: "The predominent aspects of *midbār* wilderness in the Bible give additional evidence to the unfamiliarity with and the loathing of the 'desert' which were typical of the ancient Israelite. It is the attitude of the city-dweller, the farmer, the semisedentary shepherd, even of the ass nomad" ("Desert Motif," 42–43). Cf. Norman K. Gottwald's analysis of the desert narratives in the Pentateuch as reflective of a sedentary rather than nomadic society in *The Tribes of Yahweh: A Sociology of the Religion of Liberated Israel, 1250–1050 B.C.E.* (Maryknoll, NY: Orbis, 1979) 453–63.

16. Cf. the Israelites' concern for fields (for grain production) and vineyards when they confront Moses later in Numbers 16:14.

17. The murmuring tradition may be associated with the intolerable conditions of desert life in the opinion of J, as Martin Noth has suggested in *Exodus* (Philadelphia: Westminster, 1962) 128. George Coats has argued against this view, considering the murmuring tradition to be a later tradition rising not from the desert milieu but from anti-northern polemic in the Jerusalem cult; see *Rebellion in the Wilderness: The Murmuring Motif in the Wilderness Traditions of the Old Testament* (Nashville: Abingdon, 1968).

18. Cohn, *Sacred Space*, 7–23.

19. The Elohist also highlights the theme of the preservation of the life of Israel's ancestors in Egypt (Gen. 42:2; 45:5b, 7, 11; 50:20).

20. See for example, "The Story of Si-nuhe" (*ANET*, 19) and the account of Thut-Mose III's Campaign at Megiddo (*ANET*, 237–38). Oded Borowski reviews some of this data on the Egyptians' view of Canaan in *Agriculture in Iron Age Israel* (Winona Lake, IN: Eisenbrauns, 1987) 3–5.

21. On the environment of the Nile Valley, see M. Y. Nuttonson, *The Physical Environment and Agriculture of Libya and Egypt with Special Reference to Their Regions Containing Areas Climatically and Latitudinally Analogous to Israel* (Washington, DC: American Institute of Crop Ecology, 1961) 244–452; John A. Wilson, *The Culture of Ancient Egypt* (Chicago: University of Chicago, 1951) 8–17; and Bruce B. Williams, "Nile (Geography)," *ABD* 4. 1112–16.

22. Josephus, for example, describes Herod the Great, in response to the famine of 24 B.C.E., using his private fortune—cutting up into coinage all the gold and silver ornaments in his palace—to purchase grain from Egypt; *The Works of Josephus*, trans. William Whiston (Peabody, MA: Hendrickson, 1987) 417–18 (Book 15, Chap. 9).

23. Nuttonson, *Physical Environment*, 253–61.

24. See the discussion of "Adam and Eve" in chapter 2.

25. Both Martin Noth (*Exodus*, 81) and Brevard S. Childs, *The Book of Exodus* (Philadelphia: Westminster, 1974) 159, consider Exodus 9:31–32 a secondary addition to the text. While these verses do break into the narrative of the confrontation between Moses and Pharaoh, they reflect the characteristic interests of J and are directly related to the description of the following plague (Exod 10:5, 12, 15) and of the festival of unleavened bread (Exod 34:18). For *kussemet* as emmer wheat rather than spelt, see Michael Zohary, *Plants of the Bible* (Cambridge: Cambridge University, 1982) 74–75.

26. Paula S. Hiebert, "Psalm 78: Its Place in Israelite Literature and History" (Th.D. diss., Harvard University, 1992) 85–91.

27. Weber, *Judaism*, 13; Julius Wellhausen, *Prolegomena to the History of Ancient Israel* (1878; New York: Meridian Books, 1957) 83–120. Albrecht Alt, "The Origins of Israelite Law," trans. R. A. Wilson, in *Essays on Old Testament History and Religion* (Garden City, NY: Anchor Books, 1968) 103–71.

28. The formulation of these festivals in Exodus 34 is closely paralleled in Exodus 23: 14–17, a set of ritual regulations usually attributed to the Elohist.

29. The consumption of unleavened bread, while explained in biblical tradition as the result of the hasty departure from Egypt, has been associated from the beginning of historical analysis of these texts with the consumption of the new bread baked from the first new grain. See, for example, Wellhausen, *Prolegomena*, 87.

30. For an introductory bibliography and brief review of the history of the debate over Passover's origins, see Childs, *Exodus*, 178–90; and Baruch M. Bokser, "Unleavened Bread and Passover, Feasts of," *ABD* 6. 755–65.

31. Wellhausen, *Prolegomena*, 87–93. Examples of recent studies that reflect Wellhausen's dichotomy, seeing the feasts of Passover and Unleavened Bread arising from two distinct societies, one nomadic pastoralist and the other sedentary agriculturalist, include Roland de Vaux, *Ancient Israel: Its Life and Institutions*, trans John McHugh (New York: McGraw-Hill, 1961) 484–93; Nahum M. Sarna, *Exploring Exodus: The Heritage of Biblical Israel* (New York: Schocken, 1986) 81–102; and Bokser, 756.

32. L. Rost, "Weidewechsel und altisraelitischer Festkalender," *ZDPV* 6 (1943) 205–16.

33. Several hints suggest an association in J's thought between *pesaḥ* and *maṣṣôt*: (1) leaven is not permitted with the *pesaḥ* sacrifice (v 25); (2) the legislation of the offering of the firstborn of the flocks follows immediately upon the heels of the *maṣṣôt* legislation in J's code (vv 18–20); and (3) both *maṣṣôt* (v 18) and *pesaḥ* (12:21–23) are linked to the exodus.

34. John Van Seters's analysis the festivals of Passover and Unleavened Bread in the Yahwist also challenges the nomadic origins of Passover and the pre-Israelite Canaanite origins of Unleavened Bread. He finds in Deuteronomic tradition of the seventh century the earliest statement on the Passover, and links J's emphasis on Unleavened Bread and P's emphasis on Passover with historical developments in the exilic period; see "The Place of the Yahwist in the History of Passover and Massot," *ZAW* 95 (1983) 167–82.

35. The decalogue in Exodus 20: 1–17 appears to be Elohistic tradition that has undergone editing by the Priestly Writer.

36. Cf. Deuteronomy 14:27–29; 15:1–11; 24:14–22; 26:12–15.

37. This is the same term employed by J to mean "cultivate" in the creation narrative.

38. G. Ernest Wright, *God Who Acts: Biblical Theology as Recital* (London: SCM, 1952) 43–44.

39. Walther Eichrodt, "Offenbarung und Geschichte im Alten Testament," *Theologische Zeitschrift* 4 (1948) 322 (English translation from Wright's *God Who Acts*, 43–44).

40. Sarna, *Exploring Exodus*, 1–2

41. Emil Fackenheim, *God's Presence in History* (New York: Harper Torchbooks, 1970) 8–14.

42. J. Severino Croatto, *Exodus: A Hermeneutics of Freedom* (Maryknoll, NY: Orbis, 1981) 12.

43. Ibid., 34–35.

44. Frank Moore Cross, *Canaanite Myth and Hebrew Epic* (Cambridge, Harvard University, 1973) 164, and "The Epic Traditions of Early Israel: Epic Narrative and the Reconstruction of Early Israelite Institutions," in *The Poet and the Historian: Essays in Literary and Historical Biblical Criticism*, ed. Richard Elliott Friedman (Chico, CA: Scholars, 1983) 27.

45. Translated by E. A. Speiser in *ANET*, 60–72; and by Alexander Heidel in *The Babylonian Genesis* (Chicago: University of Chicago, 1942) 1–60. On the conflict in Enuma Elish, see Thorkild Jacobsen, "The Battle Between Marduk and Tiamat," *JAOS* 88 (1968) 104–8, and *Treasures of Darkness: A History of Mesopotamian Religion* (New Haven: Yale Univerity, 1976) 167–91.

46. Translated by H. L. Ginsberg in *ANET*, 129–42; and by Michael Coogan in *Stories from Ancient Canaan* (Philadelphia: Westminster, 1978) 75–115. On the battle between Baal and Yamm ("Sea"), see Cross, *Canaanite Myth and Hebrew Epic*, 112–20, 147–63.

47. On Exodus 15 and related biblical texts, see Cross's, "The Song of the Sea and Canaanite Myth," in *Canaanite Myth and Hebrew Epic*, 112–44; 147–94. On Habakkuk 3, see Theodore Hiebert, *God of My Victory: The Ancient Hymn in Habakkuk 3*, esp. 81–128.

48. Cross, *Canaanite Myth and Hebrew Epic*, 147–169; "Epic Traditions," 27.

49. For the challenge to Baal by Yamm in the Baal Cycle, see *ANET*, 130 (*CTA* 2.1.3–45); Tiamat's challenge to Marduk is described in Tablets 2 and 3 of Enuma Elish, *ANET*, 63–66.

50. While the holy mountain is only mentioned explicitly in the E strand of this initial theophany to Moses, J clearly has Mt. Sinai in mind. This is evident in the play on the name of the tree (*sĕneh;* Exod 3:2) in which the theophany occurs and the name Sinai (*sînāy*), in the theophanic imagery of lightning that also characterizes the theophany at Mt. Sinai (Exod 3:2; 19:16a, 18), and in the reference to sacred ground in this narrative (3:5) and in the Sinai narrative later (19:12–13a, 20–25).

51. For Baal in the Baal Cycle, see *ANET*, 133–35 (*CTA* 4.3.11, 18; 4.5.68–71; 4.7.29–35; 5.2.7). For Marduk in Enuma Elish, see *ANET*, 66 (Tablet 4, lines 35–54) and Jacobsen's comments in "The Battle Between Marduk and the Sea," 106.

52. For *labbat 'ēš* as lightning, see Psalms 29:7; 105:32; Isaiah 29:6; 30:30. Cf. J's description of Yahweh's storm in Exodus 9:24.

53. For the "column of lightning and cloud" (*'ammûd 'ēš wĕ'ānān*) as a reflection of the thunderstorm imagery of the storm deity, see Thomas W. Mann, "The Pillar of Cloud in the Red Sea Narrative," *JBL* 90 (1971) 15–30; *Divine Presence and Guidance in Israelite Traditions: The Typology of Exaltation* (Baltimore: Johns Hopkins University, 1977) 130–34; and Cross, *Canaanite Myth and Hebrew Epic*, 164–65.

54. In Elohistic traditions, this pillar of cloud and fire/lightning is associated not with the battle of the divine warrior but only with the tent of meeting and the communication of the deity in the cult. See Paula Hiebert, "Psalm 78," 115–22, 135–37.

55. Terrence Fretheim, "The Plagues as Ecological Signs of Historical Disaster," *JBL* 110 (1991) 385–96.

56. *ANET*, 66–67 (Tablet 4, lines 42–48, 96–100).

57. *ANET*, 131 (*CTA* 2.4.27); cf. Coogan, *Stories*, 89.

58. Baal returns to Zaphon, nature awakens, and a temple is constructed for the victorious warrior (*ANET*, 133–34; *CTA* 4.5.6). Marduk takes up residence in his temple Esagila, built in his home by the gods, and is granted by them absolute and undisputed authority (*ANET*, 68–72; Tablets 6,7).

59. Baal (*ANET*, 134; *CTA* 4.6.35–60) and Marduk (*ANET*, 69; Tablet 6, lines 67–77) both provide lavish banquets at their new palaces following their victories. Baal brings the rainy season with the onslaught of the thunderstorm and with it the land's fertility (*ANET*, 133, 140; *CTA* 4.5.68–71; 6.3.10–11).

60. Traditionally, going back to the work of H. Gressmann, *Mose und seine Zeit* (Göttingen: Vandenhoeck & Ruprecht, 1913) 192, scholars have considered J's theophany in Exodus 19 to be dependent on volcanic imagery while E's theophany was attributed to storm imagery. See, for example, Jörg Jeremias, "Theophany in the OT," *IDBSup*, 897; *Theophanie: die Geschichte einer alttestamentlichen Gattung* (Neukirchen-Vluyn: Neukirchener Verlag, 1965) 100–11; and Noth, *Exodus*, 158–59, and *The History of Israel* (New York: Harper & Row, 1958) 131–32. Arguments against this traditional view and in favor of J's imagery as derived from the thunderstorm have been made by Cross, *Canaanite Myth and Hebrew Epic*, 169; Richard J. Clifford, *The Cosmic Mountain in Canaan and the Old Testament* (Cambridge: Harvard University, 1972) 108–23; and Mann, "Pillar of Cloud," 15–17. Volcanic activity in the Sinai ended during the Pleistocene epoch, thousands of years before the biblical period. See Efraim Orni and Elisha Efrat, *Geography of Israel* (Jerusalem: Israel Universities, 1980) 5–14, 118–19; and Michael Evenari, Leslie Shanan, and Naphtali Tadmor, *The Negev: The Challenge of a Desert* (Cambridge: Harvard University, 1971) 81, 94; cf. Clifford, *Cosmic Mountain*, 111.

61. Whether the story of water in Exodus 17:1–7 also contains J elements is difficult to say. It is largely from E. P's version is found in Numbers 20:2–13.

62. J's account of manna and quail in Numbers 11 has been interwoven with E's account of the selection of seventy representatives from the elders of Israel to assist Moses (vv 14, 16–17, 24–30).

63. William Henry Propp, *Water in the Wilderness: A Biblical Motif and Its Mythological Background* (Atlanta: Scholars, 1987); see also Paula Hiebert, "Psalm 78," 137–87.

64. Dennis J. McCarthy, "'Creation' Motifs in Ancient Hebrew Poetry," in *Creation in the Old Testament*, ed. Bernhard W. Anderson (Philadelphia: Fortress, 1984) 83–85.

65. Sarna, *Exploring Exodus*, 93.

66. U. Cassuto, *A Commentary on the Book of Exodus*, trans. Israel Abrahams (Jerusalem: Magnes, 1967) 179.

67. Cross, *Canaanite Myth and Hebrew Epic*, 143–44.

68. *ANET*, 68–72 (Tablet 6).

69. Heidel, *The Babylonian Genesis*, 10–11.

70. Thorkild Jacobsen, *Treasures of Darkness*, 189–91, and "Religious Drama in Ancient Mesopotamia," in *Unity and Diversity: Essays in the History, Literature, and Religion of the Ancient Near East*, ed. Hans Goedicke and J. J. M. Roberts (Baltimore: Johns Hopkins University, 1975) 75–76.

71. Jacobsen, *Treasures of Darkness*, 189–91, and "Religious Drama," 75–76.

72. Cross, *Canaanite Myth and Hebrew Epic*, 143–44; J. J. M. Roberts, "Myth versus History," *CBQ* 38 (1976) 7–13; Fretheim, *Exodus*, 12–14, 161–70, and "The Reclamation of Creation: Redemption and Law in Exodus," *Interpretation* 45 (1991) 354–65.

73. Jacobsen, "The Battle Between Marduk and Tiamat," 104–8.

74. This literary critical judgment goes back to J. Wellhausen's proposal that J's "ritual dialogue" in Exodus 34 must be understood as a parallel to E's "ethical decalogue" in Exodus 20; see *Die Composition des Hexateuchs* (1899. Reprint. Berlin: Walter de Gruyter, 1963) 329–35. While Wellhausen's selection of titles for these parallel codes are in certain respects misleading, his literary critical judgment remains sound.

75. A brief introduction to sacrifice, including the offering of first fruits, and to the major interpretations of it is found in Joseph Henninger's "Sacrifice," *ER* 12.544–57.

76. For example, Jacob Milgrom, *Leviticus 1–16* (New York: Doubleday, 1991) 440–41; J. J. M. Roberts, "Divine Freedom and Cultic Manipulation in Israel and Mesopotamia," in *Unity and Diversity*, 181–90; Sarna, *Exploring Exodus*, 89; Noth, *Exodus*, 102.

77. S. R. Driver, "Offer, Offering, Oblation," in *Dictionary of the Bible*, ed. J. Hastings (New York: Charles Scribner's Sons, 1900) 587.

78. Though this text is generally attributed to the Elohist, it contains a number of Yahwistic elements, not the least of which is the interest in *'ădāmâ* (v 24). Other J traits are the invoking of the divine name in worship (v 24), the reference to divine blessing (v 24), and the concern for nakedness (v 26); cf. Coote and Ord, *First History*, 261, 264.

79. For discussions of the avoidance of leaven in Israelite religious ritual, see Milgrom, *Leviticus 1–16*, 189 and Noth, *Exodus*, 191.

80. See chapter 3, "Nature and Society."

81. Gerhard von Rad, *Old Testament Theology*, vol. 1, trans. D. M. G. Stalker, (New York: Harper and Row, 1962) 218; cf. 212–19.

82. For a review of the recent debate, see Ronald S. Hendel, "The Social Origins of the Aniconic Tradition in Early Israel," *CBQ* 50 (1988) 365–82; and J. J. Stamm and M. E. Andrew, *The Ten Commandments in Recent Research* (Naperville, IL: Alec R. Allenson, 1967) 81–89; and Childs, *Exodus*, 404–9.

Chapter 5

1. H. and H. A. Frankfort, et al., *Before Philosophy: The Intellectual Adventure of Ancient Man* (New York: Penguin Books, 1974) 246–47.

2. Albrecht Alt, "The God of the Fathers," "The Origins of Israelite Law," and "The Settlement of the Israelites in Palestine," trans. R. A. Wilson, in *Essays on Old Testament History and Religion* (Garden City, NY: Anchor Books, 1968) 1–221.

3. Helmer Ringgren, *Israelite Religion*, trans. David E. Green (Philadelphia: Fortress, 1966) 42.

4. Peter Ellis, *The Yahwist: The Bible's First Theologian* (Collegeville, MN: The Liturgical Press, 1968) 31.

5. Compare the characterizations of the Yahwist by Gerhard von Rad, *The Problem of the Hexateuch and Other Essays*, trans. E. W. Trueman Dicken (London: SCM, 1966) 68–74, and *Old Testament Theology*, vol. I, trans. D. M. G. Stalker (New York: Harper & Row, 1962) 48–56; Frank Moore Cross, *Canaanite Myth and Hebrew Epic* (Cambridge: Harvard University, 1973) 261; and Robert Coote and David Ord, *The Bible's First History* (Philadelphia: Fortress, 1989) 1–7.

6. The link between David and Abraham has been discussed by, among others, Ronald Clements in *Abraham and David: Genesis XV and Its Meaning for Israelite Tradition* (Naperville, IL: A. R. Allenson, 1967).

7. For the Sumerian King List, see Thorkild Jacobsen, *The Sumerian King List* (Chicago: University of Chicago, 1939); the Epic of Gilgamesh is translated in *ANET*, 72–99, 503–7, and Agamemnon and Odysseus are the protagonists, of course, of Greece's great epic literature, the Iliad and the Odyssey.

8. This is the traditional view of the origin of the Yahwist's traditions. It has been developed in elaborate detail by Martin Noth in his *A History of Pentateuchal Traditions*, trans. Bernhard W. Anderson (Chico, CA: Scholars, 1981).

9. Wendell Berry, *The Unsettling of America: Culture and Agriculture* (San Francisco: Sierra Club, 1986 [orig. 1977]), *The Gift of Good Land: Further Essays Cultural and Agricultural* (San Francisco: North Point, 1981), and *Home Economics* (San Francisco: North Point, 1987); Wes Jackson, *New Roots for Agriculture* (San Francisco: Friends of the Earth, 1980), *Altars of Unhewn Stone: Science and the Earth* (San Francisco: North Point Press, 1987), and *Becoming Native to this Place* (Lexington, KY: University of Kentucky, 1994); Vandana Shiva, *The Violence of the Green Revolution: Third World Agriculture, Ecology, Politics* (London: Zed Books, 1991); Miguel A. Altieri, *Environmentally Sound Small Scale Agricultural Projects: Guidelines for Planning* (New York: Coordination in Development, 1988); and C. Dean Freudenberger, *Global Dust Bowl: Can We Stop the Destruction of the Land Before It's Too Late?* (Minneapolis: Augsburg Fortress, 1990).

10. Herman E. Daly and John B. Cobb, Jr., *For the Common Good: Redirecting the Economy Toward Community, the Environment, and a Sustainable Future* (Boston: Beacon, 1989) 268.

11. Wendell Berry, *Unsettling*, 97.

12. Ibid., 38.

13. Timothy C. Weiskel, "In Dust and Ashes: The Environmental Crisis in Religious Perspective," *Harvard Divinity Bulletin* 21.3 (1992).

14. Daly and Cobb, *Common Good*, 271.

15. Compare the concrete proposals of the agriculturalists listed in note 9.

16. Wendell Berry, *Unsettling*, 7.

17. For Mircea Eliade's conception of the cosmic center, see *Images and Symbols* (New York: Sheed and Ward, 1969) 27–56.

18. John Bright, *A History of Israel*, 3rd ed. (Philadelphia: Westminster, 1972) 171.

19. See, for example, Roland de Vaux, *Ancient Israel: Its Life and Institutions*, trans. John McHugh (New York: McGraw-Hill, 1961) 468–515.

20. See, for example, the recent summary of apocalyptic thought by Paul Hanson and John Collins in *ABD* 1.279–88.

21. Gordon Kaufman, "A Problem for Theology: The Concept of Nature," *HTR* 65 (1972) 353–56.

22. Gordon Kaufman, *In Face of Mystery* (Cambridge: Harvard University, 1993) 109.

23. Thomas Berry, *The Dream of the Earth* (San Francisco: Sierra Club, 1988) 129, 132–33, 219.

24. Sallie McFague, *The Body of God: An Ecological Theology* (Minneapolis: Augsburg Fortress, 1993).

25. See, for example, *Now Is the Time*, the final document and other texts from the World Convocation on Justice, Peace, and the Integrity of Creation; Seoul, 1990 (Geneva: World Council of Churches, 1990).

26. John B. Cobb, Jr., "Postmodern Christianity in Quest of Eco-Justice," in *After Nature's Revolt: Eco-justice and Theology*, ed. Dieter Hessel (Minneapolis: Augsburg Fortress, 1993) 21–22, 27.

27. J. Baird Callicott, "Genesis and John Muir," in *Covenant for a New Creation: Ethics, Religion, and Public Policy*, ed. Carol S. Robb and Carl J. Casebolt (Maryknoll, NY: Orbis, 1991) 107–40.

28. See, for example, 1 Kings 5:4,30; Isaiah 14:2,6; Leviticus 25:43,46,53; Psalms 110:2.

29. See, for example, Numbers 32:22,29(P); 2 Samuel 8:11; 2 Chronicles 28:11; Nehemiah 5:5; Esther 7:8.

30. Wes Jackson, *Altars*, 9.

31. This theme has been taken up again recently by Bill McKibben in *The Comforting Whirlwind: God, Job, and the Scale of Creation* (Grand Rapids, MI: Eerdmans, 1994).

32. Thomas Berry, *Dream of the Earth*, 50, 128, 133, 200, 218.

33. Wendell Berry, *Unsettling*, 87, 95, 98, 212.

34. See, for example, Douglas John Hall, *The Steward: A Biblical Symbol Come of Age* (Grand Rapids, MI: Eerdmans, 1990); Al Gore, *Earth in the Balance: Ecology and the Human Spirit* (Boston: Houghton Mifflin, 1992) 167–81, 238–65; and the review of the literature by Callicott "Genesis" (p. 136, n. 9).

35. See, for example, Bernhard Anderson's exegesis on Genesis 1:26–28, "Human Dominion over Nature," in *Biblical Studies in Contemporary Thought*, ed. Miriam Ward (Burlington, VT: Trinity College Biblical Institute, 1975), and J. Baird Callicott's summary of the stewardship position (*Genesis*, 110–12).

36. Aldo Leopold, *A Sand County Almanac* (New York: Oxford University, 1949) 204.

37. Callicott, "Genesis," 107–16.

38. Wes Jackson is quoted here from correspondence to supporters of The Land Institute, dated November 30, 1993 and April 1, 1994.

39. Paul Hawken, *The Ecology of Commerce* (New York: HarperCollins, 1993) 3, 15, 130–34.

Index